THE SĒMEIA
IN THE FOURTH GOSPEL

TRADITION AND REDACTION

SUPPLEMENTS TO
NOVUM TESTAMENTUM

VOLUME XXXII

LEIDEN
E. J. BRILL
1972

THE SĒMEIA
IN THE FOURTH GOSPEL

TRADITION AND REDACTION

BY

W. NICOL

LEIDEN
E. J. BRILL
1972

CONTENTS

CONTENTS

ACKNOWLEDGEMENTS

Prof. E.P. Groenewald of Pretoria inspired me to specialize in the New Testament. I am deeply indebted to prof. Herman Ridderbos of Kampen, my promotor, who suggested this interesting subject and assisted me throughout the investigation with wisdom and friendship. Prof. O. Betz and prof. E. Käsemann of Tübingen, prof. I.M.F. van Iersel of Nijmegen, and drs. Tj. Baarda of Amsterdam gave me valuable advice. Prof. J.L. Koole of Kampen read the manuscript and made useful criticisms. Mrs. E. Jonker and drs. D.A. Pauw helped me with my English, and dr. C. Willard of Princeton corrected the language of the final manuscript. I am grateful to prof. A.F.J. Klijn and the other editors of the publisher Brill for including my dissertation in the *Supplements to Novum Testamentum*. Joke, my wife, to whom this book is dedicated, corrected the proofs, not even to mention her love and care during the years of my study in foreign countries.

ABBREVIATIONS

I use those of the encyclopedia *Die Religion in Geschichte und Gegenwart*[3] (1957-62), which are listed at the beginning of each of the volumes.

For the Rabbinica, I use those of Strack-Billerbeck (*Kommentar*, volume I p. VII).

John (Johannine) = the author of the gospel.
Jn.   = the Fourth Gospel.
S   = the sēmeia traditions.
J   = the Johannine redaction of the sēmeia traditions.

Some of the standard commentaries on the Gospel have been referred to only by means of the surname of the author :

C.K. BARRETT, *The Gospel according to St. John* (1955).
J.H. BERNARD, *St. John* I+II (ICC, [7]1969; [1]1928).
R.E. BROWN, *The Gospel according to John* (Anchor Bible, 1966).
R. BULTMANN, *Das Evangelium des Johannes* (MeyerK, [18]1964; [1]1941).
C.H. DODD, *The Interpretation of the Fourth Gospel* ([8]1968; [1]1953).
E.C. HOSKYNS, *The Fourth Gospel* (1947).
A. SCHLATTER, *Der Evangelist Johannes* ([3]1960).
R. SCHNACKENBURG, *Das Johannesevangelium* I (Herder, [2]1967).
H. STRATHMANN, *Das Evangelium nach Johannes* (NTD, [11]1968; [1]1936).
B.F. WESTCOTT, *The Gospel according to St. John* (1958; [1]1880).

INTRODUCTION

1. THE SIGNIFICANCE OF THE SĒMEIA

In the course of investigation, the sēmeia proved to be an important key to the historical and theological problems of the Fourth Gospel beyond my initial expectations. They provide one of the best opportunities to study tradition and redaction in the Gospel by applying the methods of literary criticism (*Literarkritik*, in this case amounting to source criticism), form criticism (*Formgeschichte*) and redaction criticism (*Redaktionsgeschichte*). No wonder that the sēmeia have recently been a subject of very lively scientific discussion.

The historical background of the Fourth Gospel is covered in darkness — E. Käsemann lately called it the most difficult of all New Testament problems.[1] The debate about authorship proved to be fruitless (*vide infra*), and the contemporary environment of the author is very obscure. A profitable line of investigation, however, is to study the descent of the Gospel, the antecedents of the type of Christianity it represents, by examining the character of the tradition on which it is based and the way in which this tradition was redacted. The miracle stories are fruitful for such an investigation firstly because, with the possible exception of the prologue, they provide the best opportunity for source criticism in the Gospel. Secondly, form criticism may be better applied to them than to any other material in the Gospel since a number of them represent the characteristic form of the miracle story *Gattung* with some purity and may be closely compared to the Synoptic miracle stories. Thirdly, there are striking differences between the sēmeia traditions and their redaction which reveal some significant historical developments preceding the publication of the Gospel.

A few words have to be said about the way in which my investigation fits into the present state of research. Thorough work has already been done on the source criticism of the sēmeia, but I have attempted to make some contribution by applying the method of style statistics. The form criticism and redaction criticism called forth by this source criticism have not hitherto been extensively treated. Concerning the form criticism, I have had to disagree with the most general hypo-

---

[1] *Jesu Letzter Wille nach Johannes 17* (1966) 131.

thesis about the character of the pre-Johannine miracle tradition, i.e. that Jesus was regarded as a kind of θεῖος ἀνήρ. In order to explain the differences between the *Sitz im Leben* of the tradition and that of the redaction, I have ventured a hypothesis which is new in some respects.

The theological problem of the Fourth Gospel is as acute as the question of its origin. For the western mind, there is an almost unbearable tension between history and theology in the Gospel. On the one hand, John seems to be describing sensible, realistic fact; on the other hand, the main contents of the Gospel seem to be a highly developed interpretation of the life of Jesus. How can John maintain that he writes about the historical Jesus while in many respects he actually seems to be presenting the later theology of the Church concerning the exalted Christ ? It is probably more of a tension for us than it was for him, but we require some explanation in order to understand the Gospel in terms of John's first century way of thinking and believing rather than "tearing it up" with our modern prejudices.

Again the sēmeia provide a useful key because the total "tension" of the Gospel is reflected in them with even more intensity. On the one hand, John seems to stress the historicity of these miraculous events, and on the other hand, he interprets them as symbols for the work of the exalted Christ in such a way that it may seem as if their historicity is unimportant to him.

The importance of the sēmeia is clearly illustrated by the most important controversy of the last decades about Johannine theology, i.e., between Bultmann and Käsemann. Bultmann argued that John regarded Jesus as "nichts als ein Mensch" who did not manifest divinity at all but demanded that men believe the total paradox of his claim to be God.[1] Of course, the miracles form one of the greatest problems in this interpretation because they *are* manifestation of divinity. Bultmann's answer is that miracles are only allowed by John as a concession for human weakness. Käsemann more or less reversed the position of Bultmann and laid strong emphasis on the highly miraculous wonders in the Gospel. The Johannine Jesus is like a god manifesting himself on earth; he is no true man : John is a naïve docetist. Therefore, John is not interested in realistic history. Käsemann has to admit, however, that the miracle stories do contain realistic description. Obviously, an investigation of the role of the sēmeia in the Gospel

---

[1] For a full discussion of Bultmann and Käsemann, see chapter three.

should shed some light on this controversy and therefore on the deepest dimensions of Johannine Christology.

A general theological interpretation of the sēmeia has, of course, frequently been attempted, but it seems that some of the aspects of the "tension" between historical fact and meaning might be better grasped when the normal methods of exegesis are aided by the method of redaction criticism. Then the relation between history and interpretation need not be studied only "theologically" but may also be observed in practice. We can, for example, see how John interpreted his tradition by making small and large additions. This is also of wider significance because John's method of interpreting the sēmeia is an example of this total method of interpreting the earthly Jesus. In a sense, he sees the whole earthly life of Jesus as a sēmeion because in 12 : 37 and 20 : 30 he summarizes it as "performing signs". C.H. Dodd is formally right when he takes the symbolism connected to the word sēmeion as hermeneutical principle for the interpretation of the Gospel.

2. THE THREE METHODS APPLIED IN THE THREE CHAPTERS

In chapter one, I have attempted to separate the traditional miracle stories and their Johannine redaction. John was probably no eyewitness.[1] If this is so, it is obvious that he would have obtained at least most of the miracle stories from tradition. Some think that in the case of the two stories which have Synoptic parallels (6 : 1-21), the tradition must have been one of the Synoptic Gospels, but this could not have been the case. The clearest proof lies precisely in the two Johannine pericopes which bear the greatest resemblance to their Synoptic parallels, i.e., the feeding of the five thousand (c. 6) and the anointing of Jesus' feet (c. 12). In both cases, the agreement is partly with one and partly with another of the Synoptic parallels. The most likely explanation is that there must have been an independent strain of oral tradition behind John in which this kind of cross-combination of different details took place.[2]

---

[1] I regard the arguments in favour of apostolic authorship as worthy of careful consideration. The objections, however, appear to me to be insurmountable, escpecially those regarding the character of the tradition contained in the Gospel (see chapter two, 4). On the other hand, it seems quite possible that an Apostle like John played an important part in the earlier transmission of the tradition (see chapter two, 3).

[2] The debate on this matter has been very extensive but as I judge this solution to be certain, I do not enter into it. For all the new literature, see J. Blinzler, *Johannes und*

A next question is whether this tradition was still oral when John used it or whether it had, by that time, already been written down. In the first chapter, I have shown that there are some conspicious seams and style differences between tradition and redaction. These would have been smoothed out had the tradition been in a fluid oral state and freely reproduced by John. It was probably in written form,[1] and if not, it must have been in a very fixed oral state.[2]

A very serious problem is whether the reconstruction of a sēmeia source will not be so hypothetical that it is useless speculation.[3] It is clear that John did not quote his source mechanically but treated it with some freedom. His general intention would, of course, have been to present his book as a unity and to make the seams invisible. Is source criticism then to be abandoned as impossible ? Source criticism indeed often becomes so hypothetical that no one but the critic himself believes it. I regard this as an important problem and have ventured to attempt source criticism only because I became assured that it is possible to adapt the method in such a way that an acceptable degree of probability may be expected. I have given the most of my attention to style because the results of style statistics can be fairly objective. I have not attempted a full reconstruction of the source because this is impossible. My aim has not been to publish the text of the source but only to characterize it as far as possible in order to be able to evaluate John's reaction to it. Characterization can better be built on a few probable observations than on many uncertain ones. Source and redaction are sometimes inseparably interwoven, but frequently close observation discovers certain unevennesses on the basis of which one can separate the two : therefore, I term my source criticism

---

die Synoptiker (1965). The solution I accept is affirmed throughout Dodd's book, *Historical Tradition in the Fourth Gospel* (1963), see pp. 199-211 for the feeding miracle and chapter two, note 1 below, for the anointing pericope.

[1] This may be affirmed by 20 : 30f. which mentions a "book" that was "written". We shall see that it seems that these verses were traditional.

[2] An attempt was made to prove that John would have used all sources freely from memory because he quoted the Old Testament in this way — C. Goodwin, How did John treat his sources ?, *JBL* 73 (1954) 61-75. The Old Testament was, however, not really one of John's sources but rather the broad background of all his thinking; moreover, free quoting of e.g. the Old Testament was a general usage in New Testament times. B. Noack, *Zur johanneischen Tradition* (1954) gave many other arguments for the oral character of John's tradition but they are not convincing.

[3] Cf. Barrett, 16, who believes that it is probable that John used sources, but it is "useless to speculate" about such obscure matters.

"separation" rather than "reconstruction".[1] Although the results of chapter one primarily depend on strict source-critical observations (style and *aporias*), I have given them a broader base by making them dependent also upon the results of chapters two and three where I have studied the character of the source and of John's redaction of it. This is, of course, an indirect method because these two chapters partly depend on chapter one. But they also depend on much other material so that the knowledge attained in them could here and there be anticipated to help decide what words are characteristic of and would have belonged to the tradition or to the redaction. Finally, the source criticism has been put to the test in chapters two and three because there it had to be discovered whether the full picture is historically conceivable or not.

I have tried to avoid the excesses of the old liberal source criticism, but sometimes I have indeed made sharp distinctions and, for instance, have regarded a single phrase in a miracle story as a Johannine insertion. I am fully aware of the hypothetical nature of any such distinction. The reason why I have sometimes delimited so precisely is not that I know so much about source and redaction but that I know so little about it. If matters were clear, one would have been capable of quick generalizations, but since they are so obscure, one cannot offer generalizations without basing them on as exact an analysis as possible. It is conceivable that a traditional pericope may here and there contain a few Johannine words. John did not sit with the source on his desk like a modern scholar. The source was probably his "Gospel" from which he had preached for years, thus more or less knowing it by heart. When he finally started writing his own Gospel, he probably wrote down the traditional miracle stories from memory.[2] He was careful because the

---

[1] The exact reconstruction of hypothetical sources was more common in the first decades of the century than now. It is disappointing that the latest and most valuable book on Johannine source criticism again goes too far and becomes very hypothetical : R.T. Fortna, *The Gospel of Signs* (1970). Even where Bultmann finds exact reconstruction of the sēmeia source impossible, Fortna usually has no doubts about the precise wording of the source. He is even sure that nearly all the narrative in the Gospel was taken from the source, and by a complex rearrangement he can also reconstruct the original order of the source. Nevertheless, precisely on account of its exactness, the book is very useful. D.M. Smith reviewed the book in *JBL* 89 (1970) 498 ff. He agrees that Fortna "has made a strong case for the literary character of the tradition" but doubts the rearrangement and whether the Passion story would also have belonged to the source.

[2] There is ample evidence that it was customary in New Testament times to reproduce sources from memory, cf. W.G. Kümmel, *Einleitung in das Neue Testament*[15] (1967) 43.

Jesus-tradition was holy to him, but his own way of interpreting these miracle stories in the light of other traditions known to him and under the guidance of the Paraclete is occasionally almost unconsciously reflected in a few words of his own.

It must also be clear that by "sēmeia source" (S) I do not mean a source which contained only sēmeia. It would probably have contained more, even of the other narrative material in Jn. But I have limited myself to the miracles because they were probably an important and homogeneous core in the source so that the source criticism may be carried out with more certainty. It is not even certain that all the miracle stories in the Gospel originally belonged to the same source, but it will be shown in chapter two that the miracle stories form a unity under the aspect of the history of tradition. They all seem to reflect the same state of development, environment, purpose, and Christology. Basically, their common attitude towards the miraculous binds them together, and this does not apply to the other pericopes in the Gospel which also might have belonged to the source. Therefore, if one attempted to incorporate them, the danger of intermingling originally different strains of tradition would be greater.

Finally, a possible misunderstanding should be emphatically removed, namely, that the classification of a passage as Johannine implies that it is unhistorical. It has often been thought that all the typical Johannine discourses are completely unhistorical, but this is incorrect. It is often surprising to see how apparently fully "Johannine" discourses seem to be based on tradition. Dodd investigated the entire Gospel in this respect and found that there is much more "historical tradition" in it than is usually thought. I have argued that the sēmeia source contained missionary preaching for Jews. Such a book does not, of course, contain all the tradition available because some parts of the tradition are better suited for missionary preaching — in those days, especially the miracle stories. Later John used the "missionary Gospel" in order to write a more extensive Gospel for the Church. He was a man who had lived for many years in the broad stream of tradition about Jesus. The principle of his theology was revelation *in* history. The matter deserves separate investigation, but obviously it would be wrong to regard his additions to the sēmeia source as unhistorical in principle. In chapter three, I have studied a number of Johannine insertions on which symbolical interpretation is based, and the conclusion has been that John sought symbolical meaning *in* history.

In chapter two, form criticism has been applied to try to determine different aspects of the character of S. Because of the hypothetical nature of the partial reconstruction of the source, a direct exegesis of the seemingly traditional pericopes would not have sufficed to define the character and Christology of S. Form criticism, rather, functions as a test of the hypothetical source to see whether it becomes intelligible in terms of the history of tradition, whether, for example, its Christology suits its background. It is sometimes overlooked that form criticism is a prerequisite for redaction criticism because one cannot interpret the redactor's reaction to the tradition before having studied the character and *Sitz im Leben* of the tradition itself.

Form criticism may be used to attempt a reconstruction of the original history, see, for instance, the way that Bultmann tries to prove that certain Synoptic *logia* are *ipsissima verba* of Jesus[1] and that J. Jeremias tries to disprove the historicity of the nature miracles.[2] The scientific study of the historical Jesus is of course of major importance, but in this book I have used form criticism in the more limited way in which it is ordinarily applied. I have only investigated the character of the tradition and have not attempted to reconstruct the original history. Of course, the character of the tradition allows conslusions about its general reliability. If, for instance, its character were Hellenistic, it would have been of only minor historical value, but I have found it to be very Jewish so that this obstacle is removed — Jesus and the disciples were Jews so that Jewish elements in the tradition may be primitive. The reasons why I have limited my form criticism are twofold. Firstly, extensive form criticism is exceedingly difficult in the case of the Gospel of John, for it was probably of later origin than the other three Gospels. Secondly, extensive form criticism is not strictly necessary for my subject. My aim has been to study the relation between tradition and redaction, and my form criticism has therefore basically been directed forward towards John and not backwards towards the original history. Therefore, I have limited myself to the tradition which lies before us and have not tried to enter the semi-dark (but important) area behind it.

In chapter three, redaction criticism has been applied. Even more than in chapter two, the results of the source criticism were put to the test because John's attitude towards miracles can partly be established by normal exegesis with which redaction criticism, of course, had to

---

[1] E.g., *Geschichte der Synoptische Tradition*[7] (1967) 174 about Mt. 12 : 28f.

[2] *Neutestamentliche Theologie I* (1971) 91f.

harmonize. Redaction criticism has to be strictly limited; otherwise one will soon be giving a general discussion of the entire theology of the redactor. I have limited myself to John's reaction to what is the central theme of the sēmeia traditions, i.e., the miracles as events, and have discussed the *content* of his symbolical interpretation of the miracles only in so far as it illuminates his attitude towards the miraculous, towards historical events, towards the flesh of Jesus, i.e., in so far as it illuminates the relation between event and meaning. These matters could, however, not be analyzed without going further and investigating the relation between Jesus' earthly glory and his final glorification.

CHAPTER ONE

THE SOURCE-CRITICAL SEPARATION OF THE SĒMEIA TRADITIONS AND THEIR JOHANNINE REDACTION

1. The History of the Identification of the Sēmeia Source

The history of the literary criticism of John has, for the greater part, been one of failure. Most of the theories were immediately rejected; only two could hold their own : the Logos-hymn behind the prologue and the sēmeia source. In this survey we shall describe how this last theory continually gathered support and became more refined during the course of this century so that at the moment there is a consensus among some scholars.

It had already been observed in the previous century that there is tension between the narrative and the discourse parts of the Gospel. The first scientific literary criticism was done by the Göttingen philologists J. Wellhausen and E. Schwartz in the first decade of the present century. Both thought that the miracles were the backbone of the *Grundevangelium* to which the discourses were added later.[1]

A few years later H.H. Wendt detailed the tension between the narratives and the discourses with greater clarity.[2] He made the observation that 20 : 30f., the conclusion of the Gospel, seems to belong to the miracle stories and that its writer is apparently unconscious of the discourses. On the other hand, the writer of the discourses had no interest in the miracles. Wendt's hypothesis was that the discourse material was the oldest and that the miracles were added by another hand to prove the Messiahship of Jesus.

Some years afterwards, J.M. Thompson, working completely independently of the Germans, observed the same tension between the Messianic miracle-faith in the miracle stories and 20 : 30 f., on the one hand, and faith in the eternal word in the prologue and discourses, on the other. His judgement was that the signs-Gospel was the oldest layer.[3]

---

[1] J. Wellhausen, *Das Evangelium Johannis* (1908) 102; E. Schwartz, Aporien im Vierten Evangelium, in : *Nachrichten v.d. Kön. Gesells. der Wiss. zu Göttingen : Phil.-Hist. Kl.* (1908) 559.

[2] *Die Schichten im Vierten Evangelium* (1911) 36, 42.

[3] The Structure of the Fourth Gospel, *Exp* 10 (1915) 514, 523.

In 1922 A. Faure[1] carried the argument further by observing that the first two miracles seem to have belonged together in a source because they are both connected with Cana and are enumerated as first (2 : 11) and second (4 : 54). He conjectured that John took all his miracles from a "Semeia Quelle" which consisted of "kurze, schlicht sachliche Berichte": 20 : 30f. was its conclusion. The final author of the Gospel was critical of the miracle theology of his source, and for this reason he added 4 : 48f. in the second miracle story.

The next year H. Windisch published an interesting article in which he analysed John's narrative style form-critically and contrasted it with that of the Synoptic Gospels.[2] John's typical narratives are long and dramatic (especially cc. 4, 9, 11) and different from the short Synoptic-like pericopes in the Gospel which he, therefore, regarded as traditional. The first two miracles are such pericopes, and they fit so loosely in their context that they were probably taken from a collection of Galilean signs. Others of these Synoptic-like pericopes in John are 5 : 1-9 and 9 : 1-7 (two miracles). In his well-known book introducing form criticism, M. Dibelius also distinguished, on the basis of style, between the traditional miracle stories and the dialogues connected with them by John : the style of the former is "novellistisch" and contrasted to that of John.[3]

So far then, some continuity may be observed, but as these basic insights were worked out in detailed source criticism, no two scholars agreed. In 1927 R. Bultmann wrote that the only way to a more objective source criticism is to gather the style characteristics of the different layers;[4] hence, it is no surprise that style played an important part in the complex literary theory of his enormous commentary, published in 1941. He accepted all the above mentioned observations of Faure and proposed that the evangelist used mainly a sēmeia source, a passion source and a source of *Offenbarungsreden* to compose this Gospel.

Even before Bultmann's commentary was finally published, a storm began to develop in Johannine literary criticism; Bultmann's method of source analysis with the help of style criteria was turning against

---

[1] Die alttestamentliche Zitate im 4. Evangelium und die Quellenscheidungshypothese, *ZNW* 21 (1922) 107ff.

[2] Die Johanneische Erzählungsstil, in : *Eucharisterion* II (für H. Gunkel, 1923) cf. 174-189, 208ff.

[3] *Die Formgeschichte des Evangeliums*[2] (1933) 88f.

[4] Das Johannesevangelium in der neuesten Forschung, *CW* 41 (1927) 503.

itself. After others such as W.F. Howard had made small beginnings, E. Schweizer gathered thirty-three striking Johannine style characteristics and proved statistically that they are evenly distributed throughout the Gospel. He concluded carefully that although John would probably have used written traditional material, he had revised it so thoroughly "sodass sie kaum mehr mit Sicherheit herauszulösen ist."[1] This method was elaborated in 1951 by E. Ruckstuhl.[2] He extended Schweizer's list to fifty and tested Bultmann's five principal literary strata to see whether they differed from each other in style. Agressively, he went further than Schweizer and conlcuded that Bultmann was totally disproved and that John could not have used written sources.

To some this seemed final, but upon closer examination it became clear that there is a gap in this method of fighting source criticism. This was already admitted by Schweizer. He noticed that some short, Synoptic-like pericopes (the first and second sēmeia; 2 : 13-19; 12 : 1-8, 12-15) were remarkably lacking in Johannine style characteristics and concluded that they had probably been taken from a written source.[3] Later he worked this out in an article : the first two signs stood together in the source, and 4 : 48f. was an addition of the Evangelist.[4] Joachim Jeremias also applied stylistic tests and agreed that the style of the pericopes of Schweizer indicated that they consisted of traditional material.[5] He thought it probable that 20 : 30f. also belonged to this tradition and concluded that it was probably a written source because 20 : 30f. mentions a "book" that was "written".

Nevertheless, after this there were nearly two decades of silence about the literary criticism of John. It seemed as though Bultmann had done as much as was possible, and the stylistic unity was discouraging. But this unity, of course, did not dissolve the tensions and hard connections upon which the earlier literary criticism was based. The natural result was that the silence was broken in 1958 by W. Wilkens in a strange attempt to reconcile Ruckstuhl's conclusions with different literary strata : the Evangelist himself twice extensively revised his book.[6] Although Wilkens rejected the sēmeia source-hypothesis, he could not avoid admitting many of the observations upon which this

---

[1] *Ego Eimi* (1939) 87ff.; conclusion 108f.

[2] *Die Literarische Einheit des Johannesevangeliums* (1951); conclusions on pp. 218f.

[3] *Ego Eimi*, 100, 108.

[4] Die Heilung des Königlichen : Jh. 4 : 46-54, *EvTh* 11 (1951/2) 64f.

[5] Johanneische Literarkritik, *ThBl* 20 (1941) 35, 46.

[6] *Die Entstehungsgeschichte des vierten Evangeliums* (1958) 30f.

hypothesis was built. He thinks the first edition of the Gospel was a signs-Gospel with 20 : 30f. as conclusion. Afterwards, the Evangelist added the discourses in such a way that the seams were still clear enough for him to be able to separate the two layers.

Thus, in spite of the storm, some pillars of the sēmeia source-theory still remained. No wonder that recently more scholars have given their consent to some form or another of this theory. Among the German Protestants there were many.[1] This cannot be explained away simply as the influence of Bultmann because all those mentioned here rejected his *Offenbarungsreden* source. It is significant that the major Roman Catholic Johannine specialist, R. Schnackenburg, accepted the sēmeia source.[2] Also in America, quite a number have agreed.[3] None of the important recent British commentators (Hoskyns, Barrett, Dodd) did any literary criticism, but it is interesting that in his last book C.H. Dodd made many observations which may point to a sēmeia source.[4] By means of form criticism in the wider sense he tried to identify the traditional material in the Gospel. In general he regarded as traditional that material which bore more resemblance to the form and content of the Synoptic traditions than to the typical Johannine theological themes. In the case of all seven of the miracles, he thought that the

---

[1] I mention only a number of the more important ones : E. Käsemann, *VF* (1942/6) 186; E. Haenchen, Aus der Literatur zum Jhev., *ThR* 1 (1955) 303 : an "Urevangelium" with the miracles as core; G. Bornkamm, *RGG*³ II 1001; W. Grundmann, *Zeugnis und Gestalt des Johannesevangeliums* (1960) 14; W. Hartke, *Vier Urchristliche Parteien* ... I (1961) *passim*; W. Marxsen, *Einleitung* (1965) 212; H. Conzelmann, *Grundriss der Theologie des Neuen Testaments* (1968) 354; J. Becker, Wunder und Cristologie, *NTS* 16 (1969/70) 132. O Michel agreed that the first two miracles are taken from a source, Der Anfang der Zeichen Jesu, in : *Die Leibhaftigkeit des Wortes*, (Köberle Festgabe, 1958) 17. W.G. Kümmel, *Einleitung* (1963) 147, does not regard as proved that a single written sēmeia source was used but agrees that the short, Synoptic-like pericopes which Schweizer mentioned must be taken over from tradition because their style differs from that of John.

[2] *Johannesevangelium*² (1967) 51ff.

[3] E.C. Broome, *JBL* 63 (1944) 109; R.H. Fuller, *Interpreting the Miracles* (1963) 88; J.M. Robinson, in : *The Bible in Modern Scholarship*, ed. J.P. Hyatt (1965) 136; H. Köster, *HThR* 61 (1968) 232; G.W. MacRae, *CBQ* 12 (1970) 15; J.L. Martyn, in : *Jesus and Man's Hope* I (Perspective, Pittsburgh, 1970) 247ff.; S. Temple, *JBL* 81 (1962) 170 agreed about the first two miracles. D.M. Smith's entire dissertation, *The Composition and Order of the Fourth Gospel* (1965), dealt with Bultmann's literary theory; he rejected almost everything of Bultmann's theory but admitted that there was a possibility that something like a sēmeia source had been used (p. 113). Here it may be added that the Frenchmen M. Goguel, *Introduction* (1923) 396, and P. Merlier, *Le Quatrième Évangile* (1961) 407, agreed that the second miracle must have followed upon the first in a source.

[4] *Historical Tradition in the Fourth Gospel* (1965).

Evangelist used a short story from the tradition, and in many instances his divisions between the traditional and Johannine material exactly coincided with the divisions of the source criticism, as will be shown later.

So far, however, one problem remains. Although many have agreed with the hypothesis of the sēmeia source because of the unevennesses in the Gospel upon which it is based, the attack of Ruckstuhl and Schweizer was not yet answered. Bultmann wrote that the stylistic unity may be the result of the Evangelist's thorough editing of his sources.[1] But if this was done so thoroughly, how can source criticism then be possible? As long as it cannot be proved statistically that there are stylistic differences in the Gospel, the possibility of source criticism remains doubtful and many will refuse to accept the sēmeia source. Recently this was seen by R.T. Fortna who tried to indicate such differences in his dissertation.[2] According to him, not only the signs but also the basis of nearly all the other narrative in the Gospel belonged to a "Gospel of Signs". After reconstructing the source, he applied Ruckstuhl's test to it and found that thirty-two of Ruckstuhl's fifty Johannine style characteristics were wanting in it.[3] This is the main support of his conclusion that in the main, style had verified his source criticism.

Let us first admit that these numbers are probably an indication that John did not create his narrative material freely but depended

---

[1] Johannesevangelium, RGG[3] III 848f.

[2] The Gospel of Signs (Cambridge, 1970).

[3] p. 205. By criticising and modifying Ruckstuhl's list, he tried to increase the ratio from 32 : 50 to 39 : 48 (pp. 208ff.). Only three of these changes are acceptable : numbers 37 and 49 are too weak (vide infra) and it is significant that τις, πολλοί and οὐδείς with the partitive ἐκ occur twenty-five times in Jn. and never in the source. The other changes are unacceptable. The typical Johannine word ἑλκύειν occurs twice in the source, but Fortna says only its figurative use, which does not occur in the source, should be counted as typical of Jn. But of course this use will not appear in the source because the figurative sense which John gives to it can occur only in discourse material of which the source has none. 'Οψάριον also occurs twice in the source, but Fortna says there is a stylistic difference because the collective singular appears only in Johannine passages and the plural only in the source. But this is meaningless : the two Johannine occurrences could not have been plural because there the word is used not for fishes which can be counted but for fish as food (21 : 9, 13), and the reverse holds good for the three source occurrences (6 : 9, 11 ; 21 : 10). Fortna's rejection of numbers 17, 42, 48 and 50 is unfounded because although they do occur elsewhere in the New Testament, they are much more frequent in Jn. and are, therefore, typical of him. Thus, the ratio 32 : 50 can only be changed to 31 : 48 which is not a significant difference.

upon traditions. It is significant to compare Schweizer's application of his test to altogether seven hypothetical literary strata identified by Spitta, Wendt, and Hirsch : in not one of these strata do more than three of his thirty-three characteristics fail.[1] So the 32 : 50 of Fortna is remarkable. But, for two reasons, this method is surely not adequate to verify the reconstruction of an entire source.

(1) Fifteen of the thirty-two characteristics which do not occur in Fortna's source do not appear in any narrative material in the Gospel so that their absence from the source is meaningless.[2]

(2) One of the criteria which he used to identify the source is style characteristics[3] so that it is a circular argument to verify the reconstructed source with the same characteristics. There is proof that ratios like 32 : 50 can occur also with unacceptable source theories : twenty-eight of Ruckstuhl's characteristics are absent from Bultmann's *Offenbarungsreden* source, which was generally rejected.[4] At least one conclusion can be drawn from the history : Ruckstuhl still has to be answered.

J.L. Martyn[5] accepted Fortna's source as a "solid working hypothesis" although the differs from him at minor points. He applies the methods of *Religionsgeschichte* and *Theologiegeschichte* to the source and the Gospel and concludes that Fortna's hypothesis seems to be affirmed by them.

2.   The Basic Indications of the Source

When dealing with such obscure matters as hypothetical sources, one has to attempt to enhance the probability of one's reconstruction of the source by basing it on the convergence of independent indications. There are four sets of indications : form, style, *aporias* and ideological tensions. (An *aporia* is any unevenness, inconsistency or hard connection in the text resulting from — in our case — the redaction of a source). Each one is independent of the other three with this exception, that the ideological tensions are related to the *aporias* in some respects. The observations based on form are general but also fairly obvious.

---

[1] *Ego Eimi*, 104f.

[2] See p. 206f. : numbers 3-8, 10, 11, 21, 23, 25, 31-34, 41, 46.

[3] P. 18.

[4] *Literarische Einheit*, 213f.

[5] Source Criticism and Religionsgeschichte in the Fourth Gospel, in : *Jesus and man's hope* I, (Perspective, 1970) 248.

Style is the most objective indication but sometimes somewhat ambi-
guous. In a number of cases, the *aporias* yield clear-cut indications,
but they should be trusted only in combination with other indications
because the danger is great that they may depend on subjective im-
pressions. The ideological tensions are only mentioned here because they
will be investigated in chapter three.

A) *Form*

We have already seen that Windisch, Dibelius and Dodd distinguished between the long Johannine narratives and the short Synoptic-
like pericopes on the basis of form and narrative style. J.L. Martyn
generally accepted the "Gospel of Signs" as reconstructed by Fortna,
but in contrast to the latter, he found the basic argument to be the fact
that the sign stories in Jn. have the typical form of a miracle story as it
also occurs in the Synoptics.[1]

John's characteristic narrative style can be studied in cc. 4, 7, 9, 11,
18f. The narrative is dramatic, consisting of many short, powerful
dialogue scenes in a lively sequence. For instance, the trial before
Pilate in Jn. is dramatized in eight scenes while in the Synoptics it
consists of only one or two scenes. More than two persons frequently
take part in the Johannine debates while this is hardly ever the case in
the Synoptics.

In contrast to this, the form of the short miracle stories in the Gospel
(and the other pericopes which have Synoptic parallels : 2 : 13ff.;
12 : 1ff.; 12 : 12ff.) closely resembles that of the typical Synoptic
pericopes. The Synoptic miracle stories frequently contain barely more
than the basic pattern of the miracle story *Gattung*, i.e., (a) the illness,
(b) the healing, and (c) the demonstration of the reality of the healing
(e.g., Mk. 7 : 32-7; 8 : 22-6). This pattern is also basic to a number of
John's miracle stories where it is further filled in by themes resembling
those of the typical Synoptic miracle stories. The differences can mostly
be explained by form criticism (see chapter two). This creates the impression that John received these pericopes from the same general
stream of tradition from which the Synoptic Gospels grew. This is
clear in any case for the two miracle stories in c. 6 which have Synoptic
parallels and also for the healing at a distance (c. 4) which, if not a
parallel, is at least very like the healing of the centurion's boy (Mt. 8).

The healing at Bethesda (5 : 2-9b) could almost have been a Synoptic

---

[1] *History and Theology in the Fourth Gospel* (1968) 3f.

healing story. As in Lk. 13 : 16 and Mk. 5 : 25, the seriousness of the
malady is stressed by specifying its duration (v. 5). A short conversation
between Jesus and the patient preceding the healing (6 f.) is customary
in the Synoptics (cf. Mk. 1 : 40; 9 : 23 f.). The strong emphasis on the
man's helplessness is consistent with the character of S (see p. 43).
The healing word in v. 8 is identical to that in Mk. 2 : 11 : ἔγειρε ἆρον
τὸν κράβατόν σου καὶ (περιπάτει ; Mk. ὕπαγε). The demonstration
of health by carrying the stretcher also occurs in Mk. 2 : 12. On the
basis of these form-critical observations, one would be inclined to
conclude that the traditional miracle story comprises vv. 2-9b and
not vv. 9c ff. where a Sabbath conflict is narrated in a number of short,
dramatic scenes. The stylistic difference, an *aporia*, and the content
of vv. 9c ff. indeed point in the same direction. In the same way the
healing of the man born blind (c. 9) resembles the Synoptic healing
miracles. Form seems to imply that v. 7 is the conclusion of the traditional story and again it converges with style and other indications
(see p. 35). There is nothing quite like the miracle of the wine in the
Synoptics, but the general form of the pericope resembles that of a
miracle story. [1] The raising of Lazarus (c. 11) contains a number of
themes which are familiar in the Synoptics, but on the basis of form,
one would expect that the extended dialogues in vv. 7-10, 20-27 did
not belong to the traditional miracle story. This is affirmed by *aporias*
as well as content.

B) *Style*

As indicated, Schweizer noticed that his style characteristics appeared very rarely in a few Synoptic-like pericopes and he, Jeremias, and
Kümmel concluded that these pericopes had been taken from tradition
although not one of them accepted the sēmeia source-hypothesis.
This method of identifying traditional material has not yet been worked
out and I want to attempt it as an answer to Ruckstuhl. We can answer
him best if we make use of his list. He extended Schweizer's list in such
a way that more characteristics appeared in the mentioned pericopes —
but he could not hide the difference. [2]

I give Ruckstuhl's list with the figures for the frequency of the appearance of each
characteristic in the following formula : a+b/c+d where a = Jn., b = 1-3 John/c =
rest of the New Testament, but counting an expression only once when it occurs in

---

[1] Cf. Bultmann, 79; the basic features agree with e.g. Mk. 6 : 35-44.
[2] *Literarische Einheit*, 203-5.

Synoptic parallel portions, d = the total number of Synoptic parallel portions minus the one counted in c. (I have depended on Ruckstuhl or Schweizer for many of the figures in this list. My own figures depend on the concordance of Moulton and Geden, fourth impression.)

1. τότε οὖν : 4/0 (= 4+0/0+0).
2. οὖν *historicum* : 146/8. This one is difficult to define exactly. Usually οὖν has argumentative force but in Jn. it is frequently used simply as a narrative link. Sometimes it occurs in narrative material to resume a preceding name (4 : 6), a word (6 : 10), or a concept (6 : 14). Then it is a little more than merely a narrative link, and therefore Schweizer (*Ego Eimi*, 90) does not count it. But this usage is still very typical of Jn. and I shall count it although it appears in some miracle stories. (The only instances I could find which are not clearly argumentative in the Synoptics are Mt. 18 : 26, 29; Lk. 3 : 7; 19 : 12). So I take as οὖν *historicum* the whole classification no. 2 in Arndt-Gingrich, *Lexicon*.
3. ἄν = ἐάν : 5/0.
4. τὰ 'Ιεροσόλυμα : 4/0.
5. ἵνα and ὅτι *epexegeticum* : 11+12/0. (Ruckstuhl overlooked 11 : 4).
6. Asyndeton *epicum* : 39/5.
7. Inversion of previous sentence ending : 6/?
8. Article + ἐμός in attributive position : 25+1/0 (The figures of Fortna, 206).
9. Noun used as attributive : 9/1.
10. Unusual word separation : 12/?
11. Collective neuter singular : 4/0.
12. καθὼς καί : 6+2/1.
13. οὐ ... ἀλλ' ἵνα : 10+1/1 (Ruckstuhl overlooked 1 : 31; 3 : 17; 12 : 9; 12 : 47; 17 : 15).
14. οὐχ' ὅτι ... ἀλλ' ὅτι : 2+2/1.
15. ὥρα ἵνα ; ὥρα ὅτε : 8/0.
16. ἀπεκρίθη καὶ εἶπεν : 30/2.
17. Independent use of singular ἐκεῖνος : 44+6/11 (The figures of Fortna, 210).
18. ὥρα with personal pronoun : 6/1.
19. παρρησίᾳ : 7/1.
20. οὐ μὴ ... εἰς τὸν αἰῶνα : 6/1.
21. παροιμία : 4/0.
22. σκοτία (for σκότος) : 8+6/2+1.
23. λαμβάνειν τινά : 5+1/0.
24. Σίμων Πέτρος : 17/2.
25. τίθημι ψυχήν : 8+2/0.
26. μέντοι : 5/3.
27. γύναι (of Jesus' mother) : 2/0.
28. φανεροῦν with reflexive : 2/0.
29. Metaphoric μεταβαίνειν : 2+1/0.
30. μαρτυρεῖν περί τινος (of a person) : 17+2/0.
31. ἀφ' ἑαυτοῦ : 13/1.
32. τῇ ἐσχάτῃ ἡμέρᾳ : 7/0.
33. οὐ ... πώποτε : 4+1/1.
34. μικρός (of time) : 11/3+1,

35. ἀνθρακιά : 2/0

36. ἐκ τούτου : 2/0.

37. πάλιν + δεύτερος : 2/2. This is one of the two characteristics in the list which I reject. This one is not typical enough of Jn. because the only other appearance in Jn. is in 21 : 16, and it appears twice in the rest of the New Testament (Mt. 26 : 42; Acts 10 : 15). (Fortna, 211, and Schnackenburg, 'Zur Traditionsgeschichte von Jh. 4 : 46-54', BZ 8(1964)64, also reject it).

38. ἑλκύειν : 5/1.

39. ὀψάριον : 5/0.

40. ἀμὴν ἀμήν : 25/0.

41. Metaphoric ὑπάγειν and πορεύεσθαι : 20/2+1.

42. πιστεύειν εἴς τινα : 34+3/8 (Fortna, 211).

43. μετὰ τοῦτο : 4/1.

44. οὐ ... ἐὰν(εἰ)μή (or reversed) : 19/16+1.

45. Partitive ἐκ : 31+3/26+3. These are Schweizer's figures; it is not clear what they include. The characteristic is better defined by Fortna (209f.) : — quite typical of Jn. is τις, πολλοί or οὐδείς + ἐκ 25/[1]. The noun + ἐκ ("from among") occurs 3/[8] (in 4 : 7 and 18 : 3 ἐκ denotes origin), but it will also have to be counted because grammatically it is the same construction. The noun + ἐκ ("made of") : 3/[1]. The final figures are 31/[10].

46. εἶναι or γεννηθῆναι ἐκ : 22+26/11+6 (Fortna, 207).

47. (ἐ)ὰν (μή) τις : 24+4/19+2.

48. ἐντεῦθεν : 6/4.

49. ὥρα ἐν ᾗ : 3/0. I also reject this one. The analogous expression is found with καιρός, χρόνος and ἡμέρα in the rest of the New Testament so that it is surely no more than accident that it does not appear with ὥρα elsewhere (Fortna, 211).

50. πιάζειν : 8/4.

In the following table it can be clearly seen how these characteristics are distributed in the Gospel. The number of the characteristic is put in the first column next to the verse in which it appears. It was not necessary to include all the discourses because the characteristics abound in them in any case.

Conclusions from column I of the table.

At this stage, we only give attention to a few of the most striking features. In the two discourses included the highest frequencies are reached : 5 : 19-47 (an *average* of 1.0 *per verse*) and 6 : 26-59 (1.1). There are also many characteristics in a number of the narrative portions : 1 : 13-25 (0.8); 7 : 1-13 (1.0); 9 : 8-41 (1.0); 11 : 45-57 (1.0). Therefore it is striking that the most of the short miracle pericopes contain very few : 2 : 1-12 (0.3); 5 : 1-9 (0.1); 9 : 1-7 (0.4). 4 : 46-54 has 0.6 but with one exception (v. 48 which is probably J-*vide infra*) it is only οὖν *historicum*, a nearly meaningless, small word which is such a favourite of John that it could have slipped in while he was rewriting his source.

Ch.	Verse	I	II
1	1	7	
	2		76
	3		76
	4		
	5	22, 22	
	6		
	7	30	52, 65
	8	13, 17, 30	76
	9		66
	10		66, 66, 66
			74
	11		74
	12	23, 42	79
	13	46	
	14		
	15	30	77
	16		
	17		
	18	17, 33	79, 81
	19		55, 56, 65
	20		76
	21		62
	22	2	
	23		
	24	45	
	25		
	26		
	27		
	28		
	29		66, 81
	30		76, 76
	31	13	72
	32		65
	33	17	76, 79, 80
	34		65
	35		
	36		
	37		
	38		
	39	2	
	40	6	
	41	24	
	42	6	
	43		
	44		
	45	6	
	46		
	47	6	
	48	16	
	49		62, 69
	50	16	78
	51	40	

Ch.	Verse	I	II
2	1		
	2		
	3		
	4	18, 27	67, 70
	5		
	6		55
	7		
	8		
	9		
	10		
	11	42	72
	12	43	
	13		55
	14		
	15	45	60, 69
	16	48	
	17	6	
	18	2, 16	55
	19	16	
	20	2	55, 63
	21	17	
	22	2	
	23	4, 9, 42	
	24		
	25	30	76

Ch.	Verse	I	II
4	1	2	
	2		
	3		
	4		
	5	2	
	6	2, 6	
	7	6	
	8		
	9	2	55
	10	16	57, 63, 76
			80
	11		
	12		
	13	16	
	14	20	61
	15		
	16		
	17	16	
	18		
	19		
	20		
	21	15	67
	22		55
	23	15	67, 69
	24	76	

Ch.	Verse	I	II
4	25	17	
	26		
	27	26	
	28	2	
	29		73
	30	6	
	31		
	32		63
	33	2	
	34	5	54, 81
	35		
	36		
	37		53, 80
	38		
	39	10, 42, 45	52, 65
	40	2	
	41		52
	42		52, 66
	43		
	44		65
	45	2	
	46	2	
	47		
	48	2, 44	
	49		76
	50		
	51		
	52	2, 2	
	53	2	
	54		

Ch.	Verse	I	II
5	1		55
	2	4	
	3		
	4		
	5		
	6		
	7		62
	8		
	9		
	10	2	55, 76
	11	17	62, 79
	12	6	73, 76, 80
	13		
	14		69
	15	6	55
	16		51, 55
	17		54, 62
	18		51, 55

		I	II
5	19	2, 3, 17, 31, 40, 44 47	59, 79
	20	10	54, 82
	21		
	22		59
	23		
	24	29, 40	75
	25	15, 40	67
	26		
	27		76
	28		67, 76
	29		
	30	8, 8, 31	59, 76
	31	30	65, 68
	32	30, 30	65, 80
	33		65
	34		65, 71
	35	17	
	36	30	54, 54, 65 79
	37	17, 30, 33	79, 81
	38	17	79
	39	30	
	40		
	41		
	42		
	43	23, 23	
	44		
	45		80
	46	17	57
	47		
6	1		
	2		
	3		
	4	9	55
	5	2	
	6		71
	7		62
	8	24	
	9	39	
	10	2	
	11	2, 39	
	12		
	13	2, 45	
	14	2	66, 81
	15	2	

		I	II
6	16		
	17	22	70
	18		
	19	2	
	20		
	21	2	
	22		
	23	6	69
	24	2	
	25		
	26	14, 16, 40	75
	27	9	69
	28	2	
	29	5, 16, 17, 42	56
	30		54, 75
	31		
	32	2, 40	63
	33		66, 80, 81
	34	2	
	35	33, 42	
	36		75
	37	11	68
	38	8	81
	39	5, 11, 32, 45	56, 79, 81
	40	5, 32, 42	56, 75, 76 76
	41	2	55, 81
	42		
	43	16	
	44	32, 38, 44	76, 81
	45		
	46		64, 68, 79 81
	47	40	
	48		76
	49		
	50	5, 45	75, 81
	51	47	61, 66, 76 81
	52	2	55
	53	2, 40, 44	
	54	32	76
	55		69, 69
	56		
	57	12	75
	58		61, 75, 76 81
	59		71

		I	II
6	60	2	69
	61		
	62		81
	63		59, 80
	64	45	80
	65	44	76
	66	36	
	67	2	
	68	24	62
	69		
	70		62
	71		77
7	1		55
	2	9	55
	3	2, 48	54
	4	28	66
	5	42	
	6	2, 8, 17	
	7	30	66
	8		70, 76
	9		71
	10		
	11	2, 17	55
	12	10	
	13	19, 26	55
9	1		
	2		
	3	13	54, 62, 72
	4		54, 54, 81
	5		66, 69, 71
	6	45	69
	7	2	
	8	2	80
	9	6, 6, 6, 17	
	10	2	
	11	2, 17	62, 73
	12	17	
	13	6	
	14		
	15	2	76
	16	2, 6, 45	64, 69, 73 73
	17	2	
	18	2	55
	19		
	20	2, 16	
	21		
	22	47	55, 55, 71
	23		76

I		II	I		II	I		II
9 24	2	73	11 33	2	55	18 1	9	71
25	2, 17	62	34			2		
26	2	76	35	6		3	2	
27		62	36	2	55, 82	4	2	
28		69, 69	37	45		5		62
29			38	2	76	6	2	76
30	5, 16	53, 70, 75	39			7	2	76, 76
		76	40			8		62, 76
31	47		41			9	45	59
32			42		71	10	2, 24, 38	
33	44	59, 64	43			11	2	79
34	16	74	44	6		12	2	55
35	6, 42		45	2, 42, 45	55	13		
36	16, 17, 42		46	45		14		55, 73
37	17		47	2	69, 73	15	24	
38			48	42		16	2	
39		66	49	45	59, 69	17	2, 9, 17	69, 73
40	6, 45	69	50		73	18	35	
41		57	51	31	69, 71, 76	19	2	
			52	13		20	19	55, 62, 66
1			53			21		
11 2			54	2, 19	55	22		69
3	2	82	55		55	23		62, 65
4	5		56	2		24	2	
5		76	57	47, 50		25	2, 17, 24	
6	2					26		
7	43		12 1	2		27	2	
8		55, 74	2	2		28	2	
9	47	62, 66	3	2		29	2	73
10	47	71	4			30	16, 44	
11	43		5			31	2	55, 59
12	2		6	14		32		
13	9		7	2		33	2	55
14	1, 19		8			34	31	62
15	10		9	2, 13	55	35		62
16	2		10			36	7, 8, 8, 8,	55, 57, 62
17	2	69	11	10, 42	55		8, 46, 46,	66, 66, 76
18	4		12				48	
19	45	55	13			37	2, 46	62, 65, 66
20	2		14			38		55, 69
21	2		15			39		55
22			16		58	40	2	
23			17	2	65			
24	32		18	10	51			
25	42		19	2	59, 66			
26	20, 42	61, 76						
27		66, 81						
28		71						
29								
30		70						
31	2	55						
32	2	69, 76						

6 : 16-21 has 0.5 with οὖν twice. 6 : 1-15 has 0.7 — John's hand seems to have had more influence here. The total average for five of the short miracle pericopes (2 : 1-12; 4 : 46-54; 5 : 1-9; 6 : 16-21; 9 : 1-7) is 0.4. We contrast this with the five other narrative pericopes mentioned above, 2 : 13-25; 6 : 60-71; 7 : 1-13; 9 : 8-41 and 11 : 45-57, which have an average total of 0.92.[1] Thus Ruckstuhl's style characteristics appear *2.3 times* more in a few typical Johannine narrative passages than in the short miracle stories of the Gospel.

Additions to Ruckstuhl's List

This result can be tested. We may gather more Johannine style characteristics than Schweizer and Ruckstuhl. Some significant ones have been overlooked. In addition to this, we are not as limited as they were because the aim of our test is different. In the first place, they had to be very careful in their selection of characteristics because they had to consider the possibility that a later redactor could have imitated John's style. To disprove redaction hypotheses, they concentrated on "möglichst unbetonte sprachliche Kleinigkeiten"[2] and tried not to include expressions with a typical Johannine content because they are imitable. As we are not testing for such a redactor, we may include such expressions if they are characteristic enough of John. (We shall have to keep in mind that they are less conclusive than their figures seem to indicate because they are more conscious, and unconscious linguistic habits are of course better for statistical purposes). In the second place, we are able to gather more because Ruckstuhl and Schweizer drew their conclusions from the *presence* of these characteristics while we find their *absence* significant. Théy had to be very careful to make sure that their characteristics infrequently occur in the rest of the New Testament because the appearance of only a few of them had to prove that certain passages were Johannine. On the contrary, the more typical Johannine style characteristics we can gather, the better we can judge whether they are really scarce in the miracle stories. But, of course, our characteristics still have to be typical of John. For statistical purposes, I have decided on the limit that they have to occur in Jn. at least four times as frequently as in the rest of the New Testament, or as in the Synoptic Gospels if they are typical of historical material.[3]

---

[1] Afterwards I tested this figure by listing c. 18 — and it gave 1.0.

[2] *Ego Eimi*, 88.

[3] This is at least 4/7 or 6/[5].

There is one more limitation : we could not include the many Johannine characteristics which in any case do not occur in narrative material in Jn. [1]

51. διὰ τοῦτο ... ὅτι (reason) : 6+1/3.[2]
52. πιστεύειν + διά (reason) : 6/0.[3]
53. ἐν τούτῳ referring to a clause : 4+12/5.[4]
54. ἔργον or ἐργάζεσθαι for the Messianic works of Christ : 20/2.
55. οἱ Ἰουδαῖοι (pl.) : 67/[10+6] — but it occurs only four times in the Synoptics outside the combination with βασιλεύς/βασιλεία.
56. The definition-clause : τοῦτο/αὕτη + ἐστὶν + a reference to a preceding concept + an explication of it : 7+5/1.[5]
57. εἰ irrealis : 12+1/14+2.[6]
58. τὸ πρῶτον (at first) : 3/0.
59. οὐκ ... οὐδείς (or inflexions) : 15+1/15 : 1.[7]
60. The genitive before article + noun : 5/[1].[8]
61. εἰς τὸν αἰῶνα : 12+2/11+1.
62. ἀπεκρίθη(σαν) or ἀπεκρίνεται (not followed by another verbum dicendi) + direct speech : 45/12.
63. The typical misunderstandings based on dualism found in the Gospel : 10/ ?[9]
64. παρά of Jesus coming from God : 6/0.[10]
65. μαρτυρεῖν/-ία : 47+17/49.[11]

---

[1] Bultmann used a great number of characteristics to identify the hand of the Evangelist. I examined them and found the most not characteristic enough. Of the thirty-two which Smith, *Composition and Order*, 9f., lists as Bultmann's most important ones, thirteen occur too frequently in the rest of the New Testament: numbers : 5, 6, 7, 11, 12, 13, 14, 18, 20, 21, 22, 26, 31.

[2] 5 : 16, 18; 8 : 47; 10 : 17; 12 : 18, 39 + 1 Jn. 3 : 1/Mt. 12 : 13; 24 : 44; 1 Thes. 2 : 13. (The texts will only be given when they cannot easily be found in a concordance).

[3] 1 : 7; 4 : 39, 41, 42; 14 : 11; 17 : 20.

[4] Frequently the clause follows and is introduced by ὅτι (4 : 37; 9 :30; 1 Jn. 3 : 16; 4 : 9, 10, 13; Lk. 10 : 20); or by a word like ἐάν (13 : 35; 1 Jn. 2 : 3), ὅταν (1 Jn. 5 : 2), ἵνα (15 : 8; 1 Jn. 4 : 17); or without such a word (1 Jn. 3 : 10, 24; 4 : 2); sometimes the clause precedes (1 Jn. 2 : 5; 3 : 19; 1 Cor. 4 : 4; 11 : 22; 2 Cor. 8 : 10; Phil. 1 : 18). Ἐν τούτῳ is not counted when it means "therefore" (16 : 30; Acts 24 : 16; 2 Cor. 5 : 2).

[5] 1 : 19; 3 : 19; 6 : 29, 39, 40; 15 : 12; 17 : 3+1 Jn. 1 : 5; 3 : 23; 5 : 3, 4, 11/Rom. 10 : 8. Many other cases in Jn. are nearly the same construction : 3 : 16; 16 : 9ff.; 15 : 21; 1 Jn. 2 : 25; 3 : 11, 16; 4 : 9, 10; 5 : 9, 14 (cf. Bultmann, 177, 5).

[6] Number 31 in Schweizer's list. Texts given in E.A. Abbott, *Johannine Grammar* (1906) par. 2078c : 4 : 10; 5 : 46; 8 : 19, 39; 9 : 41; 14 : 7, 28; 15 : 19, 22, 24; 18 : 36; 19 : 11.

[7] Number 18 in Schweizer's list.

[8] E.g. 2 : 15 τῶν κολλυβιστῶν ἐξέχεεν τὰ κέρματα. Schweizer, number 30.

[9] 2 : 20; 3 : 3f.; 4 : 10ff., 32f.; 6 : 32ff.; 7 : 34ff.; 14 : 4f., 7ff., 22ff.; 16 : 17f. (Bultmann, 89, 2).

[10] 6 : 46; 7 : 29; 19 : 16, 33; 16 : 27; 17 : 8.

[11] Of course the instances of μ. περί τινος (Ruckstuhl, number 30) will not be recounted.

66. κόσμος : 78+24/83.
67. ὥρα in the sense of the time which God had appointed for Jesus : 13/[2+1].
68. Chiasmus : 23+2/ ?[1]
69. Word separation : 56/53+6.[2]
70. οὔπω : 12+1/13+2.
71. τοῦτο/ταῦτα referring back + *verbum dicendi* : nowhere in Mark; twice in Matthew; fairly frequent in Luke.[3]
72. φανεροῦν : 9/[3].
73. ἄνθρωπος of Jesus : 15/[7+3].[4]
74. Grammatical parataxis for logical hypotaxis, one of the typical Semitic characteristics of John's language : 14/ ?[5]
75. Conditional parataxis in a subordinate clause (also Semitic) : 13/ ?[6]
76. Remarkable repetitions are also typical of John.[7]
77. τινα λέγειν meaning saying something about someone : 6/1 (perhaps more).[8]
78. The subordinating use of ὅτι ("because" ... at the beginning of a sentence) : 5/7.[9]
79. *Casus pendens* : 27/[28].[10]
80. The periphrastic construction of ἐστίν + article + *praesens* participle (singular) :
81. 12+2/11+1.[11]
82. Formulistic participles like ὁ πέμψας με are also typical of John : 31/ ?[12]
     φιλεῖν : 13/11+1.

---

[1] Schweizer, number 33.

[2] Schweizer, number 32.

[3] 5 : 34; 6 : 6, 59; 7 : 39; 8 : 20, 30; 9 : 22; 11 : 51; 12 : 33; 14 : 25, 29; 15 : 11; 16 : 1, 4, 33; 17 : 13. It is used as transition in 7 : 9; 11 : 28; 12 : 36; 18 : 1; and also in 9 : 6; 11 : 11, 43 (in the last three instances it apparently belongs to the previous verse as transition between two literary strata; I have so categorized them). Note that identical the same construction appears with γράφειν in 1 Jn. 1 : 4; 2 : 1, 26; 5 : 13. (Bultmann, 157, 1).

[4] 4 : 29; 5 : 12; 7 : 46; 8 : 40; 9 : 11, 16*bis*, 24; 10 : 33; 11 : 47, 50; 18 : 14, 17, 29; 19 : 5.

[5] Listed by K. Beyer, *Semitische Syntax im Neuen Testament* I/1 (1962) 280 (quoted in Schnackenburg, 93) : 1 : 10, 11; 7 : 21, 22, 26, 34, 36; 8 : 52, 57; 9 : 34; 10 : 12; 11 : 8; 14 : 9; 16 : 22. Note that Barrett, 6, calls parataxis "perhaps the most striking feature of John's style."

[6] Beyer, 269 : 3 : 12; 5 : 24; 6 : 26, 30, 36, 40, 50, 57, 58; 9 : 30; 12 : 47; 15 : 10; 20 : 29.

[7] Cf. Schnackenburg, 96, 99f.; Barrett, 5. In the listed passages I took the following : 1 : 2, 3, 8, 20, 30bis, 33; 2 : 25; 4 : 10, 24, 49; 5 : 10, 12, 27, 28, 30; 6 : 40*bis*, 44, 48, 51, 54, 58, 65; 7 : 8; 9 : 15, 23, 26, 30; 11 : 5, 26, 32, 38, 51; 18 : 6, 7*bis*, 8, 36.

[8] 1 : 15; 6 : 71; 8 : 27, 54; 10 : 35, 36 (Bultmann, 50, 2; Barrett, 140).

[9] 1 : 50; 8 : 45; 15 : 19; 16 : 6; 20 : 29.

[10] 1 : 12, 18, 33; 3 : 26, 32; 5 : 11, 19, 36, 37, 38; 6 : 39, 46; 7 : 18; 8 : 26; 10 : 1, 25; 12 : 48f.; 14 : 12, 13, 21, 26; 15 : 2, 5; 17 : 2, 24; 18 : 11 — C.F. Burney, *The Aramaic Origin of the Fourth Gospel* (1922) 64. A useful definition for *casus pendens* seems to me to be : a nominative or accusative standing loosely at the beginning of a phrase and taken up in the phrase by a pronoun.

[11] 1 : 33; 4 : 10, 37; 5 : 12, 32, 45; 6 : 33, 63, 64; 8 : 54; 9 : 8; 14 : 21. I placed it lower on the list because the plural form of the construction occurs 2+1/9+3.

[12] Schweizer, 98. I used the list in E. Norden, *Agnostos Theos* (1913) 382.

To avoid a vicious circle, I have taken all the significant Johannine style characteristics which I could find and have not excluded any from this list because they appear in portions which seem to me to be from the source. The result is that twelve of these characteristics do occur in such portions.[1]

Conclusions from columns I and II

Clearly the conclusions from column I are affirmed in column II. Now that we have more characteristics, it can even without calculations be seen in a quick review of the table that the Johannine characteristics are evenly distributed in the Gospel, with the exception of some short Synoptic-like pericopes, mostly miracle stories. The following list gives the averages of the total number of Johannine characteristics per verse (with Ruckstuhl's averages in brackets) for the different pericopes. The material is roughly divided into three groups : sēmeia source (S), Johannine narrative (JN) and Johannine discourse material (JD). These divisions will be justified later.

1. 1 : 1-18	JD	1.6	(0.7)
2. 1 : 19-34	JN	1.2	(0.3)
3. 1 : 35-51	S	0.7	(0.5)
4. 2 : 1-12	S	0.7	(0.3)
5. 2 : 13-25	JN	1.3	(0.8)
6. 4 : 1-9, 16-19, 27-30, 40	S	0.7	(0.6)
7. 4 : 10-15, 20-24, 31-39, 41f.	JND	1.4	(0.5)
8. 4 : 43-5, 48f.	JN	1.0	(0.6)
9. 4 : 46-7, 50-54	S	0.6	(0.6)
10. 5 : 1-9	S	0.3	(0.1)
11. 5 : 10-18	JN	2.1	(0.4)
12. 5 : 19-47	JD	1.9	(1.0)
13. 6 : 1-15	S+J	1.1	(0.7)
14. 6 : 16-21	S	0.7	(0.5)

---

[1] The following, which occur in the source, have nearly made the list, but were rejected because they are not sufficiently characteristic : (a) ἐγγὺς : 10/15+3/1(2) (the last figure refers to the source). (b) ἴδε : 15/[12]/3(?). (c) μένειν : 40+27/51/5, but John normally uses this verb in his specific theological sense, and only thirteen times does it have the normal literal sense which also occurs in the source, so that the figures should be 13/[12]. (d) θεωρεῖν : 24+1/33/3, but the word is mostly used in historical books : in the Synoptic Gospels + Acts it occurs thirty times. (e) The temporal ὡς occurs mostly in Jn. and Luke (sixty-one times) : 19/76/6. (f) ἦν δὲ : 29/21/8, but the total figure for the Synoptics + Acts is thirty-two.

14a 6 : 22-5	S	0.75	(0.5)
15. 6 : 26-59	JD	2.4	(1.1)
16. 6 : 60-71	JN	1.3	(0.5)
17. 7 : 1-13	JN	1.8	(1.0)
18. 9 : 1-2, 6-7	S	0.75	(0.5)
19. 9 : 3-5	JND	3.3	(0.3)
20. 9 : 8-41	JN	1.9	(1.0)
21. 11 : 7-10, 18-32	JD	1.5	(0.7)
22. 11 : 1-6, 11-17, 33-44	S+J	1.0	(0.6)
23. 11 : 45-57	JN	1.9	(1.0)
24. 12 : 1-8, 12-15	Trad.	0.4	(0.4)
25. 12 : 9-11, 16-19	JN	2.0	(1.0)
26. 18 : 1-40	JN	2.0	(1.0)[1]

Again the two discourses have very high averages (1.9 and 2.4). If we take the same five other narrative pericopes which we have used for comparison in the interpretation of column I (numbers 5, 16, 17, 20, 23), the total average is 1.69 (Ruckstuhl 0.92). The five short miracle stories which we have taken (numbers 4, 9, 10, 14, 18)[2] have 0.58 as average (Ruckstuhl 0.4). Thus, the characteristics appear *2.9 times more* frequently in the first than in the last (Ruckstuhl 2.3 times).[3] *I contend that this cannot be ascribed to chance and must mean that in these five miracle stories there is evidence of the influence of a style different from that of John : he must have taken them from tradition.* Of course, he probably also followed tradition in most JN material, but in the case of these five miracles, he is apparently following it with less freedom so that an identification of this tradition might be possible to some extent.

Nevertheless, some Johannine style characteristics do appear in S.

---

[1] In general the new averages correlate with Ruckstuhl's averages : in eighteen of the twenty-six divisions they are more or less the average of Ruckstuhl multiplied by two, as would be expected. Where there are differences, it seems that the extended list is a more exact instrument for identifying John's hand. To take one independent example : in the case of numbers 6 and 7, Ruckstuhl's averages do not differ notably while the new average for number 7 is twice that of number 6. This probably points in the correct direction because there are *aporias* on the basis of which the verses of number 7 can be identified as JN. (In the miracle material, it is the same case with numbers 11 and 19).

[2] This time it is necessary to exclude 4 : 48f. and 9 : 3-5 from these pericopes because they are clearly Johannine, not only because they contain many style characteristics but also for other reasons.

[3] With the new averages, this final figure of 2.9 will hardly change when all the JN passages are included.

This is due to the fact that John did not reproduce the source in a mechanical way but probably relied upon his memory. Therefore, typical Johannine expressions could slip into the source material even where John was following S fairly faithfully. This was normal in New Testament times, e.g., the style of Luke also appears in those passages where he follows the Marcan or the Q material.[1] Moreover, John consciously made some insertions in his source, a few of which we shall be able to identify with the help of the table.[2]

C) *Aporias*

In addition to the *aporias* indicating the sēmeia source, there are many others in the Gospel. For instance, chapter 21 follows upon the conclusion of the Gospel. 14 : 31 is the conclusion of a farewell discourse so that cc. 15f. seems to be a second farewell discourse. In c. 5, Jesus is in Jerusalem while in c. 6 he is, without any explanation, assumed to be in Galilee. 7 : 21ff. refers to the miracle of 5 : 1ff. as if it had just been described. 3 : 31-6 is typical Johannine elevated discourse material, inserted without any warning in an historical scene, a conversation between John the Baptist and his disciples, in which it hardly fits. Similar examples can be multiplied. They indicate that the Gospel as

---

[1] Cf. H.J. Cadbury, The Style and Literary Method of Luke II (*Harvard Theological Studies* VI, 1920) 115-205.

[2] Some appearances of characteristics in S may, of course, be accidental because the most of the characteristics also appear in the rest of the New Testament. Two other explanations were proposed. (a) The later hand imitated the former one (E. Hirsch, Stilkritik und Literaranalyse im vierten Evangelium, *ZNW* 43 (1950/1) 129f.). (b) Both had to some extent the same style because they both belonged to the same congregation (Becker, Wunder und Christologie, 133). But with a few possible exceptions, these cannot be correct because in some passages there are practically no Johannine style characteristics.

Are there any style characteristics of S which do not occur in J ? This is not to be expected. The passages where John followed S fairly faithfully are very few. Moreover, the way of expression of S would certainly have had much influence on J for the reason that S is probably followed freely in some other portions of J and the relationship of John to S was one of inner dependence (S was part of his "Bible"). Bultmann found a number of signs that the Greek of S is Semitic (cf. Smith, *Composition*, 36) and this may have some significance, but it can hardly be used to distinguish the two because the style of the whole Gospel has Semitic colouring. Fortna (214ff.) tried to find style characteristics of his much longer source, but of the thirty-five he lists, all are unconvincing with the possible exceptions of εὐθέως, Μεσσίας, πρός + dat., κραυγάζειν, ἦν (δε) (τις). For the most part either the others are too rare in the source or their absence from J is explicable by the fact that the source contains nearly all the Synoptic-like narrative material in the Gospel.

we have it was not written down at one and the same time. Probably
the process of its composition was not completely finished so that the
diverse materials incorporated were not so fully moulded into a unity
that all the seams became invisible. If a sēmeia source was redacted,
one would expect to find traces of it.[1] Here I only mention a few of the
basic ones.

1. The healing of the officer's son is concluded by 4 : 54 : "Again
this second sign Jesus performed on coming from Judaea to Galilee."
This is a reference to "the first of the signs" (2 : 11) and seems to ignore
2 : 23 and 4 : 45, where it is said that Jesus had done other signs in the
meantime. In addition, this enumeration is not continued and seems
pointless in the present Gospel.[2] Attractive explanations of the seeming
inconsistency are that 4 : 54 really means that this was the second miracle which Jesus had performed in Cana or after a jouney from Judaea to
Galilee (which also applies to the first miracle), but neither is justified
by the text, where it is directly stated that this was the second miracle
and where the phrase "on coming from Judaea to Galilee" only specifies
the time and place of the miracle as the words "at Cana in Galilee" in
2 : 11. Could it be a solution that the enumeration stems from a source
in which these two miracles were indeed the first and second ? The
critical question may be asked why, if the source enumerated its miracles, are there no traces of this enumeration in the rest of the Gospel.
The reason may be that the first two miracles are the only ones in the
Gospel that are not immediately followed by Johannine material. In
other words, in the case of the other miracle stories, John took over
from the source before its last sentence.[3]

2. There is another probable sign that the second miracle story was
taken from a source. 4 : 48 gives the impression of being a *corpus
alienum* in this story. After the officer had asked Jesus to come and

---

[1] Probably a final editing of the material by a secondary redactor was necessary
because of its unfinished state (cf. 21 : 24f.). Many students of the Gospel have the impression that the Evangelist did not fully complete his book, e.g. Kümmel, *Einleitung*,
148f.; Schnackenburg, 60; Brown, XXXVIf.

[2] The fact that seven miracles can be counted in the Gospel hardly has any significance. If the number 7 were important, it would at least have been mentioned in the
conclusion 20 : 30f. where the principle of selection is described. (Bultmann 78, 2, and
K.H. Rengstorf, art. sēmeion, *ThW* VII 244, n. 310).

[3] As has already been indicated, not only those who accept the sēmeia source agree
with this explanation of 4 : 54 : in addition to Michel, Temple, Goguel and Merlier (see
notes 14 + 16), we can also mention F. Spitta, *Das Johannesevangelium als Quelle der
Geschichte Jesu* (1910) 70, and Brown, XXXI (he would rather think of oral tradition).

heal his son, Jesus said to him : "If you do not see signs and portents, you will never believe." These words are inconsistent with the fact that the officer's question already implies belief, that he did not ask the miracle as legitimation of Jesus, and that according to v. 50, he believed the word of Jesus without seeing anything. The point of the story is that finally the miraculous power of Jesus was proved to the officer — cf. the detailed proof of the miracle in vv. 52f. — and, therefore, he and his household believed. It seems that this whole point is partly rejected by v. 48, which implies a certain criticism of a miracle-faith. Can this verse therefore be a Johannine insertion ?[1] There are other indications that this might be the case. 'Eὰν ... οὐ μὴ is a typical Johannine style characteristic.[2] V. 48 is addressed to "you" in the plural, and this must be a reference to all the Galileans who, according to v. 45, accepted Jesus on account of his miracles. This last verse does not belong to the miracle story and the theme of the multitudes super-ficially impressed by the miracles is typically Johannine (cf. 2 : 23; 6 : 2; 11 : 45ff.). It is understandable why John might have made this critical insertion here : the story subordinates faith in the word (v. 50) to miracle-faith (v. 53), whereas John is inclined to do the reverse.

3. In 20 : 30f., the Gospel is concluded with the following words : "There were indeed many other sēmeia that Jesus performed ... but these have been recorded that you may believe ..." After c. 12, no sēmeion has been described, but all the emphasis falls on the life-giving words of Jesus. (*Only* twice are the sēmeia referred to by the word ἔργον, which sets them in a wider Johannine context and connects them with the words, 14 : 11; 15 : 24). Then it is surprising that John concluded his book as though he had been describing sēmeia from beginning to end. A possible solution is that the resurrection and appearances are also sēmeia. It is probable that the final author had some such connection in mind. But still, 20 : 30f. is strange. The meaning of sēmeion in the Gospel is a miracle which Jesus himself performs — something different from the resurrection and appearances. Surely a possible explanation is that these words were the conclusion of the source and that John adopted them because he had respect for

---

[1] Schweizer, Heilung, 65; Schnackenburg, Zur Traditionsgeschichte von Joh. 4 : 46-54, *BZ* 8 (1964) 60f.; Bultmann; Fortna; J.M. Robinson, Kerygma and History in the New Testament, in : *The Bible in Modern Scholarship*, ed. J.P. Hyatt (1965) 140, and many others.

[2] Schweizer, *Ego Eimi*, 93.

his source and wanted to emphasize that his deeper interpretation of the sēmeia and the life of Jesus was based on the tradition.[1]

There are many other *aporias* which I shall point out in separating tradition and redaction. In c. 6 there seems to be a seam between v. 25 and v. 26, dividing the traditional miracle stories from the Johannine discourse. In cc. 5 and 9, it appears that the dialogue scenes are Johannine additions to the miracle stories because the dialogues start with the theme of Jesus working on the Sabbath and this theme forms no integrated part of the two miracle stories but succeeds them as an afterthought. A final example may be that the apparently Johannine conversation between Jesus and Martha in c. 11 (vv. 20ff.) creates a few obvious *aporias* and seems to be inserted into the traditional miracle story.

D) *Ideological Tensions*

The sēmeia traditions regarded miracles as a legitimate basis for faith (2 : 11; 4 : 53; 6 : 14; 20 : 30f.), but John was critical of a faith based on miracles (2 : 23; 6 : 26) and regarded the testimony of the miracles as a way of coming to faith as being a second best (14 : 11; 10 : 38; 4 : 48). If the sēmeia source is accepted, it seems that these tensions could be historically explained.

3. THE SEPARATION OF S AND J

1. *Water changed into wine* : 2 : 1-11

Apparently John faithfully followed S, and his insight into the deeper meaning of the miracle is reflected in only a few phrases in vv. 4, 6, 9, 11.

Four of the eight style characteristics in this pericope appear in the last part of v. 4 (from γύναι ... — see the table). There is tension between the direct refusal of v. 4b and the following, where Jesus immediately performs the miracle. This phrase prepares the symbolical meaning of the miracle by using "hour" in the typical Johannine sense of hour of glorification (see p. 128). In 7 : 6, which is probably Johannine, Jesus also refuses to work miracles, saying that his "time" has "not yet" come. So at least οὔπω ... μου is quite probably J.[2]

---

[1] Schnackenburg, Traditionsgeschichte, 79; Jeremias, Literarkritik, 46; Bultmann; Fortna; Dibelius, *Formgeschichte,* 37, note 3.

[2] With the exception of Bultmann, nearly all who have worked on the source criticism of this pericope, thought so, e.g., Schwartz, Aporien (1908) 512; K.L. Schmidt, Die

In v. 6 the phrase κατὰ τὸν καθαρισμὸν τῶν Ἰουδαίων may be J[1] because the plural οἱ Ἰουδαῖοι is typical of John (it rarely appears in the Synoptics) and serves here to give the pericope the same symbolical meaning which John attaches to the cleansing of the temple in the next pericope : Jesus replaces the Jewish religion.

In v. 9 the words καὶ οὐκ ... ὕδωρ are probably J[2] because the syntax is strained by them and the οὐκ ᾔδει πόθεν apparently has the Christological sense which it frequently has in Jn. (3 : 8; 4 : 11; 7 : 27f. etc.) : the world does not know whence the Revealer comes.

S would have contained v. 11a (cf. 4 : 54) and probably also v. 11c (the typical miracle-theology). But in 11b φανεροῦν is a Johannine style characteristic, and δόξα also seems to be used in a typical Johannine sense, referring to the deeper meaning of the miracle (cf. 1 : 14 and see pp. 119ff.). Thus 11b is probably J.[3]

These four phrases are the only clues for the symbolical interpretation of the miracle. This kind of symbolism seems to be strange to the character of S (see p. 44) but typically Johannine.

2. *A Nobleman's Son Healed* : 4 : 46-54

With the exception of vv. 48f. which are apparently a Johannine critical note (see p. 28), the pericope seems to be basically traditional, especially the detailed proof of the miracle in vv. 51-3, which suits the character of S.

3. *The Healing at Bethesda* : 5 : 1ff.

In the first two miracle stories, John had to make insertions because their meaning is not explained by discourses. Here, however, a Johannine discourse follows, and indeed vv. 2-9b show no signs of John's

---

johanneische Charakter der Erzählung vom Hochzeitswunder in Kana, in : *Harnack-Ehrung* (1921) 37; Goguel, *Introd.*, 390; Dodd, *Hist. Trad.*, 226; E. Haenchen, Johanneische Probleme, *ZThK* 56 (1959) 34, note 1; Schweizer, Heilung, 65; Schnackenburg, Traditionsgeschichte, 63 ("vielleicht"). Fortna (31), Haenchen and others think the tension between Jesus' refusal in v. 4 and the rest of the story may be removed by excising at least the whole of v. 4, but some refusal would probably have been traditional because for S, Jesus is the great miracle-worker who always acts on his own initiative and whose actions are never determined by others (7 : 1-13; 11 : 6).

[1] Dodd, *Hist. Trad.*, 226; Becker, Wunder, 142; Fortna, 32.

[2] Bultmann, 82, 9; Jeremias, Literarkritik, 35; Schmidt, Charakter, 41; Faure, Zitate, 110; Fortna, 33.

[3] Bultmann, 79 (cf. *Ergänzungsheft*) and Fortna, 37.

hand. V.1 is clearly his introduction — the expression "feast (Passover) of the Jews" is typical (2 : 13; 6 : 4; 7 : 2; 11 : 55). Vv. 2-9b, however, have the basic form of a Synoptic miracle story (as we have seen — pp. 15 f.). The setting of the story in vv. 2f. is more elaborate than usual in the Synoptics, but it would not have been invented by John, for without it the reader would not have understood the dialogue in vv. 6f. (which apparently belonged to S), and, what is more, we shall see that there is archaeological evidence that there probably was such a pool in Jerusalem (p. 44). Between v. 9b and c there appears to be a seam. The point of the story as it now stands in vv. 1-18 is that Jesus healed the man on the Sabbath but it is strange that this is only mentioned in v. 9c at the end of the real miracle story — in the Sabbath conflict stories in the Synoptics, it is always stated at the beginning that it was Sabbath (e.g. Mk. 3 : 1ff. parr.). By the addition of vv. 9c ff., the point of v. 9b (the man carried his stretcher) is also changed : in the miracle story it demonstrates that the miracle is real,[1] but in vv. 9c ff. it is the reason for the conflict with the Jews. Bultmann agrees that the Sabbath theme is a secondary addition but thinks that it was added at an earlier stage and that vv. 2-16 all belonged to S. It seems clear, however, that John added vv. 9c ff. (Of course, he would have known about Jesus' Sabbath conflicts from other traditions.) Vv. 1-9 contain very few Johannine style characteristics while vv. 10-18 contain many (averages of 0.3 and 2.1 respectively !). Conflict with the Jews is a main theme of John, while it probably clashes with the character of S. In vv. 10-18 alone there are four dramatic dialogue scenes, a feature which seems to be characteristic of John's narrative style. In c. 9 a Sabbath conflict with the Jews is again secondarily connected with a miracle story, and it also contains many Johannine style characteristics as well as a great number of short scenes, and there are also other indications that it is Johannine. Therefore the conclusion is fairly obvious that only 5 : 2-9b is S.[2]

4. *The Feeding of the Five Thousand and the Walking on the Water* : 6 : 1-25

Vv. 1-15 contain more Johannine style characteristics, with an average of 1.1, than the other short miracle pericopes, although this

---

[1] Cf. Mk. 2 : 12; Bultmann, *Geschichte der Synoptische Tradition*[7] (1967) 240.

[2] Dodd, *Hist. Trad.*, 178; Haenchen, Probleme, 48f.; Schnackenburg, Traditions-geschichte, 80; Fortna, 52.

average is still lower than our average for normal Johannine narrative (1.69). It is also clear from the content that John reproduced S with more freedom.[1] Fortunately, the Synoptics contain the same basic story so that we have other means of deciding what belonged to S. All the details in this pericope which also appear in the parallel Synoptic stories were probably imparted in S although John might have narrated them in his own words. This applies to most of the details in vv. 1-3 (cf. Mt. 15 : 29-31), v. 5 (cf. Mk. 8 : 34), the bulk of vv. 7-13 (cf. especially Mk. 6 : 37-44), and v. 15b (Mk. 6 : 46). The features in these verses which do not occur in the Synoptic accounts are not conscious changes of John. In v. 2 the phrase, "because they saw the sēmeia", seems to be a Johannine wording (cf. 2 : 23; 4 : 45), but in content it does not say more than Mt. 15 : 29f. It differs from Mk. 6 parr. that Jesus takes the initiative in v. 5., but this is typical of the character of the tradition which we have in S (see p. 74), and it occurs already in the parallel in Mk. 8 : 1ff. The individualising of actors (names of two disciples; the boy) and the extensive use of direct speech are also typical of the tradition, and there is no reason why John would have created it. V. 6 is a typical Johannine parenthetical note explaining something said (cf. 7 : 39; 11 : 51; 12 : 33), but it is quite possible that something of the kind could have been part of S which frequently emphasizes Jesus' omniscience (cf. 11 : 11ff.; 1 : 42, 47ff.).

Three portions remain, and they are possibly conscious additions of John.

(a) V. 4 interrupts the narrative, contains two Johannine style characteristics, and is parallel to the many other Johannine references to Jewish feasts (e.g., 2 : 13; 7 : 2; 11 : 55). In addition to this, it seems to prepare for the symbolical explication of the miracle in the following discourse, where there is reference to the Eucharist, (which must be understood in the context of the Jewish Passover). It is fairly certain that 6 : 4 is J.[2]

(b) The last four words of v. 12 have a Johannine ring : the disciples had to collect the pieces left over ἵνα μή τι ἀπόληται. In v. 27 the material bread is called ἡ βρῶσις ἡ ἀπολλυμένη, and, as such, it is contrasted with the spiritual bread. Therefore, these four words in v. 12

---

[1] W. Wilkens, Evangelist und Tradition im Jhev., *ThZ* 16 (1960) 81-90 over-emphasized this.

[2] Many agree that 6 : 4 is inserted : Schwartz, Aporien (1908) 121; R.H. Fuller, *Interpreting the Miracles* (1963) 89; Fortna, 57; Bultmann, 156, 6 (by final redactor).

may be a conscious Johannine reference to the symbolical meaning of the bread.[1]

(c) Vv. 14-15a. The last 5 words of v. 14 are probably J (cf. 1 : 9; 11 : 27, and κόσμος is a Johannine style characteristic), but the rest of the content of this verse probably belonged to S because it is typical of S to conclude a miracle story with the positive reaction of those who experienced the miracle and the title "prophet" eminently suits S (see pp. 87 ff.). V. 15a seems to be in contrast to this. The multitude misunderstand the miracle and want to seize Jesus to make him an earthly king. This may be criticism by John of the miracle-faith of v. 14.[2] It would anticipate the rejection of miracle-faith in v. 26 (J). This seems to be affirmed by the fact that 18 : 36 reveals that John was interested in the contrast between Jesus' spiritual kingship and earthly kingship and by the fact that the normal form of a miracle story never describes the further results of a miracle.

The walking on the water (vv. 16-21). There is no sign that this pericope is symbolically interpreted by John. It contains only a few Johannine style characteristics (0.7) and there is no other indication of John's hand in it. (The ἐγώ εἰμι of v. 20 also occurs in Mk. 6 : 50).[3]

Vv. 22-5 are very confused, but one thing is clear, namely, that the verses are meant to demonstrate the miracle that Jesus crossed the sea without a boat.[4] S is always interested in demonstration so that this is one reason to accept that at least the basis of this portion is S. The other reason is that there is a seam between v. 25 and v. 26. (1) The question of v. 25b is not answered. (2) There is a superficial contradiction : according to v. 14, the multitude accepted Jesus because they had seen the sēmeion, but v. 26 says they seek him *not* because they had seen sēmeia, and in v. 30 they even ask Jesus to show them a sēmeion so that they can believe ! The cause of the contradiction is that the word sēmeion has a deeper meaning in J than in S : in vv. 26ff. it is connected to the symbolical interpretation of the miracle. (3) The seam may be affirmed by the fact that vv. 26ff. contain an abundance

---

[1] Dodd, *Hist. Trad.*, 207 ; Fortna, 60.

[2] Fortna, 60ff., regards vv. 14b+15a as J. F. Hahn, *Christologische Hoheitstitel*[2] (1964) 392, regards vv. 14f. as traditional. Bultmann, 157, and Schnackenburg, Traditions-geschichte, 81, take the entire vv. 14f. as J.

[3] So also Bultmann, 158ff. ; Dodd, *Hist. Trad.*, 196ff.

[4] Probably something like vv. 23-4 is a later addition, but it is not certain whether it was done by John (Bultmann, 160 ; Fortna, 67f.), by a final redactor (Schnackenburg, 45), or even by one of the compilers of S who wanted to clarify the demonstration of the miracle.

of Johannine style characteristics (four in v. 26, two in v. 27, one in v. 28, five in v. 29, etc.). The conclusion is highly probable that John followed S in vv. 1-25 and that vv. 26ff. are, at least to a great extent, his own composition.[1]

5. The Man Born Blind : c. 9

Vv. 1, 6-7 appear to have been part of a short miracle story in S. They show fairly few Johannine style characteristics. The features in them are customary in the Synoptic healing miracles so that John probably took them from tradition.[2] The name "Siloam" is interpreted in a Johannine sense, but this does not mean that John created v. 7 and the name because there was a pool in Jerusalem called Siloam. Only the interpretation of the name is very probably John's addition because it is an important theme in Jn. that Jesus is $\dot{\alpha}\pi\epsilon\sigma\tau\alpha\lambda\mu\acute{\epsilon}\nu o\varsigma$ by God.[3]

The controversial dialogue in vv. 2-5 appears to be extraneous to the narrative, but there is reason to think that vv. 2-3a belonged to S. In the Synoptic Gospels, dialogues are often incorporated in healing narratives, and there is at least one sign of interest in the problem of theodicy (Lk. 13 : 1-5). John, however, nowhere shows any interest in this problem. This might be the reason that the second part of the answer to the question of theodicy (v. 3b) is rather a first indication of the Johanning meaning of the miracle. Vv. 3b, 4 and 5 each contain three Johannine style characteristics.[4] V. 5 is quite clearly a symbolical interpretation of the miracle by John (cf. 8 : 12). The content of v. 3b is also Johannine (cf. 3 : 21; 10 : 32; 11 : 4, etc.). The imagery of v. 4 does not quite fit that of v. 5,[5] but it reappears in 11 : 9-10 which is probably Johannine. In v. 6, the miracle story is resumed with the typical Johannine transition $\tau\alpha\hat{\upsilon}\tau\alpha$ $\epsilon\hat{\iota}\pi\grave{\omega}\nu$ (see style characteristic no. 71 and note). The conclusion seems reasonable that John reformulated the last part of the answer in S so that vv. 3b-5 are J.[6]

---

[1] The *aporia* between vv. 25 and 26 has been recognised by many, e.g., Schwartz, Aporien (1908) 500f.; Thompson, Structure, 520ff.; Brown, 264; Dodd, *Hist. Trad.*, 219; Bultmann, 155, 161, 2.

[2] V. 1 : e.g., Mt. 9 : 27; spittle : e.g., Mk. 8 : 23-5: the cooperation of the patient : e.g., Lk. 17 : 11-19.

[3] Dodd, *Hist. Trad.*, 184; Bultmann, 253; Fortna, 72.

[4] $\dot{o}$ $\pi\acute{\epsilon}\mu\psi\alpha\varsigma$ $\mu\epsilon$ in v. 4 is also a significant Johannine style characteristic (29/0 — not in my list because it only occurs in discourse material).

[5] For this reason Dodd, 185ff., judges that vv. 3b-4 are also traditional material and only v. 5 is J.

[6] So also Schnackenburg, Traditionsgeschichte, 80; Fuller, *Miracles*, 89; Bultmann,

9 : 8ff. is clearly a different kind of narrative, and as in c. 5 the Sabbath theme is again added secondarily. Bultmann admits this (p. 249)
but argues that the bulk of vv. 8-38 was nevertheless S. This is almost
certainly wrong. I admit that it is quite possible that the miracle story
in S contained a description of the recognition of the man by neighbours
as an authentication of the miracle, and John could have reproduced
it freely in vv. 8f. In the present context, however, the neighbours are
no longer part of the miracle story but rather introduce the dramatic
development of the rest of the chapter. There are many reasons to think
that vv. 8-41 are, as a whole, a Johannine composition. (1) Johannine
style characteristics are distributed evenly throughout the whole
passage, and the average is very high (1.9).[1] (2) Consisting of six lively
changing scenes, vv. 8ff. are a very clear example of the typical dramatic
narrative style of John. The dialogue is not only between Jesus and
the Jews, as frequently in the Synoptics, but the neighbours and
parents also take part; the healed man has to fight for himself, and
Jesus finally meets him and the Jews again — features which never
occur in the Synoptic stories.[2] (3) The central theme of these verses is
conflict with the Jews, and it is worked out in a way very typical of
John. It frequently happens elsewhere in the Gospel, as in this chapter,
that the reality of the miracles is stressed in the conflict with the Jews
(e.g., 10 : 25,32, 37f.). There are many references to the fear of the Jews
(v. 22) : 7 : 13; 12 : 42; 19 : 38. In Jn. the conflict between Jesus (or his
followers) and the Jews is normally described in forensic terms, which
is paralleled by the fact that the healed man also undergoes trial here.[3]
The climax of the conflict in this chapter is the ban from the synagogue
(v. 34, cf. v. 22) which is also mentioned in 12 : 42 and 16 : 2 and seems

---

251; Fortna, 71f. Wilkens, *Entstehungsgeschichte*, 52, regards vv. 4f. as a secondary
addition.

[1] Cf. also : in v. 23 διὰ τοῦτο + *verbum dicendi* + a repetition is frequent in Jn. (6 : 65;
13 : 11; 16 : 15); in vv. 29f. the thought that the world does not know whence (πόθεν)
Jesus comes is typical of John (7 : 27f.; 8 : 14); v. 32 is parallel to 15 : 24; vv. 39-41 are
clearly Johannine (Bultmann admits it).

[2] Windisch, Erzählungsstil, 181-3, pointed this out and concluded that a typical
Synoptic miracle story would have comprised only vv. 1-7. (For the lively changing of
direct speech in vv. 8-9, cf. 7 : 12, 40f.; 1 : 21.)

[3] In the debates with the Jews, Jesus frequently uses the root μαρτυρεῖν in the context
of Jewish court proceedings (cf. especially 8 : 17; the root μ. has a basic forensic sense
in Jn. in any case, Bultmann, 30, 5). In its controversy with the Jews, the Church is
helped by the παράκλητος — a forensic concept meaning something like advocate — and
in 16 : 8-11 the Paraclete is pictured as accusing the world in a cosmic court case (O. Betz,
Der Paraklet (1963) 197ff.: J. Behm, *ThW* V 810-2).

to betray John's immediate background (see p. 144). Therefore, we may be fairly certain that only 9 : 1-3a, 6-7 is S and the rest J.[1]

6. *The Raising of Lazarus : 11 : 1-44*

This chapter is a crux for the source criticism of John, for although it is clear from a number of *aporias* that John must have used a shorter miracle story, it is difficult to make any reconstruction because he thoroughly wove his interpretation of the miracle into the original story. There are almost no significant style differences. Many attempts to analyze this passage in the beginning of the century were fruitless, and only when the principles of the sēmeia source were applied to it in the last decades, was some progress made.

I shall try primarily to distinguish conscious Johannine additions from the rest, which seems to be mostly S-content in Johannine wording.

The content of v. 4 clearly shows that it is J (cf. 9 : 3; 17 : 4).[2] A result of the insertion is that the words "when Jesus heard" in v. 4a are repeated in v. 6a. V. 5 again repeats v. 3b : Jesus loved the family. Moreover, Martha is the most important person in v. 5, just as in the Johannine addition vv. 20-27 (*vide infra*). The importance of Martha seems to be secondary. In v. 1 Mary is mentioned first and in v. 45 alone.[3] In v. 39 Martha is introduced as if she has hitherto been unknown in the story.[4] Thus vv. 4-5 are probably J. The content of v. 6 is probably traditional because both the independence of the thaumaturge and the emphasis on the marvellousness of the miracle agree with the character of S.

Vv. 7-10 are J for many reasons. V. 8 refers to 10 : 31-39 (J). These verses neglect Lazarus and Bethany and stress the Johannine theme of Jesus willingly going to his death (14 : 31; 18 : 4; cf. 11 : 53). V. 7 ("let us go") is repeated in v. 11b (S) where Lazarus is again the reason

---

[1] Vv. 8ff. are also taken to be J by Dodd, *Hist. Trad.*, 185; Schnackenburg, Traditionsgeschichte, 80; Fortna, 73; J.L. Martyn, *History and Theology in the Fourth Gospel* (1968) 3ff.

[2] Fortna, 77; Fuller, *Miracles*, 105; Bultmann, 302, 7 (he identifies a few traits of John's style).

[3] Vv. 45ff. are J but it is probable that John based v. 45 on the conclusion of the narrative in S. In v. 2 Mary is also mentioned alone, but it is not clear whether this verse is S, J or inserted by a later redactor.

[4] Agreement that the importance of Martha is secondary : Bultmann, 311, 3; Wellhausen, *Ev. Jh.*, 52f., Fortna, 77; W. Wilkens, Die Erweckung des Lazarus, *ThZ* 15 (1959) 23.

for the going. V. 11a is clearly an editorial seam, for ταῦτα εἶπεν is John's typical way of resuming his source (cf. on 9 : 6a) and the words which follow reiterate v. 7a. Finally, the contrast between light and darkness in vv. 9f. is typical of John and the image of the night as the death of Jesus also occurs in 9 : 4 (J).[1] V. 16 refers to vv. 7-10 and will therefore also be J.

It is the clearest of all that vv. 20-7 contain Johannine symbolical interpretation of the miracle. There is an *aporia* between v. 17 and v. 20. According to v. 17, Jesus had arrived at Bethany whereas v. 20 says — as is clarified by v. 30 — that Martha met Jesus outside Bethany while he was still on his way. It seems that John first keeps Jesus away from the bustle around the grave for the sake of an undisturbed theological dialogue with Martha. The Johannine character of these verses may also be revealed by the fact that Martha plays the leading role here (cf. on v. 5). Vv. 24-7 contain eight Johannine style characteristics and a number of concepts that are obviously Johannine.[2] Vv. 28-32 cannot be unravelled. They probably contain traditional elements but the placing of Jesus outside Bethany must be Johannine.

The greater part of the content of vv. 33-9 would probably have been imparted in S. The grief of those present is common to the parallels in the Synoptics, e.g., Mk. 5 : 38, and the ἐμβριμᾶσθαι of Jesus also occurs in Mk. 1 : 43; Mt. 9 : 30 (cf. Mk. 7 : 34). These verses stress the marvellousness of the miracle : neither the sisters nor the Jews have real hope for Lazarus, and they weep; Lazarus has been dead for four days and there is a stench. This eminently suits the character of S. The way in which Martha is introduced in v. 39 also reveals that this verse must be traditional.

V. 40 is probably J. It refers to vv. 20-27 and the connection of the "glory of God" with the miracle must be John's work. Possibly also vv. 41b-42 were inserted by John : the unity of the Father and the Son and the sending of the Son are Johannine themes; in v. 43a John then resumes the source with his usual transitional formula.[3]

---

[1] There is a very wide agreement that these verses were inserted by John : not only Bultmann, 301; Fortna, 78; Faure, Zitate, 114 — but also Brown, 430 (!); Broome, Sources, 114; Hirsch, *Studien zum Vierten Evangelium* (1936) 89 (vv. 9f.); Dodd, *Hist. Trad.*, 231, etc.

[2] Nearly all analysts agree that vv. 20-32 are J : Schwartz, Aporien (1908) 170; Wellhausen, 51; Bultmann, 301; Fortna, 80; Fuller, *Miracles*, 95; with some differences also : Wendt, *Schichten*, 48; Hirsch, *Studien*, 87f.; Broome, Sources, 116; Dodd, *Hist. Trad.*, 232, implies that at least vv. 21-7 are Johannine.

[3] Vv. 40, 41b-42 are regarded as J by Bultmann, 311; Fortna, 83; Fuller, *Miracles*, 105.

In our stylistic test, the average for vv. 7-10, 18-32 is 1.5, while it is 1.0 for the rest of the chapter. This difference is too small to prove anything, but it may be meaningful that it points in the same direction as the *aporias*.

7. *The Conclusion of S*

We have already seen that 20 : 30f. seem to have been the final sentence of S (p. 29). On the basis of its content, I judge v. 31b as J.[1]

Faure and Bultmann argued that 12 : 37f. were also part of the conclusion of S.[2] The only real argument is that John would not have summarized cc. 1-12 by saying only that Jesus performed sēmeia because the words were more important to him. John, however, frequently refers to Jesus' activity as one of "performing miracles" (11 : 47; 2 : 23; 3 : 2; 7 : 31), and it would only be natural if he concluded the signs-part of his Gospel with a final reference to the signs. Moreover, it seems quite unthinkable that S could state that the final result of the miracles was unbelief. Therefore, I regard these verses as J.[3]

8. *Other possible S Material*

(a) *The First Disciples : 1 : 35-51*

The bulk of this passage was probably S. In S the disciples are normally seen as the companions of Jesus (6 : 3; 9 : 1; 11 : 11ff.), and it would, therefore, not be surprising if their calling were described. Indeed, it seems as though the first miracle story is a necessary continuation of this pericope : v. 50 promises the disciples greater demonstrations of Jesus' miraculous power and the first of these is given in the miracle of the wine so that their initial faith, which is described in 1 : 35-51, is strengthened (2 : 11). The last person in this pericope is Nathanael from Cana, and the miracle of 2 : 1-11 happens at Cana, a possible sign of traditions belonging together. We have noted that the pericope contains fairly few Johannine style characteristics (average 0.7). Throughout, the theme is that Jesus is the Messiah and that the disciples are especially inspired to faith by the (miraculous) omniscience of Jesus (vv. 42+47ff.) — we shall see that this seems to suit S. V. 51,

---

[1] Bultmann, 541; Fortna, 198; Schnackenburg, Traditionsgeschichte, 79.

[2] Zitate, 99-104; *Jhev.*, 346.

[3] Schnackenburg, Traditionsgeschichte, 78; Fortna, 199.

at least, is probably an addition of John, in which he indicates the deeper meaning of the miraculous powers of Jesus.[1]

(b) *Jesus and the Samaritan Woman* : 4 : 1-42

The divisions between J and the traditional material are fairly clear : vv. 1-3, 10-15, 20-24, 31-39, 41-2 are probably mainly J while vv. 5-9, 16-19, 28-30, 40 must be basically traditional. Vv. 25-6 appear to be J, based on tradition.[2] My stylistic test seemed to confirm this analysis; the traditional material shows an average of 0.7 and J, of 1.4. There is no proof that the tradition is S, but it is noteworthy that Jesus is shown to be the Messiah by his omniscience, just as in 1 : 35ff. The redaction of John bears characteristics which are by this time well-known to us : symbolical interpretation of visible entities (vv. 10ff.) and emphasis on the word rather than on the miraculous as such (cv. 39, 41f.).

---

[1] Ἀμὴν ἀμὴν is a significant Johannine style characteristic : 25/0. The shift to the second person plural does not fit the preceding dialogue between Jesus and Nathanael (cf. 4 : 48). It cannot be decided with certainty whether v. 50 is S or J. Compare the striking reasons that Bultmann later changed his mind in favour of J in the *Ergänzungsheft* to p. 68 of this commentary. Fortna, 187, regard v. 50 as S and I tend to agree. (Becker, Wunder, 135, also judges the bulk of this pericope to be S.)

[2] See Bultmann, 127ff., and Fortna, 189ff., for the arguments — they nearly fully agree. Bultmann thinks the tradition is possibly the sēmeia source, so also Becker, Wunder, 135.

CHAPTER TWO

THE CHARACTER OF THE SĒMEIA TRADITIONS

First, we have to try to understand the message of these miracle stories, especially in comparison with the Synoptic miracles; secondly, we shall explain their typical characteristics in terms of both the religious environment and the development of the Gospel tradition; finally, we should then be able to interpret the deeper Christological motives of this layer of tradition.

1. The Apparent Characteristics of S

In a comparison with the Synoptics, the relationship between the stories in Jn. 4 : 46-54, Mt. 8 : 5-13 and Lk. 7 : 1-10 about the healing at a distance of a boy at Capernaum is conspicious. It is not completely certain that Jn. and the Synoptics refer to the same event,[1] but the

---

[1] The similarities are striking : in both cases it is a healing at a distance; the patient is a boy — παῖς (Matthew, but also Lk. 7 : 7 and Jn. 4 : 51) may mean both υἱός (Jn.) and δοῦλος (Luke); he lies in Capernaum and Luke and Jn. agree that death was near; the petitioner is closely related to the boy and is in the service of Herod Antipas; Luke and Jn. agree that the man had heard (ἀκούσας) about Jesus and asked (ἐρωτάω) him to help; both Matthew and Jn. emphasize that the boy recovered in the same "hour" when Jesus spoke the healing word. On the other hand, there are also a number of differences. Although some are minor and may be explained away (see especially Schnackenburg, 502ff.), the following are noteworthy : according to the Synoptics, the request is made at Capernaum while in Jn. the man finds Jesus in Cana. (This may be due to a special interest in Cana in the Gospel of Jn. — cf. 21 : 2; 1 : 45ff.; 2 : 1ff. — or to a tendency to emphasize the miraculous.) In Jn., the father is not a heathen as in the Synoptic account. (There are possible explanations for this — see pp. 56, 74.) The most distinct difference is that the core of the Synoptic pericope, namely, the remarkable faith of the man which invites Jesus to heal the boy at a distance, is wanting in Jn. where faith follows the miracle. The question of whether we have to do with the same event cannot be answered with absolute certainty because it is not impossible that similar events could have taken place in the life of Jesus. It has, however, to be noted that the accounts of Matthew and Luke, which certainly refer to the same event, also differ considerably. In Matthew's account there is no room for the function of either the "elders" or the "friends" of Luke. Therefore, the possibility cannot be excluded that Jn. also refers to the same event. Whether this is probable depends to a great extent on the question of whether the main difference between the Johannine and Synoptic pericopes — which concerns the relation

comparison is illuminating in any case because the stories are very similar and all stress the relationship between miracle and faith. The point of the Synoptic account is that the man believes before he has seen, and he takes the initiative for the healing at a distance; in Jn., conversely, Jesus takes the full initiative, and the point of the story is that the man believes after having seen the miracle. The Synoptics mention the miracle in only half a verse, and the main content of the story is the dialogue between the man and Jesus by which the exceptional faith of this heathen is emphasized (apparently with the Gentile missionary work in mind) so that in form-critical terms, it is a pronouncement-story rather than a miracle story. John's pericope, on the other hand, is a real miracle story in which the astonishing fact of the miracle is stressed in four full verses (51-54). In order to demonstrate the reality of the miracle, it is narrated in detail how the man discovered that his boy had recovered in the same hour that Jesus spoke the healing word, and that he and his house came to a full faith; finally it is stressed that this was a sēmeion, i.e., a miracle. Therefore, the impression is created that it is the trend of S to emphasize the miraculous as such and to shift Jesus with his unlimited power to the centre of the stage even more than in the Synoptics.

Can this also be seen in the rest of S ? S contains the most marvellous miracles of the New Testament. One man has been dead for four days, another paralysed for thirty-eight years, and another blind from birth; Jesus made about 120 gallons of wine, and in the story of the walking on the water an extra miracle is told which is not mentioned in the Synoptics : the boat was still in the middle of the stormy sea, but when they took Jesus aboard, all problems were solved "and immediately the boat reached the land they were making for" (6 : 21). Clearly it is no accident that the miracles of S are so wonderful; S is consciously interested in the miraculous. In 1 : 50b Jesus promises that Nathanael will see "greater things" than his supernatural knowledge. As in 4 : 51ff., the reality of the miracles is sometimes deliberately demonstrated, e.g., 6 : 22-25 (wanting in the Synoptics) and 2 : 9f. where the steward — ignorant of the miracle — testifies to the good quality of the wine.

Related to this is the fact that S never says Jesus performed the

---

between miracle and faith — may be explained in terms of the character of S. The majority of the newer Protestant commentators regard the pericopes as parallels, e.g., Barrett, 205; Hoskyns, 259; Bernard, 166; Dodd, *Hist. Trad.*, 194 (not with certainty). Also Schnackenburg, 506, and even Brown, 193.

miracles out of compassion. Although this is not a main theme in the Synoptic miracle stories, it is a distinct part of their message[1] : in Jesus the mercy of God became visible. In S, however, the sole aim of the miracle stories is to demonstrate the power of Jesus. In this light, it can be understood that it is the tendency to depict Jesus as acting on his own initiative and not at the request of others. In the Synoptics the miracles of Jesus are nearly always preceded by a request, while in Jn. Jesus never directly grants a request. In four of the seven miracles, he takes the full initiative, and in the other three, where requests are addressed to him, he keeps the initiative in hand by reacting differently than expected (2 : 4; 11 : 6; 4 : 50; cf. the difference from the Synoptic account). For S Jesus is so significant that his actions cannot be determined by others, and he always acts out of his own free will. This feature is especially evident in the pericope of the feeding of the five thousand (6 : 1-15). In the direct Synoptic parallel, the disciples call the attention of Jesus to the hunger of the people (Mk. 6 : 35 parr.) while in the feeding of the four thousand, the hunger of the multitude is at least mentioned as the reason that Jesus feels compassion and takes the initiative to feed them. In Jn., on the contrary, no single motive is given for the action of Jesus. The figure of Jesus is so powerful that room is hardly left for the disciples to take part in the action : of all six of these parallel pericopes, John's is the only one where they do not help distributing the food and do not gather the remainder at their own initiative but on the order of Jesus. The only role left for them is to show how helpless human beings are in the presence of the Mighty One. (Note that in vv. 7b and 9b their embarrassment is depicted in slightly stronger colours than in the parallels.) Similarly, in the passage on the walking on the water, the Synoptics say Jesus came to the disciples when he saw them struggling at the oars, while John only mentions in passing that the sea was rough and does not offer the trouble of the disciples as reason for the coming of Jesus.

No wonder that, in marked difference from the Synoptics, the only possible position for faith in these stories is at the end, i.e., as a result of the miracle. In the Synoptics faith frequently precedes the miracle,[2] sometimes even as condition, and it is never explicitly stated to be the

---

[1] Mk. 8 : 2par.; Mt. 14 : 14; 20 : 34; Lk. 7 : 13 (cf. the call for mercy in Mk. 10 : 47; Lk. 17 : 13).

[2] Mk. 2 : 5; 5 : 34, 36 (7 : 29) 10 : 52; 6 : 5f.; 9 : 23 (in the last two instances it is clearly a condition). In Matthew this feature is still more distinct.

result;[1] in S, on the contrary, faith never precedes the miracle but is rather regarded as a natural result of it (2 : 11; 4 : 53; 6 : 14a; 11 : 15, 45). The divine Jesus stands above all other human beings and needs no cooperation from them. Take for an example the healing at Bethesda (5 : 1-9). For no human reason Jesus chooses one crippled man from the crowd of sick people lying around the pool. No one tells or asks him anything because in a divine way he already knows the patient's condition. The man has so little hope left that he must be asked whether he still *wants* to be cured, to which he responds with no more than a feeble excuse for his inaction. There is not the faintest sign of faith; he does not even know who Jesus is. But Jesus heals him with a single word of power![2]

The sole theme of S is that all should see the miracles as authenticating signs (sēmeia) of the Messiah and believe. The point is the powerful deed as such; nothing more is necessary. Therefore, the narrative style of S is realistic. Detailed description is given with the intention of vivid portrayal of the event itself and not to reveal hidden symbolical meanings. Through the centuries, especially the numbers in these stories have been the prey of much speculative interpretation, but a clear indication that this is not the intention is that they are frequently not given precisely. In 2 : 6 it is two or three; in 6 : 19 again twenty-five or thirty and in 1 : 39 it says "about the tenth hour". [3] It has long been thought that the five colonnades of 5 : 2 refer to the five books of Moses, but during recent excavations in Jeruzalem, remains of five collonades have been found at the double pool of St. Anna which can

---

[1] This may, however, sometimes be implied. The usual result of the Synoptic miracles is amazement, fear, etc., but sometimes the onlookers see the miracles as the work of God (Lk. 7 : 16; 9 : 43; Mt. 9 : 8; and probably Mk. 5 : 19, where κύριος seems to refer to God, E. Schweizer, *Mk.*, NTD², 1968; E. Lohmeyer, *Mk.*, MeyerK¹⁷ 1967); sometimes they carefully express the beginning of faith in Jesus by a question about him (Mk. 4 : 41parr.; 12 : 23); and only once do they confess Jesus as Son of God (Mt. 14 : 33, but it seems to be a later development, cf. Mk. 6 : 51).

[2] To my mind, therefore, Dodd reverses the point when he says θέλεις ὑγιὴς γενέσθαι ; demands the cooperation of the patient (*Hist. Trad.*, 176), and the main motive of the story is "faith as the will to health" (p. 179). The function of the question is to elicit the answer by which the helplessness and hopelessness of the man is made clear. Dodd (p. 176) argues that the taking up of the stretcher is cooperation, but in v. 9 it is clearly stated — and stressed by εὐθέως — that the man was healed before doing anything (contrast Mk. 2 : 12 and 3 : 5 where ocoperation is not expressly excluded as in Jn.).

[3] E. Stauffer, Historische Elementen im vierten Evangelium, in : *Bekenntnis zur Kirche* (für E. Sommerlath, 1960)34.

quite probably be identified with these colonnades of Jn !¹ Many of the details of S accurately describe Jewish usages of those time (*vide infra*). Another possible proof for the realism of S is that the Synoptic accounts of the feeding miracle probably intend a hidden reference to the Eucharist by using the words λαβών, εὐχαριστέω, εὐλογέω and κλάω,² while John's account seems not to make this reference because the important Eucharistic term κλάω is wanting and the typical λαβών is replaced by ἔλαβεν.³ The final writer of the Gospel was indeed interested in the symbolical meaning of the miracles, and as we have seen in the source criticism, it seems that he had to add the clues for such an interpretation (2 : 4b, 6b, 9b, 11b; 6 : 4, 12b; 9 : 7b and the longer discourse material attached to the miracles). Besides the emphasis on the fact of the miracle, the Synoptic miracle stories frequently contain extra Christian teaching, e.g., about the nature of faith (Mk. 9 : 22) and about true discipleship as following Jesus (Mk. 10 : 52) and witnessing for him (Mk. 5 : 19f.).⁴ In S hardly anything of the kind becomes visible because the main theme dominates everything : Jesus is the Messiah !

In the Synoptic tradition the interpretation of miracles as legitimation of Jesus is limited in various ways, not only in that they are usually not followed by the faith of the onlookers, but in Mt. 11 : 20ff. par., it is even implied that the most of Jezus' miracles were answered by impenitence. If the people do not want to believe the message, Jezus does not try to convince them with miracles (Mk. 6 : 5f. even says he *could* hardly perform any !). Never are the miracles of Jesus called sēmeia in the Synoptics — only the miracles by which the eschatological false prophets try to legitimate themselves are thus described (Mk. 13 : 22 par.). Little wonder, then, that Jesus flatly refuses when the Jews ask him to authenticate himself with a sēmeion (Mk. 8 : 11 parrs.). In S, however, it seems that those legitimating signs for which the Jews ask are given in the sēmeia. So far as I am able to see, this

---

¹ J. Jeremias, *Die Wiederentdeckung von Bethesda* (1949), esp. pp. 22ff.

² See especially B. Van Iersel, Die wunderbare Speisung und das Abendmahl in der synoptischen Tradition, *NovTest* 7(1964)167-194.

³ Jn. only has εὐχαριστέω, which is the normal word for the Jewish thanksgiving over a meal (Rom. 14 : 6; 1 Cor. 10 : 30; 1 Tim. 4 : 3f.). So also Bultmann; Bernard; A. Heising, *Die Botschaft der Brotvermehrung*² (1967)78.

⁴ Mk. 1 : 44 teaches that Jesus does not break the law, and according to 2 : 10, the miracle warrants his authority to forgive sins. 3 : 1ff. contains teaching about the Sabbath, 7 : 24ff. about the heathen, and 9 : 14ff. about faith-healing. In Matthew the teaching imparted in the miracle stories is even more prominent (see p. 80).

function of the sēmeia was not criticized or limited in S. The sēmeia
of Jesus are regarded as so clear that practically everybody who is
involved believes, and this faith is regarded as adequate. The simple
facts of the miracles so directly indicate that Jesus is the Messiah that
there is no secrecy or paradox in his Messiaship.

A final difference between S and the Synoptics pertains to the
connection between miracles and Kingdom. In the Synoptics this
connection is clearly stated. In Lk. 11 : 20 Jesus says his excorcisms are
a sign that "the Kingdom of God has already come upon you"; the
same is implied in Mk. 3 : 27 parr. When asked whether he is the expected One, Jesus refers to his miracles by quoting references to the eschatological work of God from Is. 29 : 18f; 35 : 5f.; 61 : 1 (Mt. 11 : 5ff., cf.
Lk. 4 : 18ff.). In Mt. 4 : 23, the preaching of the Kingdom and the
healing of the sick are regarded as a unity. In S the miracles are solely
related to Jesus and never to the Kingdom as the final eschatological
work of God. Of course, as sēmeia they authenticate Jesus as Messiah
and as such are connected with Jewish eschatological expectations,
but they are so strongly centred around the person of Jesus that the
wider eschatological perspectives become practically invisible. The
difference between Jn. and the Synoptics is not absolute, because,
although the latter clearly connect miracles and Kingdom in the
sayings mentioned, the coming of the Kingdom is not explicitly the
main theme of the Synoptic miracle stories. The primary aim of these
stories is to demonstrate the divine power of Jesus as Son of God and
Messiah, and the wider context of eschatology — although generally
present — is revealed only indirectly.[1] But it is visible; the miracles
are seen as the work of God (p. 44, 1), and God is praised on account of
them.[2] In S, however, Jesus himself is the "Kingdom", his Person is

---

[1] Lk. 7 : 16 : ἐπισκέπτομαι refers to eschatology (see Lk. 1 : 68, 78). Mk. 7 : 37 and
μογιλάλος in v. 32 refer to Is. 35 : 5f. — both in the New Testament and in the LXX it is
a hapaxlegomenon, K. Kertelge, Die Wunder Jesu im Markusevangelium (1970)160.
Mk. 1 : 24 : ἀπολέσαι refers to the Jewish expectation of the eschatological destruction of
demonic powers (E. Lohmeyer, Mk., 37; Bill. II 2); therefore, one can say that all the
excorcisms have an indirect eschatological background; this background also becomes
visible in Lk. 13 : 11, 16. On this whole theme : H. Ridderbos, De Komst van het Koninkrijk
(1950) 69ff. The explicit point of these stories is rather to answer the question, "Who is
He ?" (Mk. 4 : 41) — He is the Son of God (Mk. 5 : 7), the Son of David (Mk. 10 : 48);
R. Bultmann, Synoptische Tradition, 234; Fuller, Miracles, 43; G. Schille, Die urchristliche Wundertradition (Arbeiten z. Theol. I 29, 1967)26; Kertelge, Wunder, 190; vs.
G. Delling, Botschaft und Wunder im Wirken Jesu, in : Der historische Jesus und der
kerugmatische Christus, ed. Ristow & Matthiae (1961) 389-402.

[2] Mk. 2 : 12; Mt. 15 : 31; Lk. 5 : 26; 18 : 43.

all-inclusive, and the wider horizons of God and his eschatological
work need not be mentioned explicitly in order to explain who Jesus is.

The climax of S is the raising of Lazarus, and we shall best be able
to grasp its majestic Christocentric message if we conclude with this
pericope. As we have seen, no exact reconstruction of the traditional
pericope is possible, but the basic story of c. 11 is so much in harmony
with the character of S, and the final author had such a high esteem
of his Jesus-traditions — he would not have changed them haphazard-
ly —, that the following is a more or less reasonable account. When
Jesus hears about the malady of his friend, he deliberately postpones
the journey thither because in divine omniscience he knows how he is
going to give the climactic demonstration of his power (v. 6). Lazarus
dies, and his sisters and their friends are plunged in deep sorrow (33);
they had believed that Jesus would heal him, but now all their faith is
destroyed (37, 39). Jesus — fully aware of Lazarus' death — is not
grieved because in his eyes human death is only sleep (11); rather, he
rejoices, because he knows the miracle will establish in his followers a
faith which *cannot* be destroyed by death (15). When he sees the
mourning (33) and hears the Jews speaking as if he can do nothing
when death has set in (37), he is filled with terrible anger at such
unbelief in his presence (33, 38)[1]. The difference between this and the
raising at Nain is illuminating. There Jesus also sees the family weeping,
and he is not filled with anger but with compassion (Lk. 7 : 13). The
Jesus of S is so divine, that there is no room for weeping in his presence,
only for faith. The corpse was already corrupted, but when Jesus, the
Almighty, calls, Lazarus emerges from the grave (this being a miracle
within a miracle because he was tightly bandaged hand and foot).
Inevitably, many believe (45).

The Synoptic miracles teach much about the *nature* of Jesus'
Messiahship, for example : the Messiah is the One through whom God
erects his Kingdom; the Messiah conquers the powers of evil; he
reveals God's compassion; he has the authority to forgive sins and to

---

[1] There has been much difference of opinion about the significance of Jesus' anger in
these vss. That it is anger at death and suffering (Brown, 435) is possible, but this contra-
dicts the fact that Jesus is glad that Lazarus has died (15) because death is only sleep to
him (11). The cause of the emotion can hardly be compassion because ἐμβριμᾶσθαι
certainly implies anger in Biblical Greek. Is the cause of the anger not clearly stated in
the text ?, i.e., remarks made in unbelief (37) and weeping (33) which is therefore probably
also seen as unbelief. Similarly : Hoskyns, 405; Dodd, *Hist. Trad.*, 231; Strathmann;
R.H. Lightfoot, *St John's Gospel* (1956) 229.

preach the message of joy; he introduces a different attitude towards
the Sabbath and the cultic law so that the mercy of God can reach
even the lepers and the heathen. The miracles in S, however, do not
reveal the nature of Jesus' Messiahship; they only demonstrate *that* he
is the Messiah. Why is this so ? Why is all the emphasis on Jesus' miraculous power as such ? Why are the miracles so marvellous, and why
should théy be the convincing signs that Jesus is the Messiah ? Does
the meaning of "Messiah" in S then amount to something like "great
wonder-worker" ?

2. The Possibility of Hellenistic Influence : Jesus as ΘΕῖΟΣ 'ANḢP

A) *The General Theory*

In pure Jewish thought, there was a clear separation between God and
man, but this was not the case in Hellenistic thought, where nearly all
extraordinary men such as sages, statesmen, prophets, and wonder-
workers were seen as partly divine, as *theioi andres* (θεῖοι ἄνδρες).
Fantastic miracles were attributed to some of these men, like Pytha-
goras, Empedocles, and Apollonius, on account of which they were
honoured as θεοί.[1] Apollonius lived in the first century A.D., and
according to legend, he travelled to many countries and impressed
people with miracles. There is good reason to believe that he was not
unique and that faith in miracles played an important part in the religious atmosphere which surrounded the writers of the New Testament[2].
Since the beginning of this century a theory which has gained popularity
was that such a large number of miracles are ascribed to Jesus in the
Gospels not so much because he did them as on account of the Hellenistic idea that the divinity of a man can be proved by his miracles. Of
course, the Johannine Jesus drew special attention. G.P. Wetter made
an extensive collection of parallels in order to prove that John strove
to convince Hellenists that Jesus was the real *theios anēr*, by emphasizing, among other things, his miracles.[3] Wetter did not even distin-

---

[1] H. Windisch, *Paulus und Christus. Ein Religionsgeschichtlicher Vergleich* (1934)
60-75; L. Bieler, Θεῖος ἀνήρ I, II (1935, 1936).

[2] D. Georgi, *Die Gegner des Paulus im 2. Korintherbrief : Studien zur religiösen
Propaganda in der Spätantike* (1964) 96-130; Origenes, *Cels.* 7, 8ff.; this is also clear
from Acts (*vide infra*).

[3] *Der Sohn Gottes* (1916) 68ff.

guish between S and J; among those who did and studied the pre-Johannine miracle traditions separately, a more or less general consensus of opinion has been reached that the Jesus of S was in some way or other influenced by *theios anēr*-ideas.[1]

The primary basis for this consensus, however, was not the general considerations of comparative religion but the rise of form criticism. It was noticed that there are certain similarities in form between the miracle stories of the New Testament and those of the Jewish and especially the Hellenistic environment.[2] All these stories tend to have a common pattern with certain typical features occurring again and again, e.g., the use of spittle; the thaumaturge meets the funeral procession; the cured patient carries his bed to demonstrate the reality of the curing.[3] The conclusion frequently reached was that many of the New Testament miracle stories had originally been Hellenistic legends which had been transferred to Jesus.

The problem is, however, that many of the New Testament miracle stories bear such clearly Jewish features that it is difficult to see how they could have been inspired by the purely pagan *theios anēr*-concept described above. The solution seemed to be that the Jews were also

---

[1] P. Wendland, *Die Urchristliche Literaturformen* (1912) 307ff.; M. Dibelius, *Formgeschichte*, 68, 88; Bultmann; E. Haenchen, Literatur, 325; E. Käsemann, *RGG³* IV 1835; R.H. Fuller, *Miracles*, 89ff., who argues that these stories contain hardly any Jewish-Christian themes and are therefore "more secular" than the Synoptic miracle stories; H. Köster, One Jesus, 232; J.M. Robinson, Kerygma, 136ff.; H.D. Betz, Jesus as Divine Man in : *Jesus and the Historian*, ed. F.T. Trotter (1968) 127; L. Schottroff, *Der Glaubende und die feindliche Welt. Beoachtungen zum gnostischen Dualismus und seiner Bedeutung für Paulus und das Johannesevangelium* (Wiss. Mon. z. ANT, 1970) 257ff.; J. Becker, Wunder, 137ff.; R.T.Fortna, 230f. (not stressed); J.L. Martyn, Source Criticism and Religionsgeschichte, 254, strongly emphasized the Jewish milieu of S although he does not reject Fortna's suggestions about the *theios anēr*.

[2] Useful collections were made : O. Weinreich, *Antike Heilungswunder* (1909); P. Fiebig, *Antike Wundergeschichten* (KlT 79², 1921); *idem, Jüdische Wundergeschichten des neutestamentlichen Zeitalters* (1911).

[3] Many possible parallels have been gathered by Dibelius, *Formgeschichte*, 78-88, and Bultmann, *Syn. Trad.*, 236-41, 247-53. Dibelius emphasized the *Sitz im Leben* of these stories : he pointed out that miracle stories were sometimes told in the Hellenistic world in order to convince people to believe in certain gods, especially Sarapis (p. 93; Cf. Georgi, *Gegner*, 197; O. Weinreich, *Neue Urkunden zur Sarapis-Religion*, 1919, 4, 14), and concluded that the New Testament miracle stories would have been used to compete with the propaganda of the Hellenistic religions. He argued that the fitting form for such propaganda would have been the "Novelle", characterized by realistic, lively, secular narrative ("Erzählersfreude", p. 73ff.) and regards many of the Synoptic miracle stories and particularly those of Jn. as typical examples of such "Novellen".

influenced by these Hellenistic ideas. There is some evidence that Jews
like Josephus and Philo tended to portray the Old Testament men
of God as divine men.[1] In Palestine Christianity, men like Moses were
seen as types of Christ, and their miracles were connected with his
(see part 6). Therefore, it is conceivable that when Christianity came
on Hellenistic soil, the *theios anēr*-concept could have entered — after
being "tamed" by the Jews — partly via the Old Testament.[2] Many
of the Jewish missionaries trying to make proselytes in the Hellenistic
world, strove to impress partly by excorcisms, magic, and other
"charismatic" activities.[3] From Acts it is apparent that the early
Christian missionaries felt the effects of the Hellenistic miracle-seeking
atmosphere — Paul was for instance twice honoured as a god on account
of his miracles (14 : 11 ; 28 : 6) — and it appears that they also competed
with the wonderworkers and *theioi andres* in their environment.

According to Acts 8, Philip convinces the Samaritans partly by his
signs (v. 6), and he has to compete with another wonder-worker,
Simon, whom the population had previously honoured as divine on
account of his "magic" (vv. 9-13).[4] Now there is a possibility that if
the Jews and Christians competed with the Hellenistic miracle-men in
deeds, they would also have done so in words and depicted their
Old Testament heroes and Jesus respectively as *theioi andres*. In this
Jewish sense the *theios anēr*-Christology is accepted as basic for S by
H. Köster, J.M. Robinson, L. Schottroff and partly by R.T. Fortna
(see p. 49, note 1).

It is clear what the possibilities of this interpretation could be in

---

[1] To mention only a few salient points : Josephus calls Moses a θεῖος ἀνήρ (*Ant.* 3, 180),
also Isaiah (10, 35) ; Solomon has θεία διάνοια (8, 34) ; Saul is described as ἔνθεος γενόμενος
(6, 76), and David had δόξα ὁμοῦ θειότητος (10, 268). Philo seems to take this further ;
although he never uses the term θεῖος ἀνήρ, he frequently calls the men of God θεσπέσιος
ἀνήρ (Windisch, *Paulus*, 110) ; he writes of Moses' θεία πρόνοια (*Vita Mos.* 1, 12) and
says that as a friend of God, he partook in the miraculous powers of God (1, 155ff.).
The Jewish apologist Artapanus (3, 6) says that the Egyptian priests regarded Moses as
worthy ἰσοθέου τιμῆς. (Cf. especially Georgi, *Gegner*, 147ff. ; also Bieler I 18 and II 27-36).
Agreement about this : F. Hahn, *Christologische Hoheitstitel* (1962) 293ff. ; E. Schweizer,
ThW VIII 356f. ; J. Jeremias, *ThW* IV 860.

[2] Hahn, *Hoheitstitel*, 295 ; Schweizer ThW VIII 357 ; M. Smith, Prolegomena to a
discussion of Aretalogies, Divine Men, the Gospels and Jesus, *JBL* 90 (1971)192.

[3] Jos. *Ant.* 20, 142 ; 8, 46ff. ; Juvenal, *Satires* III ; Orig., *Cels.* 7, 8ff. ; cf. Acts 13 : 6ff. ;
19 : 13ff. (Georgi, *Gegner*, 114-130).

[4] Cf. Acts 6 : 8 ; 13 : 6ff. (Paul is stronger than the Jewish magician Elymas and
blinds him) ; 19 : 11ff. (the miraculous powers of Paul — even sticking to his clothes ! —
inspire Jewish excorcists to try his "magic" name Jesus). See Georgi, 210-218.

explaining the differences between S and the Synoptics. Hellenistic divine-men concepts could be the reason that the Jesus of S is so divine and his miracles so wonderful and that the Kingdom and other elements of specific Jewish-Christian teaching are absent. It seems plausible that, for instance, R.H. Fuller thinks S is more Hellenistic than the Synoptic miracle stories.

B) *An Investigation of the Evidence in S*

In order to prove the Hellenistic character of these miracle stories, it is not sufficient to show that Jesus is described as a remarkable wonder-worker. This and related general considerations are not insignificant, but one would also expect to find more specific traces of Hellenistic influence in these stories if they depict Jesus as *theios anēr*. Nor does it suffice to point out that the general form of some of the miracle stories in S agrees with that of the Hellenistic environment, i.e., (a) the malady, (b) the healing, and (c) the attestation, because this is the natural pattern for a short miracle story in any case. [1] It must be demonstrated that this pattern contains specific features which are distinctly Hellenistic. This is what Bultmann in particular tries, and this is what we have to examine.

Many use, as one of the basic arguments for Hellenistic influence, the supernatural knowledge of Jesus in Jn. : according to 1 : 42, 47f.; 4 : 17-19 (possibly parts of S), Jesus knows and sees through the strangers whom he meets, and according to 11 : 11-14 he knows what happens elsewhere. There are clear Hellenistic parallels about *theioi andres* like Apollonius.[2] But this sort of supernatural knowledge was not strange in Judaism. It occurs in the rabbinic writings, in the Old Testament and in Synoptic pericopes which are quite probably Palestinian. [3] This feature alone cannot prove Hellenistic influence and our evaluation of it will have to depend on the Jewish or Hellenistic character of the context in which it appears.

---

[1] V. Taylor, *The Formation of the Gospel Tradition* (1933) 128; H.v.d.Loos, *The Miracles of Jesus* (1965)119f.

[2] Bultmann, 71, 4; Wetter already stressed this (*Sohn*, 69-72); Käsemann, *RGG*³ VI 1835; Hahn, *Hoheitstitel*, 381.

[3] T. Pes. 1, 27f.; Lv. R.21(120c); Berakh. 34b — a prophet is one who knows what happens elsewhere; 1 Sam. 9 : 19; 2 Kgs. 4 : 27. The ability to know the future is not quite the same, but related — attested for the Essenes by Jos. *Bell.* 2, 159; 1QpHab. 7, 1-5; it was given to many Old Testament prophets. Mk. 2 : 8; Mt. 12 : 25; Mk. 10 : 21 are clearly Palestinian (Bultmann, *Syn. Trad.*, 13, 41); cf. Mk. 12 : 15, 43; Lk. 7 : 36-50; 9 : 47; 19 : 5.

An important role was also played by the striking Hellenistic
parallels to the miracle of the wine. It was believed that each year on
the festival of Dionysus, three empty vessels were miraculously filled
with wine at Elis and fountains flowed with wine at Andros and Teos.
The date of the festival was 5 and 6 January and the old church had a
tradition that Jesus had performed the miracle of the wine on the
6th of January.[1] There are, however, also many Jewish parallels to the
idea of wine as sign of the Messiah, and we shall not be able to resolve
this difficult matter until a later stage.

We have seen that demonstration of the reality of the miracle frequently occurs in S. There are many Hellenistic parallels but many
Jewish ones as well,[2] as could be expected from such a natural feature.
The specific form of demonstration in 5 : 9b — the healed man carrying
his bed — has, however, exact Hellenistic parallels[3] while I can find
no Jewish ones; therefore, it *might* betray Hellenistic influence. The
same applies to the specification of the duration of the malady in
5 : 5 (9 : 1).[4] For the spittle of 9 : 6 there are many Hellenistic parallels,
but many Jewish ones too, and the Jews regarded spittle as particularly
suitable for eye-trouble.[5] I know, however, of only one Hellenistic
parallel to the use of clay on blind eyes (Petronius, c. 131). Bultmann
(*Jn.* 84, 4) mentions a few Hellenistic parallels to the "hour" of the
thaumaturge in 2 : 4, and that is the reason why he differs from the
most literary critics in thinking that this phrase is also S. A few scholars
thought that the anger of Jesus in 11 : 33ff. is parallel to the Hellenistic
feature that the thaumaturge must work himself up for the miracle.[6]
Although it is not impossible that this was the origin of this rather
strange feature, we have seen that the context of S seems to demand
another interpretation.

We shall be able to judge the conclusiveness of these features only
after having examined the specific Jewish features in S.

---

[1] H. Noetzel, *Christus und Dionesos* (1960) 27ff.; Bultmann, 83. Noetzel (31ff.)
thinks the date is not significant because this miracle was only secondarily connected to
it on the basis of local customs in Egypt adopted by the Church.

[2] Berakh. 34b (hour, and water asked); Jos. *Ant.* 8, 48; 2 Kgs. 4 : 35.

[3] Lucian, *Philopseudes* 11; *IG* IV 951, 105ff. — A. Oepke, *ThW* III 206 also finds
it significant.

[4] Philostratus, *Vita Apoll.* 3, 38; more parallels in Bultmann, *Syn. Trad.*, 236.

[5] Weinreich, *Ant. Heilungswunder*, 97f.; Bill. II 15ff.

[6] Bultmann, *Jh.*, 310, 4, and Fuller, *Miracles*, 96; both following C. Bonner, *HThR* 20
(1927) 171-180.

3. The Jewish Features in S

Taken separately, the most of them do not exclude the *theios anēr* at all, but we have to treat them together and study each pericope as a unit before we can finally evaluate them.

1. *Water Changed into Wine : 2 : 1-12*

A few points may indicate that the story had a Palestinian origin. Wine was drunk at Jewish wedding festivals, and it could certainly have run short as sometimes the feast lasted seven days, and new guests could arrive any day.[1] The sort of big stone pots mentioned here, have been excavated,[2] and they would have been regarded as particularly fitting for purification purposes since the Jews believed that stone did not attract uncleanness.[3] We have already noted that the passage about the first disciples and Nathanael who came from Cana (21 : 2) and the first two miracles which are connected to Cana seem to have belonged together in S. A possible reason for this is that these traditions had their ultimate origin in that vicinity. It is fairly certain that this Cana is today Chirbet Kana which lies thirteen kilometers north of Nazareth so that it would have been natural for Jesus and his family to have been invited to the feast.[4] Michel *op. cit.*, (p. 16) points out that conservative Jewish morality prevailed in the territory surrounding Cana so that it is improbable that the Dionysus cult would have exercised any influence there. In fact, although Antiochus IV Epiphanes attempted to introduce it in Palestine, it seems that the Jews managed to resist it since the only traces of the cult found in the country were excavated in non-Jewish cities such as Caesarea.[5]

It is quite possible that τί ἐμοὶ καὶ σοί (v. 4) is a quotation of the same words addressed to Elijah in 1 Kgs. 17 : 18 (**LXX**) by the mother just before he raised her son from the dead. One is inclined to think so because there are several other indications that S connects the miracles of Jesus with those of Elijah and Elisha (*vide infra*). V. 5b *might* be a reference to the words of Pharaoh to the Egyptians. When the

---

[1] Bill. II 400f.

[2] Schnackenburg, 336.

[3] Bill. II 406. Michel points out that the fact that Jesus' mother is mentioned here before her son is in agreement with Jewish custom (Der Anfang der Zeichen Jesu, 1958, 16).

[4] Michel, Anfang, 16; Schnackenburg, 331.

[5] Noetzel, *Chr. u. Dionesos*, 40.

bread was exhausted (as here the wine), he referred the nation to
Joseph and ordered them : ὅ ἐάν εἴπῃ ὑμῖν, ποιήσατε (Gen. 41 : 55).[1]
In v. 11 σημεῖον is connected to πιστεύω ; this is thoroughly Jewish,
and exact parallels can be found in the LXX (vide infra).

Finally, we approach the question of the wine. Although we know of
no similar stories in Judaism, the Jews expected that there would be
an abundance of wine in the Messianic time, Is. 25 : 6; Joel 4 : 18;
Am. 9 : 13, and especially Gen. 49 : 11. This last verse is discussed in
Keth. 111b, 30 with particular emphasis on the wine, e.g. : "Du wirst
(in der messianischen Zeit) keine einzige Weintraube haben, in der
nicht 30 Krüge Wein wären";[2] also Gn. R. 51 (32d); Keth. 111b, 28;
Syrian Apocalypse of Baruch 29, 5-8 (connected with manna, cf.
Jn. 6 : 1ff. !). The same connection of the Messianic time and wine is
echoed in Mk. 2 : 22 parr., the parable of wine and wineskins, where
the new wine bears on the newness of that which has come into the
world with Jesus.[3] Moreover, the wedding feast is a favourite symbol
for the Messianic time both in Judaism and in the New Testament.[4]
Therefore, it seems possible that the intention of this narrative in S was
that the wine is the sign that the final "wedding feast" between God
and his people has begun in Jesus. This might be suggested by the last
words of the miracle story proper (v. 10b) : ἕως ἄρτι — in the ears of a
Jew they could have an eschatological ring, the "now" of God's final
coming.[5] The immediately preceding καλὸν οἶνον would them emphasize that now the real wine is there, and we may perhaps add, the
real joy since the marriage feast (cf. 3 : 29) and wine are connected
with joy in the early Jewish-Christian thought.[6] (Whether this Jewish
interpretation is certain will depend on the question whether S appears
to be Jewish or Hellenistic in our further analysis).[7]

---

[1] Fortna, 32, regards it as certain.

[2] Bill. IV 951; cf. for this material Noetzel, Chr. u. Dionesos, 43f.

[3] Schweizer, Mk.; C.E.B. Cranfield, The Gospel according to St. Mark (1963).

[4] Bill. I 517ff.; Mt. 22 : 1-14; 25 : 1-13; cf. Lk. 12 : 36; Mk. 2 : 19; Jn. 3 : 29.

[5] John uses νῦν in this sense in 4 : 23 and 5 : 25, and Paul uses it very frequently,
e.g., Rom. 3 : 26; 5 : 9, 11; Col. 1 : 22; 2 Tim. 1 : 10.

[6] Pes. 109a.

[7] Significantly, Haenchen (ThLZ 93, 1968, 246ff.) and Schnackenburg, 343, totally
reject the Dionysus parallels, yet they remain striking and men like Barrett, 159f.;
Jeremias, Neutestamentliche Theologie, 92, and Dodd, Hist. Trad., 225, think they played
a role at the origin of the story although they do not think this excludes the fact that
the wine also has a Jewish-eschatological meaning.

2. *A Nobleman's Son Healed* : *4* : *46-54*

As we have seen, this pericope and the healing at a distance in Matthew and Luke are possibly parallels. Of the three pericopes in S which have Synoptic parallels, this one deviates the most from the Synoptics, especially because the miracle is treated with much more emphasis — so that if S was a Hellenistic development of the old tradition, we would certainly expect to find traces of Hellenism here. The fact is, however, that although the Q pericope is clearly Jewish, the S pericope contains a number of Jewish features which do not even occur in the former while the latter bears no single sign of Hellenism.

Thrice the healing of the boy is referred to by the word ζάω (vv. 50, 51, 53) instead of a more common Greek expression for healing like ἰάομαι, which occurs in the parallels (Mt. 8 : 8, 13; Lk. 7 : 7; also Jn. 4 : 47). This is Jewish, because the Jews had no special word for healing and regularly used "live" for it.[1] The words of Jesus in v. 50a might be an indirect quotation of the words addressed by Elijah to the widow after he had raised her son from death : Βλέπε, ζῇ ὁ υἱός σου (1 Kgs. 17 : 23 — the same pericope from which the possible quotation of 2 : 4 was taken).

In Berakh. 34b there is a story about R. Chanina b. Dosa who healed the *son* of Rabban Gamliël at a *distance* by prayer. After Chanina had prayed, he said to the messengers : "*Go* (= πορεύου, Jn. 4 : 50), because *the fever has left him* (= ἀφῆκεν αὐτὸν ὁ πυρετός, 4 : 52)". The messengers made a written note of the *hour* and *afterwards ascertained* that the boy was cured in the same hour (note that Matthew and Luke do not specify that the hour was afterwards checked). The story immediately following this one in Berakh. 34b is also a healing at a distance, and there "live" is used twice in the sense of being healed. Surely, the resemblance between the stories of S and Berakhot is striking.[2]

---

[1] Berakh. 34b (beneath); Num. 21 : 8; 2 Kgs. 1 : 2; 8 : 8; Jos. *Vita* 1, 421 (cf. Bultmann, 153,2, and P. Fiebig, Die Wunder Jesu and die Wunder der Rabbinen, *ZWTh* 54, 1912, 172).

[2] At the beginning of the century there was a lively controversy about Jewish miracles in the first century, and it seems that full clarity has not yet been reached. A. Schlatter, *Theologie des Neuen Testaments* (1909) I 260ff., wrote that there were no wonder-workers among the Jews of the first century, and, therefore, Jesus would really have performed miracles because the environment did not supply the reason that miracle stories would have been created for him. P. Fiebig differed radically from Schlatter and argued that

In the Synoptic accounts the father is said to be a heathen and the question of missionary work amongst the Gentiles plays a role while nothing of this appears in S. Could it be because S has a purely Jewish *Sitz im Leben*?

3. *The Healing at Bethesda* : 5 : 2-9b

We noted that the structure with five colonnades was probably excavated.

V. 7 (the idea of water being moved by visitation) — I find no Hellenistic parallels, but there is a Jewish one in Lv. R. 24 (122d) : the presence of spirits at a pool could be noticed by the movement of the water. Faith in the healing power of water is, of course, universal, but there is a very near Jewish parallel in Lv. R. 22 (121b) : a man went bathing in a lake at the moment when the fountain in the lake flowed, and he was healed[1] (cf. also on 9 : 7).

-----

the Jews of the time regarded their rabbis as having miraculous powers (*Wunder Jesu*, 158-179; *Jüd. Wundergeschichten*, 72). Schlatter immediately answered in *Das Wunder in der Synagoge* (1912) : the supernatural experiences recorded about the rabbis of the time are not miracles wrought by their own powers (as with Jesus) but deeds of God who answered their prayers; they are men of prayer and not wonder-workers (especially pp. 76ff.). Many agreed with Schlatter, e.g., H.W. Beyer, *ThW* III 129; A. Oepke, *ThW* III 202; Fuller, *Miracles*, 33; Smith, Prolegomena, 190; but some did not completely accept his thesis, e.g., J. Klausner, *Jesus of Nazareth*, 266; E. Lohse, *RGG*³ VI 1834; R.M. Grant, *Miracle and Natural Law in Graeco-Roman and early Christian Thought* (1952) 171; Van Der Loos, *Miracles*, 150; Michel, Anfang, 18; Bultmann, *Syn. Trad.*, 248. I am inclined to judge that in general Schlatter is right, but he has overstated his case. Most of the stories referred to by Fiebig either portray God as the subject of the miracle or have to be dated after 200 A.D. Therefore, Jesus with his miraculous powers would have been a unique appearance in the Palestine of his time. He connected his miracles with the Kingdom (e.g., Mt. 12 : 28par., which is historical, cf. Bultmann, *Syn. Trad.*, 174) while the rabbis saw their "miracles" mainly as proof of the merit of the pious man. It is, however, not possible to make such an absolute division between the miracles of Jesus and those of his Jewish environment as Schlatter did. In Mt. 12 : 27par. the power of Jesus to exorcise is compared to the power of Jewish exorcists, and in Pes. 112b (a tannaitic passage), Channia ben Dosa commands the demon 'Agrat without praying. According to Berakh. 33a (tannaitic), Chanina miraculously kills a water-snake, and no prayer is mentioned. Although the healing at a distance of Berakh. 34b is effected by prayer, the story itself bears traits of a miracle story (the hour; the thirst of the boy as demontration), and it cannot be denied that the resemblance to the story in S is significant.

[1] It is notable that Haenchen (Probleme, 48) calls 5 : 2-9b a "judenchristliche Heilungsgeschichte".

4. The Feeding of the Five Thousand : 6 : 1-14a

Mk. 6 : 35-44, the nearest parallel, is already thoroughly Jewish,[1] but still there are a number of Jewish traits in S which do not appear in Mark.

V. 5 — ἐπάρας τοὺς ὀφθαλμοὺς ... καὶ θεασάμενος : this is a Jewish expression, cf. Gen. 13 : 10 ; 2 Sam. 18 : 24 ; 1 Chron. 21 : 16 ; Shab. 113b.[2]

V. 9 — κριθίνους and παιδάριον : this is probably reminiscent of the feeding miracle of Elisha (2 Kgs. 4 : 42-44). The story is a very close parallel to the New Testament feeding story : Elisha also receives the food from another and orders his servant to feed the people ; the latter protests like the disciples ; the people eat, and some of the food is left over. Elisha's servant Gehazi is normally called παιδάριον in 2 Kgs. (e.g. 4 : 12, 14, 25, 38, immediately preceding the feeding story), and the bread is specified as κριθίνους (one of the four uses of the word as adjective in the LXX). These two words occur nowhere else in the New Testament save in the feeding story of S. This can hardly be accidental.[3]

V. 10 — ποιήσατε ... ἀναπεσεῖν reflects the Semitic causative.[4]

V. 14a — the connection of sēmeion and prophet is completely Jewish (vide infra).

---

[1] It is Jewish custom to have the main meal in the evening (Mk. 6 : 35) ; to have bread and fish ; to praise God before commencing (v. 41) — cf. Lohmeyer, Mk., 125, who also mentions a number of Semitisms in the language. The groups of a hundred and of fifty (v. 50) may be a reference to Ex. 18 : 13-27, where Moses had to divide the nation in groups of 1000, 100, 50 and 10, cf. 1Q Sa. 1f. (especially 1, 14f. ; 2, 17) where this typology is clearly applied to the Messianic meal. Then, the Marcan narrative would portray Jesus as the new Moses who gives the manna in the desert (v. 35). (Hahn, Hoheitstitel, 351 ; Kertelge, Wunder, 133 ; Schweizer, Mk., "vielleicht".) Contrast the other feeding story in Mk. 8 : 1-10, which seems to be less Jewish, especially because εὐλογήσας αὐτὰ is not Jewish : a Jew does not bless the food but God for the food (H.W. Beyer, ThW II 760 ; Van Iersel, Speisung, 185). Nothing of the kind appears in S. Even those who think that the feeding story was secondarily transferred to Jesus have to admit that the Jewish parallels to the miracle as such are the closest and that the story would be of Jewish origin (Bultmann, Syn. Trad., 255 ; O. Perels, Die Wunderüberlieferung der Synoptiker, 1934, 99). The closest parallel is 1 Kgs. 4 : 42ff., but it cannot be used to explain fully the origin of the story because no fish occurs in it. Cf. Bill. I 687f. for other parallels.

[2] Note the typical Hebrew tautology which also occurs in the analogous expression : "open mouth and speak" (Mt. 5 : 2 ; Dan. 10 : 16 ; "... and eat", Ez. 2 : 8 ; "open mouth" alone occurs frequently in the Old Testament, e.g., Ps. 77 : 2 ; Prov. 13 : 3 ; Ez. 3 : 27).

[3] Dodd, Hist. Trad., 206 ; Hoskyns ; Haenchen, Probleme, 33 ; Brown, 246.

[4] Schlatter ; Bultmann, 155, 5 ; the same construction occurs in Rev. 13 : 13.

5. *The Walking on the Water : 6 : 16-25*

Bultmann[1] gives a number of instances of Greek writers describing
demons and divine men as walking on water and concludes that this
story must be of Hellenistic origin. There are, however, a number of
Old Testament parallels which are at least just as clear. Job 9 : 8 reads
that God περιπατῶν ὡς ἐπ' ἐδάφους ἐπὶ θαλάσσης.[2] Sir. 24 : 5f. says
of Wisdom that she walks ἐν βάθει ἀβύσσων and has power ἐν
κύμασιν θαλάσσης.[3] Ps. 28(29) : 3 reads κύριος ἐπὶ ὑδάτων πολλῶν,
while God is said to walk through the sea in Ps. 76(77) : 20 — emphasized in Ex. R. 25 (86c) — and also in Is. 43 : 16; Job 38 : 16.

V. 20 — ἐγώ εἰμι ... μὴ φοβεῖσθε. The *ego eimi*, which also appears
in Mark, is primarily an ordinary identification in this context.[4] But
possibly there are some overtones. Jesus actually appears to his
disciples here, and in the Old Testament God frequently says μὴ φοβοῦ
when he appears : Gen. 15 : 1; 26 : 24; 28 : 13; Jud. 6 : 23; cf. also
such Jewish parts of the New Testament as Lk. 1 : 13; 2 : 10; Mt. 17 : 7;
Rev. 1 : 17. God frequently identifies himself with *ego eimi* ... in the
O.T., also when he appears : Gen. 17 : 1; 26 : 24; 28 : 13; Ex. 3 : 6;
Ez. 20 : 5. As here in S, the two formulae occur together in Gen. 26 : 24,
28 : 13 and also in Rev. 1 : 17. The problem is, however, that in all these
instances, the *ego eimi* is followed by a divine name while it is not the
case in this story. If we wish to hear an overtone of divine epiphany
in v. 20, we should actually be able to indicate that the absolute *ego
eimi* can also have divine meaning. Although we ought not to read
John's theology into S, it is nevertheless interesting that John uses the
absolute *ego eimi* a number of times : 18 : 24, 28, 58; 13 : 19; 18 : 5, 6.
Many attempts have been made to indicate Hellenistic and Gnostic
parallels of this absolute "I am", but the only good examples appear
in the Old Testament.[5] God frequently assures his people that he is
their God by using the absolute *'ani hu'*, especially in Deutero-Isaiah,
and this is always translated as *ego eimi* : Is. 41 : 4; 43 : 10; 46 : 4;
48 : 12; also Dt. 32 : 39. Whatever the exact meaning of John's

---

[1] *Syn. Trad.*, 251f.

[2] Preferred by Haenchen, Probleme, 32; Grant, *Miracle*, 169.

[3] Preferred by Lohmeyer, *Mk.*, 135; Schweizer, *Mk.*, 79.

[4] Bernard and Barrett take it only as such.

[5] H. Zimmermann, Das absolute *'Ego Eimi'* als die neutestamentliche Offenbarungs-
formel, *BZ* 4 (1960) 54-69, 266-76; Brown, 535ff.; Barrett, 282f.; Dodd, *The Interpretation of the Fourth Gospel* (paperback 1968) 93-95; E. Stauffer, *ThW* II 350f.; even
Bultmann, 265, 6, quotes the texts from Isaiah as nearest parallels to the absolute use.

absolute *ego eimi* may be, it is clear that in some way it reflects this solemn Hebrew self-indentification of God. Now the question is whether there is any reason to think that this divine meaning could already have been intended in the older tradition. According to Mk. 13 : 6 the false Christs will try to deceive many by saying *ego eimi*. The context does not supply any predicate and the most probable solution is that the expression itself has Messianic meaning in Jewish ears.[1] It is clear that the phrase ἐγώ εἰμι ... μὴ φοβεῖσθε was the climax in the traditional story of the walking on the lake. The denouement is narrated very briefly, and with the exception of the obvious περιπατοῦντα ἐπὶ τῆς θαλάσσης, it is the only phrase which occurs in both Mark and S.[2] I find it difficult to think that it *only* meant : "Never mind, it is I, not a ghost". There is even more reason to accept the divine interpretation for S because it is not mentioned as in Mark that the disciples did not recognise him or thought he was a ghost. Jesus does not merely reassure them; he reveals himself as divine.[3]

V. 21b — the miraculous landing which only occurs in S, is perhaps a reminiscence of Ps. 106(107) : 30. The psalm praises God for his miracles (θαυμάσια : vv. 8, 15, 21, 34, 31) : He gave food and drink to those who were hungry in the desert (4-9), and he healed them (20); when they were on sea, he sent a storm but stilled it again (23-29) καὶ ὡδήγησεν αὐτοὺς ἐπὶ λιμένα θελήματος αὐτῶν (30) [4].

V. 25 — ῥαββί : this word and its equivalent ῥαββουνί occur nine times in Jn. and only nine times in the Synoptics. As it is a direct transliteration of the Aramaic word and easily replaced by other Greek titles such as ἐπιστάτης (Lk. 9 : 33) and διδάσκαλος (Luke never has ῥαββί), it can be taken as a sign of the influence of Palestinian tradition.[5]

6. *The Man Born Blind : 9 : 1-3a, 6-7*

V. 2 — ῥαββί again. The idea that illness is the result of sin, even of one's parents, is *thoroughly Jewish.*[6]

---

[1] Lohmeyer, *Mk.*; Cranfield, *Mk.*; Stauffer, *ThW* II 351.

[2] Kertelge, *Wunder*, 147.

[3] This is accepted for Mark in the commentaries of Lohmeyer, Schweizer, and Cranfield; for Jn. : Brown, 538; Bultmann, 159; Stauffer, *ThW* II 350.

[4] Barrett; Brown, 255; Hoskyns, 291.

[5] Lohse, *ThW* VI 964. W.F. Allbright, Recent discoveries in Palestine and Jn., in : *The Background of the New Testament and its eschatology* (for C.H. Dodd, 1956) 158, mentions archaelogical evidence that the title was normal in the time of Jesus.

[6] Bill. II 193ff.; 527ff.; Bultmann, 251, 2; cf. Barrett for the Jewish idea that antenatal sin is possible.

V. 7 — there was a pool called Siloah in Jerusalem and later the Jews believed that it had healing power.[1] The man has to go and wash himself in order to be healed — the nearest parallel is 2 Kgs. 5 : 10ff., where Naaman must wash himself in the Jordan.

7. *The Raising of Lazarus* : c. 11

V. 6 — Jesus tarries. This need not be explained by the independence of the thaumaturge (Bultmann on 2 : 4) because it is also a Jewish notion that God's will cannot be determined by man and therefore he frequently answers requests in his own way; man often has to wait.[2]

V. 17 — Lazarus has been dead for four days. This becomes significant in the light of the Jewish belief that the soul stays near the body for three days.[3]

It is possible that S mentioned the comforting of the Jews (vv. 19, 31), the general weeping (33), and Mary's weeping at the grave (31), which are all attested as Jewish customs of the time.[4]

Vv. 33ff. — Jesus' anger at unbelief is in harmony with the Jewish notion that God's wrath rests on unbelief.[5]

V. 38 — A cave sealed with a stone used as grave — well attested.[6]

V. 41 — Lifting the eyes up to heaven for prayer : this was not the general custom, but there are examples.[7]

V. 44 — A σουδάριον (face cloth) was used for the dead. There is no direct evidence of κειρίαι (bandages), but the attested custom is close enough : the corpse was wrapped up in several pieces of cloth.[8]

---

[1] Bultmann, 252, 4.

[2] 2 Kgs. 5 : 10f.; Ps. 42 : 10f.; in Ta'an. 19b, they have to wait before the rain comes for which Choni has prayed.

[3] Bill. II 544.

[4] Bill. IV 592ff.; Schlatter; Sap. Sal. 19, 3.

[5] Ps. 78 : 21f.; Num. 14 : 11f.; 20 : 12 — each time in the context of God's great deeds (sēmeia) to redeem his people from Egypt.

[6] Bill. I 1049-51.

[7] Bill. II. 246.

[8] Bill. II 545; O. Michel, *Calwer Bibellexicon*[5] (1959) 660, judges that we can trust Jn. at this point and refers to Chrysostom who says the bandaging of the dead was customary in his time. There are a number of probable Semitisms in the language of the story : ἔρχου καὶ ἴδε (34); the absolute ἀποστέλλειν (3); ποιεῖν ἵνα (37); φωνῇ μεγάλῃ (43) — cf. Bultmann, 301, 2; Schlatter.

8. Other possible parts of S

a) 1 : 35-50

This passage is so clearly Jewish that we may be brief. The point is that the true Israelite (47) recognises Jesus as Messiah. Messiahship is described by different Jewish expressions (41, 45, 49; in whichever way one takes the lamb of God in 35, it is Jewish). The Aramaic word *Messiah* occurs only twice in the New Testament, here in v. 41 and in 4 : 25, (possibly S!) and v. 42 contains the only instance in the Gospels of the Aramaic name Cephas.[1]

b) c. 4

Jesus journeys through Samaria — this was the usual road according to Josephus (*Ant.* 20, 118). Sychar is probably the modern Askar; the well of Jacob and the plot of Joseph can also be identified.[2] V. 9 probably means that the Jews and Samaritans did not use vessels in common, and this is historical as well as the implication of v. 27 that it was not customary that men converse with women.[3] The "miracle" of Jesus' supernatural knowledge makes the woman think that he is a prophet (19) or even the Messiah (29). Bultmann interprets "prophet" as a Hellenistic title for *theios anēr*, but a Jewish interpretation is more probable because the Jews connected "prophet" with supernatural knowledge,[4] and in the story the woman's confession of Jesus as prophet is a step towards her confession that he might be the Christ (29). The eschatological Redeemer *Ta'eb* which the Samaritans expected on the basis of Dt. 18 : 15ff., had prophetical characteristics. There is no

---

[1] In vv. 37, 38, 40, 43 the ἀκολουθέω seems to imply discipleship — this would be rabbinic terminology (Bultmann, 68, 5). "Come and See" in vv. 39, 46 is Semitic (Schlatter) as well as πόθεν in v. 48 (Barrett). 'Εν ᾧ δόλος οὐκ ἔστιν (v. 47) may be a reference to Ps. 31 (32) : 2 (Schnackenburg; Schlatter). "Under the fig tree" (v. 50) may be interpreted in various ways, all Jewish.

[2] Jeremias, *ThW* VII 94; Schnackenburg; R.D. Potter, Topography and Archaeology in the Fourth Gospel, *Studia Evangelica* (1959) 331, remarks that the well of Jacob is the deepest in Palestine (cf. v. 11 "the well is deep") and that both Mt. Gerizim and the corn fields in the vicinity can be seen from the well (cf. vv. 20, 35). Jeremias points out that the aorist προσεκύνησαν in v. 20 is based on good tradition because there was no Samaritan cult any more on Mt. Gerizim in the time of Jesus. It is strange that the woman comes to the well at noon, but this is probably because she as a sinner avoids contact with others.

[3] Jeremias, *ThW* VII 92; Barrett.

[4] Berakh. 34b; R. Meyer, *ThW* VII 823ff.; G. Friedrich, *ThW* VII 845, note 400; cf. Lk. 7 : 39.

reason that "he will tell us everything" in v. 25 may not be taken as a correct reflection of this Samaritan "Messianology" because Dt. 18 : 18 says the prophet "will tell them everything which God commands", and the Samaritan source Memar Markah IV, 12 expects that he will reveal the truth.[1] The Samaritan expectations were related to those of the Jews, and, as we shall see later, it may be that this is a reflection of one of the pillars of the Christology of S : the miracles are connected to the Messiah via the prophet. Surely it is striking that there are so many details in this chapter which appear to be in harmony with the circumstances in Palestine in the first century.

9. *The Word Sēmeion and its Context.*

It seems that sēmeion emphatically means "miracle" in S. It is never used in any other sense (not even in J). The miracles are not sēmeia in the sense that they are signs which point to some meaning behind them; the miracle itself is significant, demonstrating the power of Jesus and causing many to believe. A definition of the meaning of sēmeion in S may be : an event which is, by its miraculous character, a legitimizing sign of the Christ. That this is so is verified by J. As we shall see, John adopted the theology of S to such an extent that almost all the passages where he uses sēmeion reflect the preaching and even *Sitz im Leben* of S. According to 9 : 33; 3 : 2 and 7 : 31, the sēmeia legitimize Jesus as παρὰ θεοῦ, as the Christ.

This use of the word is peculiar. The Greek word sēmeion does not normally mean miracle, and the Synoptics never use it to denote the miracles of Jesus. The normal Synoptic word for the miracles of Jesus is δύναμις, which is used for the miracle of a god in the popular Hellenistic literature,[2] but according to Formesyn (p. 882), it does not occur for "miracle" in the LXX or other Jewish-Hellenistic literature. Therefore, it is probable that its prominence in the Synoptics is at least partly due to its Hellenistic use.[3] Can the same be said of sēmeion ?

---

[1] Schnackenburg. It is improbable that v. 19 intends "*the* prophet" in an eschatological sense as 6 : 14; 7 : 40 because the article is wanting, and v. 25 implies that the woman does not yet see Jesus as Messianic, but the relation between vv. 18f., 25 and 29 (also 1 : 48f.) makes it clear that there must be some link between prophet and Messiah.

[2] Grundmann, *ThW* II 290f.; R. Formesyn, Le sèmeion johannique et le sèmeion hellenistique, *EThL* 38 (1962) 882.

[3] Formesyn, Sèmeion, 878, and Kertelge, *Wunder*, 123, think the word was directly taken over from Hellenism. To my mind this is going too far. The ultimate background of the word seems rather to be the Jewish concept of the power of God cf, Ps. 117 (118) :

Formesyn pointed out that the miraculous is never an essential complement of a sēmeion in Hellenistic Greek.[1] The nearest to the Biblical use of the word is its meaning as foretoken. Practically anything could serve as foretoken and be interpreted symbolically by μάντεις in predicting the future. Miraculous events were also frequently foretokens, but the miraculous element then merely stressed the importance of the event and did not have any significance in itself — interpretation was still necessary. In Hellenism, sēmeion is never used for a legitimizing miracle as in Jn. The Hellenistic words for miracle which we would have expected if S depicted Jesus as *theios anēr* are θαῦμα, ἀρετή, and δύναμις.

There are, however, traces of the sort of use which S made of sēmeion in the immediate environment of S, and these traces may be followed back to their origin. In Acts, the miracles of both Jesus and the apostles are often called σημεῖα καὶ τέρατα (or τέρατα καὶ σημεῖα, 2 : 22; 2 : 43; 4 : 30; 5 : 12; 6 : 8; 14 : 3; 15 : 12; σημεῖα καὶ δυνάμεις in 8 : 13), and σημεῖον alone is used in this sense in 4 : 16, 22; 8 : 6; Lk. 23 : 8. As in Jn., the sēmeia are regarded as divine authentication of Jesus and the apostles (2 : 22; 14 : 3) and result in faith (9 : 42; 13 : 12; cf. 9 : 35; 8 : 6). The Hebrew expression *'otot wemophetim* is always translated σημεῖα καὶ τέρατα in the LXX. These expressions occur frequently in the Old Testament and almost always refer to the mighty deeds of God when he led Israel out of Egypt.[2] In Acts 7, Moses is described as type of Christ (*vide infra*), and, in v. 36, τέρατα καὶ σημεῖα refer to the events of the Exodus. It appears that Acts points to the Exodus story as origin of this use of sēmeion.[3] This might be corroborated by Mk. 13 : 22 par., which says that in the end, false messiahs and false prophets will try to deceive the people by doing σημεῖα καὶ τέρατα. The implication is the same as in S. The Jewish expectation is that the final envoy of God has to be authenticated by sēmeia, and the verse is certainly a quotation of the warning against false prophets in Dt. 13 : 2. When the author of Mk. 13 quoted the

---

14ff. where God is called ἰσχύς and his saving deed δύναμις ; a miracle is called ἰσχύς in Dt. 3 : 24 (Grundmann, *ThW* II 302); Q (Palestinian) also uses δύναμις for the miracles of Jesus (Mt. 11 : 21-4; Lk. 10 : 12-15); God and the Spirit is called δύναμις in Mk. 14 : 62par.; Lk. 24 : 49; 4 : 14; δύναμις is associated with the coming of the Kingdom (Mk. 9 : 1), the Second Coming (Mk. 13 : 26) and God's power to raise the dead (Mk. 12 : 24). Moule, *Miracles*, 237, agrees.

[1] Sèmeion, 861-868.

[2] K.H. Rengstorf, art. sēmeion, *ThW* VII 214, 219.

[3] C.F.D. Moule, *Miracles* (1965) 236.

words σημεῖον and τέρας from Dt. 13, he probably had in mind the
Jewish expectation that the Mosaic era and the σημεῖα καὶ τέρατα
which are usually connected with it in Deuteronomy would return in
the end.[1]

The evidence from the writings of Josephus and Philo also points in
the direction of the LXX as origin of the use of sēmeion as legitimizing
sign. According to Formesyn (p. 869f.), they both frequently use
the word sēmeion in different Hellenistic senses like Josephus' foretokens for the fall of Jerusalem,[2] but it only means demonstrative
miracle in their writings when they directly or indirectly refer to the
LXX. This indicates that the latter meaning of the word did not belong
to the ordinary Jewish Greek of the time but only to the sacred biblical
language. Josephus stresses the relation between God's sēmeia and
faith (Ant. 2, 274, 276, 283). In Ant, 20, 167f., he tells about false
prophets who persuaded the people of Jerusalem to follow them to the
desert where they would show them τέρατα καὶ σημεῖα. The implication is probably that the sēmeia would legitimize them as prophets.[3]
The fact that they go to the desert and that others of these false prophets mentioned in Ant. 20, 97 and 169f. promised to do such miracles
of the Hexateuch as parting the Jordan and causing Jerusalem's
walls to fall down, indicate that they expected a return of the Mosaic
times.[4]

Let us therefore turn to the LXX. The Hebrew 'ot is always translated
by sēmeion.[5] In the Old Testament these words are used for many
kinds of signs which are not miraculous or need not essentially be so.
When, however, they refer to an event which demonstrates by its
miraculous character that God is participating, they mostly refer to the
Mosaic events. If we take the LXX as we have it and as the writer of
S would have studied it, the development of this use of sēmeion begins
in Ex. 4 : 1ff. God sends Moses to go and redeem Israel, but Moses
fears that the people will not believe that he is God's representative.
Therefore God gives him two miracles to authenticate himself, and they
are called sēmeia (Ex. 4 : 8bis, 9, 17, 28, 30). As in S, the aim of these

---

[1] Rengstorf, sēmeion, 239. There are a few other examples in the New Testament of
the use of sēmeion as legitimizing sign : Rev. 13 : 13f; 19 : 20; 2 Thes. 2 : 9; Rom. 15 : 19;
2 Cor. 12 : 12; Mk. 16 : 17, 20; Heb. 2 : 4; Mk. 8 : 11 parr.

[2] G. Delling, Josephus und das Wunderbare, NovTest 2 (1958) 294.

[3] Bill. II 480.

[4] Rengstorf, sēmeion, 223; R. Meyer, Der Prophet aus Galiläa (1940) 85.

[5] Formesyn, 871.

sēmeia is explicitly faith (Ex. 4 : 1, 5, 8, 9, 30; cf. Num. 14 : 11), and they are not merely given by God, they are worked *(ποιέω)* by Moses (4 : 17, 30; 7 : 10). With the same meaning, sēmeion is also applied to the plagues (Ex. 10 : 1f.; 11 : 9f.) and, after Exodus, to all the mighty works of God to save Israel from Egypt (Num. 14 : 11, 22; Dt. 4 : 34; 6 : 22; 7 : 19; 11 : 3; 26 : 8; 29 : 2; 34 : 11; Ps. 77 : 43-52; 104 : 27-36; 134 : 9; Sap. 10 : 14-20; Neh. 9 : 10). In a certain sense the recollection of the great deeds of the Exodus was the centre of the Old Testament faith; note that they are the core of the important credo of Dt. 26 : 5-9. Therefore, it is quite natural that S would have related the miracles of Jesus in terms which refer to the spectacular Mosaic sēmeia of God.

There are a few other indications that this was the intention. Can it be completely without significance that Deutheronomy ends by referring back to the sēmeia of Moses (34 : 11) while S seems to have ended with a similar reference (20 : 30f.)? In 6 : 14 the people who saw the sēmeion confess Jesus as "the prophet", and it is probable that the eschatological prophet-like-Moses, whom the Jews expected on the basis of Dt. 18 : 15, 18, is meant *(vide infra)*.[1]

It is probable that S took the sēmeia as proofs that Jesus is ὁ Χριστός (20 : 31; 1 : 41; 4 : 29). Originally this title had the full Jewish meaning of "the Anointed One, the Messiah", but because this was not completely understood in the Hellenistic churches, Χριστός soon became a proper name for Jesus, a "fossil" with its Jewish connotations forgotten, for example, frequently in the letters of Paul.[2] If S was a development of the old tradition on Hellenistic soil, we would certainly have expected something of the sort — but the exact opposite is true : there is hardly a book in the New Testament where Χριστός is used in

---

[1] Many have agreed that the Mosaic signs are the basic background of sēmeion in Jn.: L. Cerfaux, Les miracles signes messianiques de Jésus et œuvres de Dieu, selon l'Évangile de S. Jean, in : *L'attente du Messie* (Recherches bibl., 1954) 133; D. Mollat, Le sèmeion johannique, in : *Sacra pagina* II (1959) 214f.; Rengstorf, sēmeion, 254ff.; Formesyn, Sèmeion, 886; Brown, 529; Schnackenburg, 355. In the Synoptic apocalypse, sēmeion is used for apocalyptical foretokens of the end (Mk. 13 : 4 par.) The background is the late Jewish apocalyptical expectations; cf. Rengstorf, sēmeion, 230; S. Hofbeck, *Sēmeion. Der Begriff des "Zeichens" im Johannesevangelium unter Berücksichtigung seiner Vorgeschichte* (1966) 39. It is of course attractive to say the sēmeion-concept of Jn. has such apocalyptical associations which emphasize his message of realising eschatology (so Barrett, 64; Brown, 528; Hofbeck, Sēmeion, 38). But there is no proof for this, and as we shall see in part 6, there is much evidence that the eschatological meaning of the sēmeia in S has to be connected to Exodus (the same applies to J).

[2] O. Cullmann, *Die Christologie des Neuen Testaments* (1966) 135; W.C. Van Unnik, The Purpose of the Fourth Gospel, in : *Studia Evangelica* (1959) 391.

a more pronouncedly Jewish sense than in S. Nowhere is it a proper
name. S contains the only two instances in the New Testament where
the Aramaic original "Messiah" is given (1 : 41; 4 : 25), and in both
cases Χριστός is added as translation. The Christ is the One of whom
the Law and Prophets wrote (1 : 45), the King of Israel (1 : 49). The
title Messiah was certainly customary among the Jews at the end of
the first century A.D.[1]

As in Ex. 4, the result of the sēmeia is that people believe. This is not
only wanting in the Synoptic miracle stories, but there the normal
result is rather some form of amazement : θαυμάζω, ἐξίσταμαι, θάμβος,
ἔκστασις, etc.[2] I can find no Jewish parallels to these words, but they
are typical of the reaction of man to a miracle in Hellenistic literature.[3]
In S, however, there is no trace of amazement. The fear of the disciples
when Jesus appears on the lake (6 : 19) is Jewish because in Jewish
literature fear is the normal reaction when God appears.[4] S has nothing
of the shouting and astonishment of the Marcan account of the walking
on the water (Mk. 6 : 49, 51).

10. *Evaluation*

The mentioned Jewish features may be classified according to a
scheme of increasing conclusiveness. In the first place, we have found
a great number of reflections of a remarkable knowledge of Palestinian
geography and customs. There are striking Aramaic words like Messiah
and Cephas. The first bearer(s) of this tradition must have been a
Palestinian Jew — quite possibly John the son of Zebedee — and S can
certainly be regarded as an important and independent source to the
life of Jesus of Nazareth.[5] These traits, however, have but little weight

---

[1] Schnackenburg, Die Messiasfrage im Jhev., in : *Neutest. Aufsätze* (Festschr. J.
Schmid, 1963) 241; Bill. I 6f.

[2] For a complete list see Bultmann, *Syn. Trad.*, 241.

[3] E.g. *Vit. Apoll.* 4 : 20 : after Apollonius had performed an exorcism in Athens,
there was an undescribable θόρυβος and the people ἐκρότησαν ὑπὸ θαύματος. Many more
examples are given in E. Peterson, *Εἷς Θεός* (1926) 193-5, e.g., *Apul.* 10, 13 (*mirantur*);
IG 11, 1299 *(θάμβεω)*; *P. Oxyrh.* 10, 1242 *(θαυμάζω)*; cf. also G. Bertram, *ThW* III 4, 28.
It cannot but be significant that Matthew reduced this trait : it does not appear in his
parallels to the following verses in Mark : 5 : 15, 20, 33, 42; 6 : 51.

[4] Gen. 28 : 17; Ex. 3 : 6; 34 : 30; cf. Dt. 5 : 5 and Iud. 6 : 23. Ex. 4 : 31 (after a
miracle). Lk. 1 : 12; 2 : 9. Mt. 9 : 8 and 16 : 6 have it while it is wanting in the Marcan
parallels.

[5] The main aim of Dodd's *Hist. Trad.* is to prove this. He found that the whole pre-
Johannine tradition bears strong marks of Palestine, cf. especially pp. 424-426. He
agrees that there are a number of signs of later development in the tradition but contends

to prove a Jewish *Sitz im Leben* for S — Hellenists could also have obtained Palestinian tradition and remodelled it to fit their own ideas without dropping features of this kind.

In the second place, we have found a number of indications of the influence of Jewish linguistic usages in the Greek of S. The sentence structure of S is Semitic : the sentences are frequently short with the verb at the beginning; they are connected in a simple way, with the asyndeton, καί, δέ or οὖν (no μέν) [1]. The author must have been a Jew, but the question remains, how Hellenistic were his ideas ?

S seems to quote the LXX a few times, especially portions concerning Elijah and Elisha. This is not conclusive in itself (Philo also quoted the LXX), but it might be meaningful if we can show that the theology behind these references is Jewish.

Finally, S reflects a number of distinct Jewish ideas. There is the notion of sin as the cause of illness in 9 : 2 and the expectation of the eschatological prophet in 6 : 14. If one compares 4 : 46-54 with the rabbinic healing at a distance, one is left with the impression that the narrator cannot be far removed from the spirit of the rabbis. The title Christ is applied in a very Jewish way. Thoroughly Jewish features appear in S in the place of traits which may betray Hellenistic influence in the Synoptic miracle stories : δύναμις in the place of sēmeion ; astonishment in the place of faith. We shall later (p. 93f.) show that the Synoptic miracle stories are not so Hellenistic as has often been thought. In any case, it seems fair to say that S is even more Jewish than the Synoptic miracle stories; there is less reason to argue for Hellenistic influence.

Is there reason at all ? We have seen that the miraculous knowledge can be interpreted as either Hellenistic or Jewish. On the basis of the rest of S and especially the pericopes concerned (1 : 35ff.; c. 4), I am now inclined to think that it is not a Hellenistic trait at all. At least as far as S is concerned, the wine of the first miracle must be that of Jewish Messianic expectations. The only two possible Hellenistic traits left are the thirty-eight years illness and the carrying of the bed in

---

that "it is more remarkable how comparatively little the traditional narratives have been affected by late, non-Palestinian influences, and how much has come through, even in the report of the teaching, in which we can recognize the authentic atmosphere of early Palestinian Christianity" (p. 427).

[1] Bultmann 68, 7; 78, 3; 131, 5; 155, 5; 177, 4; 301, 2. He concludes S must have been written by a Semite (68, 7). Fortna, 223, regards linguistic arguments as the most important to prove the Jewishness of his source.

5 : 5, 9. Then there are the more general arguments. Why are the miracles so astonishing and the Wonder -Worker so central ? Is this not an indication of indirect Hellenistic influence ? Part of this may, however, be explained in another way, i.e., by the tendencies of the development of the tradition.

4. THE SETTING OF S IN THE HISTORY OF TRADITION

S is different from the Synoptics, and we are looking for an explanation. Basically there are two factors which could cause change in the
early Christian tradition : external influence like Hellenism or internal
development. So far, the first possibility has appeared questionable as
explanation for the characteristic emphasis on the miracles in S. If we
should succeed in explaining the character of S partly in terms of the
internal development of tradition, the door might be opened to a more
internal, i.e., theological, interpretation of the pervasive Christo-
centricity.

A) *Some Tendencies of the Early Christian Tradition*

The Apostles and other early bearers of the tradition about Jesus,
experienced this tradition as the living Word of God which had to be
preached and taught in the power of the Spirit. Therefore, they differed
from their Jewish brothers, the rabbis, in the way they transmitted
oral tradition. For the rabbis their tradition was law and they trained
their memories to transmit it in such a mechanical way that even
though centuries passed, a minimum of change took place in the
halakha. The Christian preachers believed that God had revealed himself in concrete history in Jesus of Nazareth and therefore, of course,
did not arbitrarily change their historical tradition, but because they
preached it with the purpose of leading people to faith and not to
scientific knowledge, some "life", some change, is evident.[1] This is
taught us by the Bible itself if we compare the four Gospels.

Some of the differences between them can be explained in terms of
the general tendencies of the development of any human tradition.
The best way in which these tendencies may be studied for our purpose
is probably to examine the development of the Christian tradition

---

[1] Cf. H.N. Ridderbos, *Heilsgeschiedenis en Heilige Schrift van het Nieuwe Testament*
(1955) 130, where he speaks of the "relative freedom" with which the Evangelists reproduced the tradition.

itself in the post-canonical period. Fortunately this has recently been
done by E.P. Sanders with an voluminous collection of material from
the textual tradition, the early fathers, and the apocryphal Gospels.[1]
This is the first systematic examination of the matter. He established
that the criterion of increasing length, which was frequently loosely
used by form critics, cannot be verified, but that the other criteria can,
although they are not hard and fast rules (pp. 272ff.). For reasons which
will soon become clear, it is not so easy to find evidence for these
tendencies in the Synoptic Gospels, but if the two-document hypothesis
is accepted on other grounds, some evidence may be found, and many
differences become explicable.[2]

The following possible tendencies are of the most important ones and
may appear significant if we later test them by applying them to S to
see whether they produce any intelligible result :

1. The clearest is that indirect discourse tends to become reported
directly. In the post-canonical tradition, Sanders found many examples
and no exceptions (p. 259). In the Synoptics, Matthew frequently uses
direct where Mark has indirect speech and Luke also occasionally
changes Mark to direct speech.[3]

2. The tendency to individualize characters by naming them is also
fairly clear. In the post-canonical tradition this tendency is "strong".[4]
The Synoptic evidence is not quite unequivocal because Mark sometimes
has a name where the others do not have it : 10 : 46 (Bartimaeus);
1 : 26; 11 : 21; 16 : 7 (thrice Peter); 1 : 29 and 13 : 3 (short lists of
disciples). The threefold occurrence of Peter, however, may be explained
by the possible connection between the Gospel and Peter, and the

---

[1] *The Tendencies of the Synoptic Tradition* (1969).

[2] Like W.R. Farmer, who introduced him to the Synoptic problem, Sanders doubts
this nearly generally accepted hypothesis. Therefore, he does not look for criteria on the
basis of the two-document hypothesis like Bultmann but applies the criteria which he
has found in the post-canonical field to the Synoptics to see whether the hypothesis is
verified. The result of the experiment is that the two-document hypothesis is not verified
at all, nor any other Synoptic hypothesis (pp. 276ff.). It seems that the most important
reason for this negative result lies at hand : if the hypothesis is correct, there is a specific
literary relationship between Matthew and "Mark" — Matthew deliberately abbreviated
the narrative of "Mark" — which has nothing to do with the spontaneous development of
tradition.

[3] E.g., 16 : 22; 15 : 15, 22, 25; 17 : 9 — see Sanders, 260f., and Bultmann, *Syn.
Trad.*, 340f. In general, however, Luke has much less direct speech than the others proba-
bly because changing direct to indirect was part of his avoidance of the vernacular
(Sanders, 261, referring to Cadbury).

[4] Sanders, 275, cf. 170f.; Bultmann, 71f.; 256; 338.

fact that the short lists of disciples are absent from the others, by the inclination of Matthew and to a lesser degree of Luke to abbreviate Mark. It is, then, probably significant that new names of persons or groups appear in Lk. 8 : 45; 22 : 8 (cf. 9 : 10 geographical) and Mt. 3 : 7; 8 : 19; 12 : 24, 38; 15 : 15; 16 : 1; 18 : 21; 22 : 41; 16 : 8 (cf. 15 : 12-14; 16 : 14).[1] All names are not significant for this criterion, probably not even every single one mentioned in these verses, because names could have been remembered.

3. Sanders also classifies as "strong" the tendency of the post-canonical tradition to add small, novelistic features in order to make the narrative more attractive (pp. 274f.; 143). Applied to the Synoptics, he finds that this criterion supports the order Matthew, Luke, Mark (p. 187). But we who believe the two-document hypothesis can answer that it is quite comprehensible that Matthew and Luke, who had much more logia to report, abbreviated Mark's narratives. If this hypothesis is accepted, there are a number of examples to which this criterion is applicable in the Synoptics. Here the greatest care is necessary. The more critical form critics like Bultmann were inclined to evaluate nearly every detail in this light. Especially V. Taylor opposed this and attempted to demonstrate with form-critical arguments that detail is usually reproduced from memory.[2] It cannot but be significant that Mark has the most details and what could be called "lifelike touches" (Taylor). For instance, many scholars, even the more critical amongst them, would today agree that the apparently true-to-life story about Peter's mother-in-law (1 : 29-31) seems to be Petrine.[3] The following verses may, however, offer examples of novelistic development :

---

[1] Bultmann, 54f., 71. The lists of Sanders on pp. 170ff. are not completely satisfactory because his definitions of the different criteria are so grammatical that the meaning of the various details is forgotten. The result is that (a) many examples are included which have nothing to do with individualizing, especially the many instances where a proper name appears instead of a pronoun in another Gospel but where it is clear from the context that the pronoun refers to the same person; (b) as far as I can see many of the examples mentioned in the text which have the same meaning and should therefore be included do not appear in the lists — apparently because they are not grammatically so easily comparable. (The result of these narrow definitions might limit the value of the whole book, cf. the fact that a number of the instances of direct speech in Luke mentioned in Bultmann, 341, are wanting in the list on p. 261 and that the most of the novelistic features in Luke and Matthew listed beneath do not appear in the list on pp. 182f.).

[2] *The Formation of the Gospel Tradition* (1933) 41ff.; *The Gospel according to St. Mark* (1959) 135. He has, however, to admit that the reverse is sometimes true, e.g., in the cases of Mt. 19 : 22 and Lk. 18 : 18 (*Formation*, 66).

[3] E.g., Schweizer, *Mk.*; Fuller, *Miracles*, 35; for the arguments, see Lohmeyer, *Mk.*

Lk. 6 : 6; 7 : 4f.; 8 : 42; 9 : 38; 18 : 18; 22 : 50; Mt. 5 : 29f., 39; 19 : 20.[1]

4. In the course of time, the miraculous power of Jesus seems to have received more emphasis. The different apocryphal acts of the Apostles abound in fantastic miracles,[2] but this is of minor significance for our present purpose because these books depict the Apostles as divine men under influence of the Hellenistic-gnostic environment,[3] and, therefore, do not prove much for the inherent tendencies of the tradition. There are, however, a number of possible Synoptic instances of which the same cannot be said (note, for instance, that the most are from Matthew). There are general references to Jesus' miracles of healing in Mt. 14 : 14; 19 : 2 and 21 : 14 which do not appear in the Marcan parallels. After both feeding miracles, Matthew emphasizes that the women and children were not even counted (14 : 21; 15 : 38). While Mk. 1 : 32-34 says all who were ill were brought and many healed, Mt. 8 : 16 says many were brought and all healed and, Lk. 4 : 40, all were brought and all healed. Similarly, in Mk. 3 : 10 many are healed, in Mt. 4 : 15 all, and in Lk. 6 : 19 the crowd try to touch him because power went out from him and cured them all. Mk. 6 : 5a reads : ''He *could* work *no* miracle there, except that he put this hands on a few sick people and healed them''; Mt. 13 : 58 weakens this to : ''He *did not* do *many* miracles there.'' J. Jeremias also mentions Mt. 8 : 28; 20 : 30 where two are healed instead of one.[4] Some of these examples may be debatable, but I find it difficult to deny them all. It is remarkable that all these possible enhancements of the miraculous are very small. Surely, in comparison with the fantastic miracles of the post-canonical tradition, the Synoptic tradition is marked by admirable restraint. (But how must we explain the extra miracle in Mt. 14 : 28-32 ?)

5. If later tradition is inclined to lay more stress on the miraculous power of Jesus, one might expect that it would also have a tendency to portray him as the One who take the initiative. I find, however, very little evidence of this.[5] Only the comparison of the two feeding miracles in Mark might give some light. In contrast to Mk. 6, Jesus takes the

---

[1] For a fuller treatment, see Bultmann, 72, 305f. 340.

[2] H. Schlingensiepen, *Die Wunder des Neuen Testaments* (1933) 12-24. (Sanders did not examine tendencies 4-6).

[3] *Op. cit.*, 14, 22.

[4] *Theologie*, 90.

[5] Bultmann, 69f., mentions a number of examples from apophthegmata in Mark., but I do not feel competent to judge the relative state of development of the pericopes concerned. It is noteworthy that Jesus takes the full initiative in the apocryphal Lk. 6 : 5D.

full initiative in Mk. 8, and the latter seems to be more developed than
the former. In Mk. 6 only one day is involved, while Mk. 8 : 2 says the
people have been without food for three days (!) while they followed
Jesus (so that Jesus' power of attraction receives more stress). Not
only the hunger of three days but also the remark in v. 3, that the
people would faint if they were sent away, may be evaluated as slightly
enhancing the miraculous. In v. 2 σπλαγχνίζομαι is direct speech, while
it is reported in the third person in Mk. 6 : 35. The story of Mk. 6 is
thoroughly Jewish, but the blessing of the food in 8 : 7b is not Jewish
and probably Hellenistic (cf. p. 57, 1).[1]

6. A final criterion may be called common sense. Where details in
parallel accounts differ, one is sometimes more realistic than the other,
and one would tend to judge it as older. Development might be dis-
closed by expressions or ideas which seem to belong to a later time, by
adaptation to the normal form of a miracle story, etc.

Not one of these tendencies can be regarded as a law of evolution, and
they can only have meaning when a number of them occur together.

B) *An Examination of S in the Light of these Tendencies*

We shall now mention some features from our material which might
be significant in the light of these criteria. Frequently it is not possible
to evaluate a specific detail with certainty. Additional names or details
in S may be late but may also be from memory. Therefore, it is necessary
first to obtain a full picture.

It will be useful to begin with the anointing pericope (12 : 1-8).
Although John certainly took the bulk of the pericope from tradition,[2]
it cannot be proved that it belonged to S. The names Lazarus, Mary,
and Martha, however, probably indicate that it was not too far removed
from S in the stream of the tradition. Therefore, features in this pericope
may shed light on similar ones in S.

There appear to be three different anointment stories, one each
in Mark (and Matthew), Luke, and Jn. The stories in Jn. and Mark are
very similar. Both describe a meal in Bethany (Jn. 12 : 1; Mk. 14 : 3);
in both a woman anoints Jesus with a quantity μύρου νάρδου πιστικῆς
πολυτελοῦς (= πολυτίμου, Mk. 14 : 3; Jn. 12 : 2); in both the

---

[1] Cf. Lohmeyer, *Mk.*, who finds that this story "der literarischen Sphäre nähergeruckt
ist"; Schweizer, *Mk.*; Van Iersel, Speisung, 186; Bultmann, 232.

[2] Cf. Fortna, 149ff.; Bultmann, *Jh.*, and my table of style characteristics in chapter
one.

disciples protest with the words, πραθῆναι ... δηναρίων τριακοσίων
καὶ δοθῆναι (τοῖς) πτωχοῖς (the two infinitives are indicatives in
Jn. 12 : 5; Mk. 14 : 5), and Jesus answers ἄφετε (Jn. singular) αὐτήν
... πάντοτε γὰρ τοὺς πτωχοὺς ἔχετε μεθ᾽ ἑαυτῶν ... ἐμὲ δὲ οὐ πάντοτε
ἔχετε, mentioning his ἐνταφιασμός (Jn. 12 : 7f.; Mk. 14 : 6ff.). But
there are also some striking agreements between Jn. and Luke. In
both a woman anointed (ἀλείφω) Jesus and dried (ἐκμάσσω) τοὺς
πόδας of Jesus ταῖς θριξὶν αὐτῆς (Jn. 12 : 3; Lk. 7 : 38). Mk. 14 : 3
and Lk. 7 : 40 agree that the event took place in the house of one
named Simon and that it was a γυνή who anointed Jesus with
ἀλάβαστρον μύρου (vv. 3; 37).

For the rest, however, the stories of Mark and Luke are different, and
I find it difficult to see them as parallels. More probably there were
originally two different stories, one about an anointing in Bethany and
the other about a woman who wept at Jesus' feet in Galilee, but because
the two basic scenes were so similar, some small details of the one
slipped into the other in the course of tradition.[1] The agreements
between Jn. and Mark compel us to see them as parallels. It seems that
the similarities between Luke and Jn. cannot be accidental and that
the story of Luke influenced that of Jn. in the course of tradition,
especially because the hair and the feet which fit well in the former,
make the latter hard to understand. It was very immodest for a woman
to untie her hair in public — this would fit the sinner of Luke, but
would it fit Mary ? The anointing of the head was customary, but not
of the feet, and it is especially hard to explain why the costly perfume
would then have been wiped of.[2] Therefore, one is inclined to think
that John's story is later than the two stories in the older Gospels.
Perhaps the following details are then significant. In the older Gospels
the characters are unknown while in Jn. the familiar names of Lazarus,
Mary and Martha appear. The protest is voiced by τινες in Mark.
οἱ μαθηταί in Matthew and Judas in Jn.

Let us now first take the three stories in S which may be compared
to similar Synoptic pericopes. In the case of the healing at a distance,
it is striking that 4 : 53 mentions a household conversion, something
which never occurs elsewhere in the Synoptics but was familiar in the

---

[1] A. Legault, An Application of the Form-Critique Method to the Anointings in
Galilee and Bethany, CBQ 16 (1954) 143ff.; Brown, 449ff.

[2] Legault, 137ff.; Brown; Barrett. Haenchen, Probleme, 51, adds that the costly oil
of nard was sold in "small bottles" (so Mk. 14 : 3, New English Bible) and that the λίτρα
(327 gram) of Jn. looks like exaggeration.

later missionary work of the Church (Acts 10 : 2; 11 : 14; 16 : 15, 31; 18 : 8).[1] The Synoptic account makes it clear why Jesus did not enter the man's house : a Jew was forbidden to go into the house of a heathen. In Jn., however, it is not stated that the man was a heathen; the Gentile question, which was not so acute any longer towards the end of the first century, receives no attention. Jn. emphasizes the miraculous much more than the older Gospels in this pericope.

The feeding miracle in S contains more direct speech than the one in Mk. 6 (Jn. 6 : 10, 12). The details παιδάριον and κριθίνους in vs. 9 do not occur in any of the parallels, and we found that they reflect 2 Kgs. 4. In the older Gospels, the dialogue is between Jesus and the disciples in general, but in S the names of Philip and Andrew appear.[2] The account of S concludes with a "Chorschluss" (v. 14) which does not appear in the Synoptics but is a typical feature of a miracle story (e.g. Mk. 1 : 27; 2 : 12; 4 : 41; 7 : 37). It seems as though there is a relation between these points and the fact that the initiative of Jesus and the helplessness of the disciples are stressed more in S than in the parallels.

In the pericope on the walking on the water, we have to admit, the evidence may point in the opposite direction in some respects. S does not narrate the miracle of the stilling of the storm which is mentioned in Mk. 6 : 51. Some say this means that the story of the walking is the original and the motive of the storm is secondary so that S has an older form than Mark. They argue that there are some indications in the Marcan account which may show that the storm motive entered later from the story of the calming of the storm (Mk. 4 : 35ff.).[3] On the other hand, S also has an extra miracle, a very marvellous one which is not even mentioned in the rest of the Gospel tradition — the miraculous landing. Moreover, the pericope is concluded by an extra scene (vv. 22-25) in which the reality of the miracle is demonstrated.

If 1 : 35-50 belongs to S, it seems to point in the same direction.

---

[1] Barrett and even Brown, 196, and Dodd, *Hist. Trad.*, 195, think that this is a late feature.

[2] The names and the boy are taken as signs of development by Barrett and Dodd, *Hist. Trad.*, 206.

[3] Mk. 6 : 48 "he wanted to pass them" seems to have belonged to a story in which Jesus did not come to help the disciples; the stilling of the storm is mentioned very briefly in the denouement. For further signs, see Lohmeyer, *Mk.*; similarly Bultmann, *Hist. Trad.*, 231; Schweizer, *Mk.*; Brown, 254.

The disciples immediately confess Jesus as Messiah which seems to be theological development (cf. Mk. 8 : 27ff.). The healing miracles of Bethesda and Siloam portray Jesus as the Only One who takes initiative. Perhaps it is significant that the story of Lazarus is elaborate in details, and 11 : 1 seems to imply that Mary and Martha were not regarded as the sisters of Lazarus in an earlier form of the story. The miracles of the wine and Lazarus are so unusual and so different from that which we are accustomed to in the rest of the Gospel tradition, that many say they are late, legendary developments from beginning to end. We must, however, keep in mind that the only three miracles in S to which we have Synoptic parallels have not really become more marvellous. Therefore, the observable development does not warrant such a statement.

If the conclusion should be that in general, the Synoptic miracle stories represent a more primitive stage of the tradition than S, a number of the characteristics of S can be explained. The fact that S deviates from the Synoptics in calling the miracles of Jesus sēmeia may then be connected with the impression which we received from Acts and Paul and the rest of the N.T. that sēmeion later became a normal word for miracle in the Church. The theme of S, that miracles lead people to faith, may then also be related to the fact that this theme is explicitly stated in Acts (9 : 42; 13 : 12; cf. 9 : 35) but not in the Synoptics. We can probably rely on the Synoptic tradition that Jesus himself was very reluctant to use his miracles as legitimizing sēmeia.[1] If he had done this during his life, the danger would have been that the people would have regarded him as wonder-man. After the crucifixion, this was no longer a danger, and it seems that the later Church, at least as far as Acts and Jn. are concerned, had the tendency to develop towards the idea of miracles as sēmeia. The great importance of the miracles themselves in S, stressing the dominating centrality of the powerful Jesus alone and resulting in the virtual absence of Jewish-Christian ideas such as the Kingdom, need then not be understood as the result of Hellenistic influence, but may be explained as theological development inside the Church. Could it be that the concentrated Christology of S is already nearing the "high" Christology of John ? An additional reason for the absence of the Kingdom could then be that the the eschatological expectations were no longer so acute towards the end of the first century.

---

[1] See p. 6 *supra*; G. Bornkamm, *Jesus von Nazareth*[8] (1968), 121ff.; W.G. Kümmel, *Die Theologie des Neuen Testaments* (1969) 52ff.; E. Schweizer, *Jesus Christus* (1968) 46.

On the basis of all these considerations, we must now reach a conclusion about S. It is improbable that *all* the possible indications of development which we have mentioned are indeed late features. Nobody can prove that while the five colonnades of Bethesda could be remembered, it could not also have been remembered that Jesus spoke to Andrew and Philip before the feeding of the multitude. But if all the differences between S and the Synoptics are kept in mind, it is difficult to argue that S is more primitive or even as primitive as the Synoptic miracle stories.[1] Some are inclined to speak in rather negative terms about the developed state of the pre-Johannine tradition : Haenchen stresses its "deutlich zersagte Gestalt"[2] and Käsemann calls it "eine verwilder-

---

[1] Cf. R. Schnackenburg in : *Jesus and Man's Hope I (Perspective*, 1970) 226 : "We have to do with a highly developed stage of tradition throughout the Johannine material"; Fortna, 227. *Note about authorship.* Not one of the Synoptics were written by an eye-witness, so it would be hard to argue that the miracle stories of Jn. had an eyewitness as author. As these stories form one of the least developed parts of the Gospel, an explana-tion of how the whole of Jn. could have been written by an eyewitness would be extremely difficult. The theology of the Gospel is very developed, and it is imparted in long speeches of Jesus which are so different from the Synoptic logia and are written so clearly in the style of John (which we also find in the speeches of John the Baptist and in 1 John) that we are forced to conclude they are not the *ipsissima verba* of Jesus (H.N. Ridderbos). The central theme of the preaching of Jesus was the Kingdom; a principal way in which he taught was by parables; a major part of his miracles were exorcisms — but John omits all these. The account of John the Baptist in which he points Jesus out as Son of God seems very theological (cf. Mt. 11 : 2ff.). The question about the setting of the raising of Lazarus as climax of the life of Jesus while it does not appear in the Synoptics, has to be answered by an *ignoramus* (E.P. Groenewald). An eyewitness would hardly have used sources, but the Gospel abounds in possible traces of the use of tradition. The primary objection against John the son of Zebedee as author is, therefore, the apparent distance between the Gospel and the history. If the author had been an eyewitness, one would have to conclude that he treated history very freely. Obviously, however, the theological intention of the author was one of intense interest in history because he sought meaning in the concrete events of Jesus' life. I find it most difficult to see how this man, if he had been an eyewitness, could have written a Gospel which seems to be so distant from the history. I would here mention the careful and valuable commentary of R.E. Brown. He attempts to prove the historical value of Jn. in every possible way (p. XLVIIf.), and *therefore*, he is interested in the history of tradition. His conclusion is that in some instances, the tradition is developed, and this is his principal objection against John the son of Zebedee (p. XCIXf.). "For instance, is it really conceivable that an eyewitness was responsible for the *final* form of the story of how Mary anointed Jesus (12 : 1-7) ?" R. Schnackenburg has similar positive interests, and he also finds the devel-opment a decisive objection (p. 79), so also W.F. Howard, *The Fourth Gospel in recent Criticism and Interpretation*[4] (revised by C.K. Barrett, 1955) 7.

[2] *Probleme*, 51.

te überlieferung"[1] But if one compares S with other miracle stories of the time and of the later Church, one is rather struck by its restraint. In spite of the fact that S shows indications of having been transmitted for many years, it still contains many apparently historical features (see part 3),[2] and has a deeply historical interest in the concrete miracles of Jesus.

And now, what about the *theios anēr*? If S was a development under Hellenistic influence, surely Hellenism had enough time to leave some clear marks on the material! Why is S *still* so clearly Jewish? But before we can come to final conclusions about the apparent Jewish *Sitz im Leben* of S, we must add two further links to the chain of the argument. What then would the purpose of S have been and would it have fitted into the Jewish expectations of the times?

5. THE PURPOSE OF S

We have already seen (p. 49) that miracle stories were frequently used as an aid in missionary work in the Hellenistic world, e.g., for Sarapis. We also noted that the Jewish missionaries of the time performed "miracles" to convince; they also used miracle stories for propagandistic purposes, e.g., in the Jewish Sibyllen and in Ps. Phocylides. The later Church had the same aim with the miracle stories in many of the apocryphal Acts of the Apostles.[3] From Paul (Rom. 15 : 9; 2 Cor. 12 : 12) and Acts it is clear that the miracles of the missionaries were important in the early missionary work, and according to Acts 2 : 22; 10 : 38, the miracles of Jesus were stressed in missionary sermons.

The use especially of the words sēmeion and *Christos* in Acts is significant. We saw that the origin of the use which Acts and S make of sēmeion is Ex. 4, where the word means a sign which must inspire faith in unbelievers. The word sēmeion is used ten times in Acts, always in the context of the Jewish missionary work. In 14 : 10ff.; 28 : 5ff.

---

[1] *Jesu Letzter Wille nach Johannes 17* (1967) 68.

[2] In general I am not contradicting Dodd because I am answering a different question. My question is how long is the road between Jesus and S; he asks how much of the historical Jesus has been brought along, however long the road; I am looking for signs of development which he does not deny (*Hist. Trad.*, 195, 206); he seeks traces of constancy which I welcome. But he emphasizes the historical tradition so exclusively that a one-sided impression is created by the book.

[3] Peterson, *Εἷς Θεός*, 200ff.

miracles among heathens are described but not called sēmeia. When-
ever *Christos* is used in Acts, not as a proper name but in its full force
as "the Messiah", it is in the context of the proclamation to the Jews.[1]
In contrast to this, the message to the heathen is usually that Jesus
is the κύριος : 10 : 36; 11 : 20[2] (the first two instances of missionary
work amongst the gentiles in Acts); 16 : 15, 31. The question of the
historicity of the speeches in Acts may be under discussion, but it is
clear that Luke is differentiating between Jewish and Gentile missionary
work (cf. the fact that the speeches addressed to Jews usually refer to the
Old Testament while those to Gentiles do not). Therefore, we may
conclude that at least according to Luke, who wrote Acts more or less
at the same time as S must have been written, sēmeion and *Christos*
belong to the Jewish missionary work.[3]

S forcefully emphasizes the miracles as legitimizing signs of the
Messiah — why would this have been necessary if S were addressed to
people who were already believers? The faith of the onlookers is
stressed so explicitly that it seems that they are held up as examples
for the unbelieving hearers. This might be corroborated by 4 : 53,
where it is said that the man "and all his household became believers" —
words which we found reminiscent of the missionary terminology of
the Church as reflected in Acts (cf. 10 : 2; 11 : 14; 16 : 15, 31; 18 : 18).
20 : 31, the probable conclusion of S, reads : "These (sēmeia) have been
recorded in order that you may believe that Jesus is the Christ..."
Although the words cannot be used to *prove* a missionary aim as some
have done, they would at least be a very fitting conclusion for a missionary book. In 1 : 35-50 it is described how five different people come
to faith in Jesus, four by the intermediation of others — this creates the
impression of "Propaganda" (Bultmann 76, 6). Nathanael is the true
Israelite because he believes Jesus is the King of Israel (vv. 47ff.) — is
this not a call to all Jews to recognise their King ?[4] The narrative about
Jezus' Samaritan "missionary work" in c. 4 may also betray a missiona-

---

[1] These are all the instances of the title with the article in Acts, plus 2 : 36; 3 : 20
where it is clear from the context that the anarthrous *Christos* has the full meaning.
Cf. 5 : 42; 9 : 22; 17 : 3; 18 : 5, 28.

[2] The Ἕλληνες must be heathen because they are contrasted to the Greek-speaking
Jews in v. 19, E. Haenchen, *Apostelgeschichte*[5] (1965); H. Windisch, *ThW* II 507; Arndt-
Gingrich, *Lexicon, s.v.*

[3] This is also emphasized by W.C. van Unnik, The Purpose of the Fourth Gospel, in :
Studia Evangelica (1959) 395ff, 400; F.L. Cribbs, A Reassessment of the Date of Origin
and the Destination of the Gospel of John., *JBL* 89 (1970) 49f.

[4] Schnackenburg, Messiasfrage, 247.

ry interest[1] (cf. the fact that the woman is also portrayed as witness like Andrew and Philip in c. 1). Concerning the general character of S, one is struck by the dominance of the single theme *that* Jesus is the Messiah while all additional Christian teaching and symbolism are absent. Would this not fit exceedingly well in a Jewish missionary situation where there is only one question in dispute, namely, is Jesus the expected One ? Unbelievers would not understand the Eucharistic symbolism which appears in all the Synoptic accounts of the feeding miracle — is this not why it seems to be wanting in S ?

If this is so, it must be verified by the Johannine redaction, because John would surely have known the purpose of his source. There are a number of indications of Jewish missionary work in Jn. so that some scholars have argued that the Gospel as a whole is a missionary tract for the Jews.[2] In the next chapter I shall show that this is improbable; the preaching in the Gospel is meant for believers; there is hostility between the Church and the Synagogue; it seems as though a new situation has arisen in which the Church is hardly doing Jewish missionary work any longer. The traces of Jewish missionary work which Van Unnik and others discovered in Jn. are due to the fact that the author used a book containing missionary preaching as source, and his work still reflects the former situation of Jewish missionary work in many respects. (see pp. 145ff.)[3]

6.   THE BACKGROUND OF JEWISH EXPECTATIONS

If S incorporated the preaching of Jewish Christians to Jews, that Jesus is the Messiah whom they expected, one would anticipate an attempted demonstration that Jesus corresponds to the Jewish expectations about the Messiah. At first sight, this seems not to be the case.

A)   *The Problem : The Messiah and Miracles*

The Jews did not expect the Messiah to be a wonder-worker or one legitimized by signs. He would be a normal human being who would

---

[1] Van Unnik, Purpose, 408.

[2] Van Unnik, Purpose; J.A.T. Robinson, The Destination and Purpose of St. John's Gospel, *NTS* 6 (1959/60) 117ff.

[3] Fortna (225) is of opinion that his "Gospel of Signs" was a missionary tract for Jews.

bring political unity and freedom to Israel. It was expected that illness and death would be abolished in the Messianic time; there would be abundant fertility of the earth, plenty of wine and manna — but all these would be given by God and were not regarded as miracles of the Messiah.[1]

It appears that the Jews were not so interested in wonder-workers as the Hellenists. We have seen (pp. 55f.) that there were no men who were regarded as real wonder-workers in the Palestinian-Jewish world. Although Josephus tries to convince the Hellenistic world of the significance of the Jewish nation and likes to stress the Old Testament miracles to this purpose, he mentions only a few exorcisms dating from the first century A.D. and no other real miracle stories.[2] Q, which is one of the most Palestinian parts of the Synoptic tradition, mentions only one miracle — in a pericope which cannot be called a real miracle story because the main content is dialogue (Mt. 8 : 5ff. par.). Matthew is the most Jewish of the Synoptic Gospels. The author abbreviated the miracle stories of Mark, omitted some and emphasized the logia of Jesus. He went further than Mark in attaching theological themes to the miracle stories : in 15 : 28 he added the theme of faith; in 8 : 17 and 12 : 18-21, of the fulfilling of God's promises and of God's compassion.[3]

---

[1] Bill. I 593-6; J. Klausner, *The Messianic Idea in Israel* (1954) 502-8. Those who differ from this, always refer to Pesiq. R. 36 where it is stated that the Messiah will stand on the pinnacle of the temple and say to Israel : "Ihr Geplagten, die Zeit eurer Erlösung ist da; und wenn ihr es nicht glaubt, so sehet auf mein Licht, das über euch aufstrahlt" (Bill. I 641). The passage is tannaitic (E. Bammel, "John. did no miracle", in : *Miracles*, ed. C.F.D. Moule, 1965, 188f.), and the light is a legitimizing sign, but it is not explicitly stated that it is a sign which the Messiah performed, and it is the only reference of the kind among the thousands of rabbinical references to the Messiah. Therefore, it seems to be rather a case of the exception proving the rule. Recently E. Bammel again contended that the Messiah was expected to perform miracles and quoted Pesiqtha Rabbathi and Threni R. ad Lam. 2 : 2 where it is told that Akiba believed in the Messiahship of Bar Kochba on account of his miracles (*op. cit.*, 188f.). The significant fact is, however, that it was not normally reported of Bar Kochba that he had performed miracles. The majority agree that the Messiah was not expected to be a worker of miracles, e.g., G. Delling, Botschaft und Wunder, 390; E. Lohse, *RGG*³ VI 1834; E. Schweizer, *Jesus Christus*, 127; J.L. Martyn, *History and Theology in the Fourth Gospel* (1968) 85ff. (On Qoh.R.1 — *vide infra*).

[2] Schlatter, *Wunder*, 54.

[3] Cf. H.J. Held, Matthäus als Interpret der Wundergeschichten, in : G. Bornkamm-G. Barth-H.J. Held, *Überlieferung und Auslegung im Matthäusevangelium* (1960) 284 : while Mark used the miracle stories for manifestation, Matthew used them for Christian teaching. He goes further and says that in the miracle stories of Matthew, the interest is

How could S then, if Jewish, emphasize the miracles so much ? We have already noticed that Josephus tells about people who gave themselves out as prophets and promised to legitimize themselves with sēmeia. It might prove worth while to explore this connection.

B) *The Prophet and Miracles*

Occasionally in the dense forest of Jewish eschatological expectations, traces are evident of popular expectations of some prophetic figure, and unlike the Messiah, this figure is frequently associated with miracles. Mal. 4 : 5 promises that the prophet Elijah will come before the day of the Lord, and it is clear that in different forms this became a very lively expectation in late Judaism.[1] Elijah was one of the wonder-workers of the Old Testament and the late-Jewish expectations sometimes refer to this. According to Pirqe Maschiach 72, he would show Israel seven signs "like Moses" to convince them to believe, among other things by bringing people back to life and showing them the manna.[2]

Moses, the major figure of the sēmeia, was regarded as a prophet in the Pentateuch by the layers E and D.[3] (Cf. Dt. 34 : 10, where it is said, "there has never yet risen in Israel a prophet like Moses", and in v. 11, his signs are propounded as evidence.) In Dt. 18 : 15 Moses promises : "The Lord your God will raise up a prophet from among you like myself", and in V. 18, it is added that God will put all his words in the mouth of this prophet who will convey all his commands. These verses are very seldom referred to in the late Jewish literature, but there are a few indications that a prophet like Moses was expected to return. According to 1QS 11,9ff., the community of Qumran had to keep all the commandments "until the prophet and the Messiahs of Aaron and Israel come". 4Q Test. 5ff. makes it clear that the expectation of the

---

never in the miracle itself, and, therefore, they should rather be seen as paradigmata (p. 230f.). This seems to me to go too far. Compare, for instance, the fact that Matthew sometimes enhances the miracles of Mark (p. 71 *supra*) and that the full confession of 14 : 33 is inspired by the miracle itself.

[1] Jeremias, *ThW* II 930ff.

[2] Mekh. Ex. 16 : 33 says Elijah will restore to Israel the manna and the flask with oil which will remain undiminished until he anoints the Messiah with it. It was also expected that Elijah would play a part in the resurrection of the dead (Sotah 49b; p. Scheq. 47c, quoted by Klausner, *Messianic Idea*, 456).

[3] G. von Rad, *Theologie des Alten Testaments I*[6] (1969) 305f.

prophet was based on Dt. 18.[1] Also with Dt. 18 in mind, the Samaritans
expected Moses to return. They called the figure *Ta'eb* and he would
repeat the great signs of Moses.[2] The Samaritan impostor whom
Josephus mentions in *Ant.* 18, 85f. must be understood in this light.
In approximately 35 A.D. he persuaded the Samaritans to accompany
him on to Mt. Gerizim where he would show them the holy objects
buried there by Moses — this is apparently meant as authenticating
miracle. Then they would commence the holy war.[3]

Josephus mentions a number of Jews with similar pretentions.
Ant. 20, 97 : under Fadus (44-46 A.D.), Theudas persuaded many to
follow him to the Jordan which he would part with his word, προφήτης
γὰρ ἔλεγεν εἶναι. The Romans immediately killed them all (also
mentioned in Acts 5 : 36). *Ant.* 20, 167f. : under Nero betrayers in
Jerusalem lured a multitude to come with them to the desert where
they would show them τέρατα καὶ σημεῖα (the parallel account in
Bell. 2, 259 has σημεῖον ἐλευθερίας). *Ant.* 20, 169f. : under Felix, an
Egyptian, προφήτης εἶναι λέγων, called the people to follow him on
to the Mt. of Olives (the parallel account in *Bell.* 2, 261ff. says they
first went to the desert) from where he would let the city walls of
Jerusalem fall by his word (also in Acts 21 : 38). *Ant.* 20, 188 : a deceiver
promises the people happiness if they would follow him to the desert.
Bell. 7, 437ff. : 73 A.D. in Cyrene a certain Jonathan persuaded a
crowd to follow him into the desert where he would show them signs
and portents. The legitimizing signs, the expression τέρατα καὶ
σημεῖα, the repeated appearance of the desert, the content of the
signs — all make it clear that in some way or other all these prophets
had in mind the Jewish expectations concerning the return of Mosaic
times.[4]

In 1 Macc. 14 : 41 a preliminary decision is taken to be in force
ἕως τοῦ 'αναστῆναι προφήτην πιστόν ; the same in 4 : 46. This
prophet is not explicitly stated to be *the* eschatological prophet, but an
implicit connection with Moses and Dt. 18 : 18f. is probable where it is
said that the prophet will convey all God's commands.[5]

---

[1] See especially R. Schnackenburg, Die Erwartung des "Propheten" nach dem
N.T. und den Qumran-Texten, in : *Studia Evangelica* (1959) 631-6.

[2] W.A. Meeks, *The Prophet-King, Moses Traditions and the Johannine Christology*
(1967) 246ff.; Martyn, *Hist. and Theol.*, 96.

[3] Meyer, *Prophet*, 83; Hahn, *Hoheitstitel*, 362.

[4] Hahn, *Hoheitstitel*, 361f.; Jeremias, *ThW* IV 866; Meyer, *Prophet*, 85; Rengstorf,
ThW VII 223.

[5] Jeremias, *ThW* IV 862; R. Schnackenburg, Erwartung des "Propheten", 631f.

A number of other passages stress the strong association between any prophet and authenticating miracles. We have already seen that according to Dt. 13 : 22, the typical false prophet will try to deceive Israel by giving σημεῖον ἢ τέρας. In Ps. 74 : 9 the post-exilic complaint is : "We do not see our signs (sēmeia); there is no longer any prophet." According to S. Dt. 18 : 19 the words of a prophet may be accepted if he performs miracles. This statement must date from the first century because Akiba and Jose had a discussion which presupposes it [1] (Sanh. 90a and S. Dt. 13 : 3) — they both accept the basic rule; similarly p. Sanh. 18 (30c), Sanh. 89b. In Sanh. 98a, R. Jose b. Qisma (around 110) prophecies when the Messiah will come and authenticates his words with a sign : the water of the caves of Pameas change to blood. This recalls the signs of Moses.

C) *The Prophet and the Messiah*

Clearly, if we can prove that S intended to answer these and similar expectations, we have gained much. The only problem is that S preaches Jesus as Messiah while none of the figures referred to above is called Messiah, and in the case of Qumran the eschatological prophet is even clearly distinguished from the Messiah. Would the preachers of S gain anything by showing the Jews that Jesus corresponds to their expectations about the prophet ? Are there any indications in Jewish thought of a possible identification of the prophet with the Messiah ?

A connection between the two might become indirectly visible in the false prophets of Josephus. Their aim was deliverance from the Romans, which corresponds with Jewish Messianic expectations. The "Prophet Moses" whom the Samaritans expected had some Messianic traits : he was sometimes called king and would destroy the opponents of God;[2] we saw that the Samaritan prophet whom Josephus mentions wanted to revolt against the Romans.

There is, however, a much broader basis for the connection of ideas about the prophet and the Messiah. For the Jews, the salvation from Egypt was the prototype of the Messianic salvation. According to Klausner, the ideas about Exodus and Moses were the ultimate source of the Messianic idea in Judaism,[3] and according to Bill. I 85, they had a stronger influence on Jewish eschatology than any other idea. A few

---

[1] Bammel, "John did no miracle", 190.
[2] Meeks, *Prophet-King*, 249, 251.
[3] *Messianic Idea*, 18.

examples will suffice. According to Micah 7 : 15, God will redeem his
people and show them θαυμαστά as in the days of the Exodus. In
Is. 48 : 21 God miraculously supplies Israel with water from the rock
when he leads them out of bondage. Pesiq. 67b expects that God will
punish the Romans by miraculous plagues just as in the times of old.
One would expect this typology also to be applied to the Messiah, but
this is surprisingly seldom the case. The oldest rabbinical instance of
the Moses-Messiah typology is Tanch. 7b : R. Aqiba (90-135) foretold
that the Messiah would lead Israel into the desert for 40 years like
Moses.[1] After this, no word was said about this typology until about
300 A.D. when R. Isaac made a statement which was often repeated :
Qoh. R. 1, 8 : "As the first redeemer was (= Moses), so shall the latter
Redeemer be", namely he will give manna, let water gush forth, etc.
In one of the later repetitions of this basic sentence in Pirqe Maschiach
72, the passage is added to which we referred earlier when we commen-
ced this discussion : Elijah appears with the Messiah and shows the
Israelites seven signs "like Moses".

The conclusion may be that although the expectations of a prophet and
the Messiah are not usually identified, the possibility of such identification lay inherently in Judaism because the Mosaic times and Moses,
the first prophet, were placed in a typological relationship to the
Messianic time and even sometimes the Messiah himself. As far as the
sēmeia in S are concerned, the hypothesis which has to be tested can
then be that S could use the miracles of Jesus to proclaim them as
sēmeia, not because the Jews expected sēmeia from the Messiah, but
because they had many ideas about a (final) prophet authenticated by
signs, and these ideas had the inherent possibility of being connected to
Jewish Messianic expectations.[2]

D) *New Testament Examples of the Signs of the Prophet connected
with the Messiah*

These examples cannot prove anything for S, but they can help
prepare us for a full understanding of its Christology. The Moses-Messiah
typology is important in the New Testament, and there are also many
references to expectations of a prophet. We take a brief look at the
passages where these expectations are connected with miracles.

According to Mk. 6 : 14f. par. (cf. Mk. 8 : 27f. par.), Herod and the

[1] Jeremias, *ThW* IV 865.
[2] Cf. in particular Hahn, *Hoheitstitel*, 219.

people were struck by the miracles of Jesus[1] and wondered whether he could be John the Baptist, Elijah or "a prophet like one of the prophets" (Luke : one of the old prophets). All three possibilities are prophetic figures. The last is no explicit reference to the eschatological prophet, but some basic connection cannot be denied.[2]

We have already discussed the σημεῖα καὶ τέρατα of the false prophet of Dt. 13 : 2 and its citation in Mk. 13 : 22. Note that ψευδόχριστοι is added to the quotation — a striking appearance of our basic triangle signs-prophet-Messiah. In the parallel in Matthew, the next verse (24 : 26) adds that the Church should not be deceived when they say ἰδοὺ ἐν τῇ ἐρήμῳ ἐστίν, which also reflects the Mosaic typology.[3] In Rev. 11 : 3-12 two witnesses or prophets (v. 10) appear who have the power to shut up the sky so that no rain falls (cf. Elijah) and to strike the earth with many plagues such as turning water into blood (cf. Moses). Finally they will be taken up into heaven (cf. Elijah). These two prophets are probably meant to be Moses and Elijah and it is probable that Jewish tradition is adopted here because it was not the usual Christian expectation that Elijah would appear again, and there is a very similar expectation in the Coptic Elijah-apocalypse 163ff.[4] The same Jewish expectation is reflected in the transfiguration scene where Elijah and Moses appear to legitimize Jesus as final prophet (note that Dt. 18 : 15 is partly quoted, Mk. 9 : 7).[5]

We have seen that it is especially Acts which uses the word sēmeion in the "Mosaic" sense, and we would expect clearer examples of the Moses-typology in this book. Twice Dt. 18 : 15 is applied to Jesus : 3 : 22 and 7 : 37. The speech of Stephan in c. 7 is particularly interesting. He describes the life of Moses with Jesus continually in mind.[6] The Israelites rejected Moses (vv. 25, 35, 39) as the Jews now reject Jesus (v. 51). As Jesus, Moses came to the Israelites as λυτρωτής (v. 35) to bring them σωτηρία (v. 25). Moses worked τέρατα καὶ σημεῖα like Jesus (2 : 22); he was δυνατὸς ἐν λόγοις καὶ ἔργοις. More or less

---

[1] In the Lucan parallel (9 : 7) it seems to be explicitly stated that the different identifications were made on the basis of Jesus' miracles (Jeremias, ThW II 938).

[2] Cullmann, Christologie, 34, thinks the eschatological prophet is meant; Jeremias, ThW IV 862, and Hahn, Hoheitstitel, 223, think it possible; it is denied by Lohmeyer, Mk., and Schnackenburg, Erwartung, 627.

[3] Jeremias, ThW IV 866.

[4] Jeremias, ThW II 942; E. Lohse, Offenbarung (NTD,[2] 1966); E. Lohmeyer, Offenbarung (HNT[2], 1953); R.H. Charles, Revelation (ICC, 1920).

[5] Hahn, Hoheitstitel, 337; Jeremias, ThW IV 873.

[6] Hahn, Hoheitstitel, 382ff.; Jeremias, ThW IV 873.

the same words are used of Jesus in Lk. 24 : 19 where it is said that he
was a προφήτης δυνατὸς ἐν ἔργῳ καὶ λόγῳ. In v. 21 it is added that
they hoped he would λυτροῦσθαι τὸν ᾽Ισραήλ (cf. Acts 7 : 35). It is
clear that Jesus is the eschatological prophet like Moses.[1] After the
greatest miracle described in the Synoptics (the raising at Nain), the
onlookers proclaim Jesus as προφήτης μέγας (Lk. 7 : 16). The final prophet is probably meant because it is added that God visited his people.[2]
Lk. 7 : 15 quotes from the raising miracle of Elijah (1 Kgs. 17 : 23).

We saw (p. 57) that Mk. 6 : 40 relates the feeding miracle to Moses :
Jesus is the new Moses who gives the eschatological manna. It
might be just possible that the ten miracles which Matthew relates in
the section cc. 8-9 are meant as a hidden parallel to the ten plagues of
Moses[3] — especially because Matthew comprises many other examples
of an implied Moses-Messiah typology.

One of the most important *logia* about Jesus' miracles is Mt. 11 : 4f.
John the Baptist asked whether Jesus is the One who was to come, to
which Jesus simply refers him to his miracles. These words do not in
the first place fit the specific Jewish expectations about the Messiah.
Jesus rather supposes general Jewish expectations for the time of
redemption[4] — but the list is ended by a specific reference, namely, to
the calling of the prophet in Is. 61 : 1. In Jesus' sermon in Lk. 4 : 18-27
the words of Is. 61 : 1f. are quoted in full. Jesus says they are fulfilled
in him : he is a prophet (v. 24) of whom miracles would be expected.
He explains the fact that he does not do miracles in Nazareth, by
referring to Elijah and Elisha. Is. 61 : 1 is also quoted in Acts 10 : 38
and related to the miraculous power of Jesus.

Finally, the incident of the Pharisees seeking a sign from Jesus
(Mk. 8 : 11ff. par.) must be understood against the background of
this whole complex of ideas. They would not have had in mind the
authentication of a rabbi nor directly that of the Messiah but rather the
legitimation of a prophet, or probably the final prophet.[5] An attestation
of this is that in Jn. 6 : 30f. the Jews demand a sign from Jesus and
refer to the manna as example of such a sign.

---

[1] G. Friedrich, *ThW* VI 847; Hahn, *Hoheitstitel*, 387ff.

[2] K.H. Rengstorf, *Lk.* (NTD[14], 1969) 97; Friedrich, *ThW* VI 847f.

[3] Friedrich, *ThW* VI 848. Schnackenburg, 637, and Hahn, *Hoheitstitel*, 400, say it is
perhaps so.

[4] Jeremias, *Theol.*, 107.

[5] Hahn, *Hoheitstitel*, 391; Kertelge, *Wunder*, 26; Schlatter, *Der Evangelist Matthäus*[5]
(1959) 414f., refers to the prophets of Josephus.

Our conclusion can be that the New Testament adds strong evidence
that the Jews of the first century expected the coming of an eschatological prophet who would be authenticated by signs, and it is clear that
the early Christian preachers made use of the possibility in Jewish
thought of connecting this expectation with Messianic ideas by proclaiming Jesus, the Messiah, as final prophet. Is this the reason why S
so strongly emphasizes the miracles of Jesus as sēmeia ?

7. CONCLUSION : THE DEEPER MOTIVES OF THE CHRISTOLOGY OF S

A) *Miracles — Prophet — Messiah*

The indication that we are now approaching from the right direction
for penetrating to the heart of S is that S and the rest of Jn. contain the
clearest references to the eschatological prophet in the New Testament.
According to Jn. 1 : 19ff., a Jewish deputation asks John the Baptist
who he is; when he denies that he is the Messiah, they thereupon ask
whether he is Elijah or "the prophet". In 7 : 40f., it is narrated that
many Jews held Jesus for "the prophet", others for the Messiah. It is
clear that Elijah and the prophet are meant as eschatological figures,
and in the light of the Jewish expectations which we have examined,
it seems probable that the prophet is the one of Dt. 18.[1] This will
become clearer as we proceed. In 9 : 17 the first confession which the
formerly blind man makes on the basis of the miracle is that Jesus is a
prophet, and the Samaritan woman says the same in 4 : 19 after Jesus
has revealed his miraculous knowledge. These are not explicit references
to the eschatological prophet, but we have already seen that the
writer(s) of c. 4 seems to have known enough about the Samaritans to
realize that "prophet" is very near to "Mosaic prophet" on the lips of
a Samaritan. In both 4 : 19 and 9 : 17, growing faith is described, and,
therefore, "a prophet" was possibly used somewhat pregnantly.[2] 4 : 19
was perhaps part of S. In any case, the only confession directly following
a miracle in S is that Jesus is the prophet (6 : 14). Bultmann (158, 2)

---

[1] Schnackenburg; Brown; Jeremias, *ThW* IV 862. Barrett, 272, rejects this because
the prophet is distinguished from the Messiah — he overlooks the fact that the point is
precisely that the prophet is *not* in the first place a Messianic figure. (He accepts the
Mosaic prophet for 6 : 14.)

[2] Similarly Meeks, *Prophet-King*, 34, and Hahn, *Hoheitstitel*, 397. Martyn, *History*,
109, thinks both actually refer to *the* prophet; Rengstorf, *ThW* VII 243, thinks so of
4 : 19.

thinks the Mosaic prophet cannot be meant because the next verse seems
to imply that the crowd took Jesus as Messiah since they wanted to
make him king, and, according to Bultmann, the Mosaic prophet was
not expected as king.[1] It is indeed striking that Jn. clearly distinguishes
between the prophet and the Messiah in 1 : 21 and 7 : 20, while he
seems to identify them here (6 : 15 is probably J).[2] But the arguments
for the Mosaic prophet in 6 : 14 preponderate. We have seen that the
early tradition probably connected the feeding miracle to Moses and
the manna (Mk. 6 : 40), and although there is no such reference in the
pericope of S, John is apparently conscious of this meaning of the
feeding miracle because in 6 : 30f. he interprets it in relation to the
manna. Add to this 1 : 21 and 4 : 19, and we may be confident that
6 : 14 refers to the prophet of Dt. 18. In other words, we have here
another instance of the unusual, the identification of the prophet with
the Messiah.[3] 6 : 14f. is then an instance of the triangle, miracle —
prophet — Messiah, on which the Christology of S is based. One would
expect more instances of the Moses-Messiah typology in Jn., but in
spite of many attempts to find some others, the only ones are 6 : 14, 30.[4]

---

[1] He prefers to take "prophet" as Hellenistic title for *theios anēr* (p. 138); similarly
Wetter, *Der Sohn*, 68ff.; Becker, *Wunder*, 140, and H.M. Teeple, *The Mosaic Eschatological Prophet* (1957) 120.

[2] The extensive monograph of W.A. Meeks, *The Prophet-King, Moses Traditions and
the Johannine Christology* (1967), takes this problem as starting-point. His solution is
that the "king" of 6 : 15 does *not* refer to the Messiah but to the kingly traits of the figure
of Moses in late-Jewish thought (especially Philo, the Samaritans, etc.). After having
examined all the Jewish material, he finds many traces of Moses' kingship in Jn. It
seems to me, however, that the basic exegesis of 6 : 15 is incorrect. (a) He underestimates
the early signs of the connection between the prophet and the Messiah (Josephus, Akiba)
and especially the basic possibility for such an identification (the Mosaic time-Messianic
time typology). (b) John usually identifies "king" and Messiah : 1 : 49 (cf. the whole
pericope); 12 : 13ff., where "the King of Israel" is connected to the king of Zech. 9 : 9,
and there is extensive evidence that the latter passage was interpreted Messianically
(Bill. I 842-4). The parallels in Matthew and Mark explicitly understood "King of Israel"
in the Davidic sense. (Barrett and Bultmann agree about Jn. 12 : 13.)

[3] Jeremias, *ThW* IV, 863; Hahn *Hoheitstitel*, 370.

[4] Jeremias, *ThW* IV, 866 and Rengstorf, *ThW* VII, 256. G. Ziener, Weisheitsbuch
und Johannesevangelium, *Bib.* 38 (1957) 396-416, tries to prove that John relates the
seven sēmeia to seven of the miracles in Exodus by comparing the way in which the
Wisdom of Solomon treats the sēmeia of Exodus. The last attempt of the kind was made
by R.H. Smith, Exodus Typology in the Fourth Gospel, *JBL* 81 (1962) 329-342. He
rejects the earlier hypotheses of Enz, Hunt, and Sahlin and tries to show that the seven
sēmeia are in typological correspondence to seven of the plagues. I mention only two of
the instances which *might* make some sense. Sahlin and Smith (p. 334) proposed that the

In Acts, the words σημεῖα καὶ τέρατα sometimes explicitly refer to Moses, but in S this is not the case, although the Exodus-typology is the background for the use of the word sēmeion in S. There are some indirect indications that this typology is always there as foundation.

We have seen that there were actually two eschatological prophets expected, Moses and Elijah. The latter is mentioned along with the prophet (Moses) and the Messiah in 1 : 21, and there are a number of parallels in S to the miracle stories of Elijah and Elisha in 1 and 2 Kings (see the notes in part 3 on 2 : 4; 4 : 50; 6 : 9). It cannot be wholly accidental that the kind of miracles which S describes agree with those of Elijah and Elisha : the multiplication of bread (2 Kgs. 4 : 42-4, cf. the multiplication of oil, 4 : 1-7); raising from the dead (1 Kgs. 17; 2 Kgs. 4 — both concern a *boy*, cf. Jn. 4 : 46ff.); changing of bad water to good water (2 Kgs. 2 : 19-25 — cf. changing water to wine); washing oneself to be healed (2 Kgs. 5 : 10 — the closest parallel to Jn. 9 : 7, cf. Jn. 5 : 3). Like Kings, S contains no exorcisms.[1] Is it then the intention to cast Jesus as the second Elijah ? This is never explicitly stated as of the other two figures in 1 : 21. Probably the best interpretation of the thought of S is possible when we do not too sharply distinguish between Elijah and Moses. The two figures could become more or less amal-gamated[2] as prototypes of the eschatological prophet and founders of the Old Testament miracle tradition. The feeding miracle of S refers to both Moses (6 : 14) and the book of Kings (6 : 9). The key word of S. sēmeion, has its parallel only in the Mosaic miracles and not in those of Kings, but most references in the miracle stories themselves are to Kings. If the kinds of miracles in S are parallelled by those of Kings, they agree nearly as much with those of Moses because Kings already shows many parallels to Moses. Like Moses, Elijah also went through the desert to Horeb where God appeared to him (1 Kgs. 19); like Moses at Marah, Elisha also changed bad water to good (2 Kgs. 2 : 19-25, cf. the fact that Moses also changed water into blood); Moses gave manna while Elisha multiplied bread; Moses crossed the Red Sea and his successor Joshua, the Jordan, as also Elijah and his successor Elisha (cf. Jesus' walking upon the water ?). We have also seen that Moses and

---

first miracle of the wine is related to the first plague of the changing of water into blood. It is often suggested that Jesus' walking on the water must be parallelled to the crossing of the Red Sea, e.g., Brown, 255, and O. Betz (orally).

[1] Cf. Michel, Anfang der Zeichen, 19 : "Die Vermehrung, die Verwandlung und die Auferweckung sind die drei Stoffe die an die Urzeit (= Elijah) erinnern."

[2] Brown, 235.

Elijah are sometimes associated with each other in Jewish expectations.[1] Therefore, the intention of S is interpreted correctly by O.
Michel : "Man hat Jesus als den endzeitlichen Moses und Elias ange-
sehen, der die Wunder der Urzeit wieder lebendig machte".[2] This must
not be understood in the sense that S intended an explicit typological
relationship between certain miracles of Jesus and certain ones of
old Israel. The typology is rather at work beneath the surface; it is the
barely visible foundation of the whole Christology of S, namely, the
expectation that there would be a correspondence between the final
salvation and the salvation of Israel of old, between the Messianic time
and the Mosaic era — including the "Mosaic" figure of Elijah. The
Jews expected that there would be miracles in the Messianic time,
that the prophet would be legitimized by them, and the prophet
could be identified with the Messiah. *Therefore*, S could proclaim the
miracles of Jesus as authenticating sēmeia of the Messiah.

B)   *The Divine Jesus*

The primary driving force behind this whole chapter was the attempt
to explain the massive concentration on Jesus' miraculous power in S.
J.L. Martyn recently argued that S shows "a single-minded focusing on
Christology. ... The reader ... is *not* told that a new age has dawned or
is about to dawn. He is *not* taught that suffering and sin are now
destroyed (Jesus does not perform miracles in order to alleviate
suffering or to attack sin and evil). ... He *is* told again and again who
Jesus is : the Christ, the Messiah of Israel".[3] (Of course, this is a slight
overstatement.) In a certain sense S is monotone, providing only the
miracles as proof *that* Jesus is the One and nothing more. We have seen
that there are some arguments for the theory that this dominance of
the thaumaturge must be due to influence of the Hellenistic *theios anēr*-
ideas and that nearly all those who have specifically studied S accept it.
Thus far we have, however, been led by the evidence to explain the
character of S along other lines. Let us recapitulate in order to see
whether S has been fully explained.

We have found that miracles as such are meaningful to Jews,
especially in the light of their eschatological expectations, and the

---

[1] E.g., Pirqe Maschiach 72, where Elijah performs seven signs "like Moses", *inter alia*
by giving manna; in Rev. 11 : 6 they can *both* close the heaven and cnange water into
blood; cf. Mk. 9 : 4.

[2] Anfang, 19.

[3] Source Criticism and Religionsgeschichte, 253.

fact that the wonders of S are very miraculous need not point to
Hellenistic influence because, like all ancient Orientals, the Jews were
also interested in the miraculous, and they frequently magnified it.[1]
The single-minded concentration on Jesus' power and the faith which
it should evoke may be an indication that S reflects heated missionary
debating in which there was really only one issue : "Who is Jesus?"
The virtual absence of teaching on the nature of Jesus' Messiahship may
also be due to the fact that Jewish listeners could fill in the contents of
the Messiahship for themselves from the Old Testament. We saw that
another reason for the strong emphasis on the astonishing miracles and
the divine centrality of Jesus is probably that S seems to incorporate a
fairly developed, theological form of the tradition. It is clear from the
whole New Testament and the history of the early Church that the
divinity of Jesus was confessed with increasing clarity as the decades
passed by.

Can these considerations satisfactorily explain the Jesus of S? I do
not yet feel quite convinced of this. The reason may be that we have
thus far only searched for *historical* explanations for the character of
S — the influence of the environment and the tendencies of the tradition. Human thinking is, however, not something mechanical which
can be fully explained by external factors (may we add? : especially
when this thinking is inspired by the Holy Spirit). In the last analysis,
we should be willing to understand the character of S as the result of
conscious theological effort by believers. The preachers of S intentionally
wanted to lay strong emphasis on the divinity of Jesus. Therefore,
while they preached that the miracles were the signs that Jewish
eschatological expectations were fulfilled in Jesus, they did
not, as the Synoptics did, say the miracles were the marks of the
coming end, the Kingdom, because they meant that the miracles were
the signs that Jesus *Himself is* the End, the Kingdom. Everything is
centred on Jesus and therefore the miracles cannot be separated from
him as though they were only "credentials" which he gave away ; the
message of S is not the miracles but Jesus, and in the miracles one sees
who Jesus is. What does one see? *Sēmeia* can actually only be worked
by God. In the Synoptics the Jews ask Jesus a sign *from heaven* hoping

---

[1] In Keth. 106a the 100 men who were fed in 2 Kgs. 4 have become 2200. Miracles
were especially frequently magnified in Mechilta (Fiebig, *Jüd. Wundergeschichten*, 73).
A. Guttmann, The Significance of Miracles for Talmudic Judaism, *HUCA* 20 (1947) 401,
stresses the importance of the Biblical miracles for the rabbis — "the general tendency was
to exalt the Biblical miracles."

not for a miracle performed by him but a sign given by God.[1] In the
Pentateuch God is always the author of the sēmeia even if he sometimes
authorizes Moses to perform them. In Acts, it is not said that Jesus
or the apostles performed sēmeia before it is clearly stated that it is
actually God who works them: 2 : 22; 4 : 29; 14 : 3; 15 : 12.[2] Moreover,
we have indicated (p. 44) that in the Synoptics the miracles of Jesus
are sometimes seen as the work of God. In S, however, Jesus performs
all the sēmeia by his own authority, and God is never mentioned —
Jesus himself stands in the place of God. It is difficult for us to realize
the holiness of a miracle for ancient man. When he saw a wonder, he
trembled because he saw God acting. In S "Messiah" comes very near
to being equal to "God". Jesus is everything, and therefore the meeting
with him is all that is needed. No extra Christian teaching need be
added. When Jesus meets a sinful woman in Lk. 7 : 36ff., he gives
teaching on the forgiveness of sins and assures the woman that hers
are remitted. In Jn. 4, however, Jesus has a long conversation with
the Samaritan sinner but says no word of forgiveness; he only guides
the woman step by step to the insight that he is the Messiah. When
Jesus calls his disciples in Mk. 1, it is in the context of the preaching of
the Kingdom and he promises to make them fishers of men. On the
contrary, in the longer calling pericope in Jn. 1 : 35ff., there is only one
theme, namely, that they all should meet Jesus as the Messiah. The
most profound intention of the miracle stories of S is revealed in the
ἐγώ εἰμι of Jesus appearing on the water (6 : 20). We have seen
(pp. 58f.) that the connection between this formula and the solemn self-
revelation of Jahwe in the Old Testament can hardly be denied. The
miracles reveal that Jesus is the One in whom God came. It seems that
the basic message of S approaches the "high" Christology of John, of
which the ἐγώ εἰμι is one of the most elevated expressions. John
apparently understood 6 : 20 in this way because the walking on the
water seems to be the only miracle story to which he added no deeper
interpretation, not even by the insertion of words or phrases. Thus,
even the highest branches of John's Christology have direct roots in
the old Jesus-tradition — the ἐγώ εἰμι also appears in the Marcan
parallel!

Do we still need the *theios anēr*? I do not think so. The positive
evidence is not convincing because the few possible indications of

[1] Lohmeyer, *Mk.*; Hahn, *Hoheitstitel*, 391.

[2] The same in Rom. 15 : 19; Heb. 2 : 4; Jos. *Ant.* 20, 168 : τέρατα καὶ σημεῖα κατὰ
τὴν τοῦ θεοῦ πρόνοιαν γινόμενα.

Hellenistic influence seem to melt away when they are placed next to the numerous Jewish features of S.[1] S is developed, but even in the

---

[1] This result causes doubt about the alleged Hellenistic character of many of the *Synoptic miracle stories*. We have seen that there is a tendency among form critics to think that the more a miracle story stresses the miracle itself as epiphany, the greater the possibility that such a story is Hellenistic. The miracle stories of S, however, are the most miraculous epiphanies of the New Testament, and yet they proved to be completely Jewish. This is not the place to give a complete treatment of the vast problem of the Synoptic miracle stories, but a few remarks might be helpful to others who have to orient themselves. The first major form critics did not deny that there are some Jewish features in these stories but argued that they are predominantly Hellenistic, Bultmann by emphasizing the Hellenistic features (*Syn. Trad.*, 255) and Dibelius the Hellenistic *Sitz im Leben* (*Formgeschichte*, 93). In general form criticism has become less confident about the predominant Hellenistic colour of these stories. It is true that many cautious scholars think that the idea of the *theios anēr* had some influence, e.g., E. Schweizer, *Mk.*, 221f.; Hahn, *Hoheitstitel*, 292ff.; Kümmel, *Theol.*, 108f. But when it comes to the detailed form-critical investigation of the stories themselves, it seems that most no longer think that the Hellenistic features preponderate. O. Perels, *Die Wunderüber-lieferung der Synoptiker* (1934) 82ff., classified the features and found that in only five stories do enough significant features appear to justify our regarding them as Hellenistic : Nain (Lk. 7); the deaf-mute (Mk. 7); the blind of Bethsaida (Mk. 8); the Gerasene demoniac (Mk. 5); and the epileptic boy (Mk. 9). V. Taylor, *The Formation of the Gospel Tradition* (1933) 128, rejected the parallels of Bultmann and others by simply saying they *all* only reflect the natural way in which miracle stories are always told. In his trustworthy commentary on Mark (1936), Lohmeyer does not deny the Hellenistic traits but regards them as not predominant. In his article "*iáomai*" in *ThW* III (1938) 205ff., A. Oepke criticized the position of Bultmann especially by pointing out the differences between the Hellenistic and New Testament miracles : in the New Testament there is more restraint and simplicity; less egoism. The valuable (though short) study of R.H. Fuller, *Miracles*, 30ff., regards the majority of the Synoptic miracle stories as Palestinian because of the Jewish-Christian language and other features they contain; Hellenistic exceptions : the same five stories which Perels mentioned (pp. 34f, 54, 61, 64). Kertelge, *Wunder*, 40-3, Schweizer, *Mk.*, and Jeremias, *Theol.*, 92ff., are also critical of Bultmann without rejecting all of his Hellenistic parallels.

Many more scholars could be mentioned, but let us rather turn to a few of the salient points in the material itself. (a) The healing of the deaf-mute (Mk. 7 : 31-7) is frequently regarded as a very typical example of a Hellinistic miracle story (Jeremias, 94; Fuller, 34; Perels, 85); but we saw (p. 46) that $\mu o\gamma\iota\lambda\acute{a}\lambda o\varsigma$ (v. 32) and v. 37 refer to Is. 35 : 5f. and therefore, Lohmeyer seems to be justified in saying that the story is Jewish. (b) The story of the Gerasene demoniac (Mk. 5) is also held up by many as a specimen of secular, Hellenistic style (Perels, 85; Kümmel, *Theol.*, 108f.; Fuller, 35, 54). The fact is, however, that the most "secular" motif, the one of the swine, has its parallel in Jos. *Ant.* 8, 48 where an exorcism is demonstrated by the fact that the demon turns over a cup of water; for this and other reasons, Schweizer speaks of a "jüdische Erzähler". (c) Lohmeyer regards the narrative of the epileptic boy (Mk. 9) as Jewish because scribes are mentioned. These three examples causes one to doubt some of the alleged Hellenistic features on the basis of which these stories are judged. Take as test case the healing of the blind man at development itself it becomes clear that it is thouroughly Jewish and has developed — and become enriched — on the line of the authentic Jahwe-faith of Moses, Elijah and the Lord Jesus.

Bethsaida (Mk. 8 : 22-6). It is usually regarded as the very best example of a Hellenistic miracle story (Jeremias, 94; Kümmel, *Theol.*, 53; Fuller, 34); even Lohmeyer partly agrees. It is true that all the emphasis lies on the miracle itself, and there are no Jewish features. But what are the Hellenistic ones ? Jeremias, 94, mentions four : (a) the avoidance of the public — but Bultmann, 239, has to mention mostly Old Testament parallels to the basic motive that one may not see God working; (b) the manipulation — but this also occurs in Jewish stories, especially with spittle which was regarded as suitable for eye trouble, cf. Bill. II 15; 1 Kgs. 17 : 21; 2 Kgs. 4 : 34; Berakh. 5b; p. Kil. 9, 32b, 23. 35; (c) the difficulty of the cure — he refers to Bultmann, 237, who mentions only *one* Hellenistic example from Tacitus; (d) the gradual recovery of sight — but Bultmann, 240, can quote only two modern examples. Note also that this story is *very* similar to the apparently Jewish story of the deaf-mute. Is not the reason for the absence of Jewish-Christian features rather that the story is so short ? (Cf. the fact that the short story of the healing of Peter's mother-in-law, Mk. 1 : 29-31, also appears to have a perfect Hellenistic *Topik* — but we noted that it probably has to be judged an eyewitness report.)

There are, however, a number of Hellenistic features in the Synoptic miracle stories which I find very hard to dismiss : we have already noted the duration of the illness and the carrying of the bed as demonstration (p. 52); amazement (p. 66); the importance of the word δύναμις (p. 62); and the εὐλογήσας of Mk. 8 : 7 (p. 57); there may be more. I would add the striking parallels to Lk. 7 : 11-17 in *Vit. Apoll.* 4, 45; Apul. *Florida* 19, and also mentioned by Pliny and Celsus (Weinreich, *Antike Heilungswunder*, 173) — cf. Jeremias, 92; even Taylor, *Formation*, 125, regards this story as late. (But note that a number of traits in the Lucan pericope recall the raisings of Elijah and Elisha.) These single features cannot, however, do away with the fact that tnere is a basic difference between the extravagant atmosphere of the Hellenistic miracle stories with their numerous manipulations, signs of magic and crude fantasy, and the sober atmosphere of the Synoptic miracle stories where Jesus Christ is the Lord.

CHAPTER THREE

THE JOHANNINE REDACTION OF THE SĒMEIA TRADITIONS

We are now faced with the question, to what extent John agreed with the massive Christological emphasis on the miraculous in S and based his theology on it. The answer cannot be simple because there is extensive evidence which may be used to argue that John criticized a faith based on miracles, while on the other hand it is hard to deny that miracles play an important role in the Gospel. Their symbolical interpretation lead to the first two and the fifth of the seven basic sayings combining ἐγώ εἰμι with a predicate (6 : 35, 51 ; 8 : 12 cf. 9 : 5 ; 11 : 25, "I am the bread, the light, the life") by which it is clear that this symbolism must have been an essential element in the growth of John's theology. The problem is whether John really built this symbolism upon the miracles or whether he only used them as arbitrary illustrations for what he wanted to say anyway because they happened to belong to the tradition he had to use. This leads us directly into the central problem of Johannine theology, i.e., the relationship between event and meaning, history and interpretation, the earthly σάρξ of Jesus and the δόξα of the living Christ.

These questions may be approached in three different ways. In the first place, the results of the preceding chapters may be used in order to apply the method of *Redaktionsgeschichte* in the strict sense of the word : how did John edit the source ? In the second place, the conclusions of this method will have to be verified by a standard exegesis of some of the central concepts and portions in the Gospel. (These two approaches are not treated strictly separately.) In the third place, I shall attempt to make this whole book intelligible by a historical reconstruction of the change which must have taken place in the circumstances of the Johannine community between 80 and 90 A.D.

In order to secure clear insight into the depth of our problem, we shall first take a brief look at two interpretations of John which eminently illuminate the field in which we have to labour.

1. THE CONTROVERSY BETWEEN BULTMANN AND KÄSEMANN

The interpretations of these two scholars more or less embody the extremes of what is possible as far as the above questions are concerned. According to Bultmann, John rejected the miracle-theology of his source to a large extent while the radical reaction of Käsemann, his pupil, implies that John accepted and developed the image of Jesus as a divine worker of wonders. This does not mean that we can simply work out a middle course between the two because the interpretation of one is much closer to the truth than that of the other, and they basically agree on one vital point where it seems necessary to disagree with both. Reference is only made to those aspects of their interpretations with which we shall have to wrestle in the rest of the chapter.

Bultmann found John the best witness for his existential interpretation of the New Testament. For him the key to the Gospel is 1 : 14a : the word became flesh. This means that Jesus was "nichts als ein Mensch" (*Jhev.*, 40). The glory was totally concealed in the flesh; the revelation in Jesus was without any "Anschaulichkeit" (*Theol.*, 394)[1], never in "demonstrativen Aufdringlichkeit" (398). Nevertheless John preaches that this mere human being was Gods revelation — this is a total paradox ,"Ärgernis" (*Jh.*, 40). In order to accept this message, man must be willing to give up all his own standards and "den Anspruch seiner Selbstherrlichkeit". This frees him from the world and brings him to himself and to God (41).

It is clear that there can be no room for miracles. He stresses that "die σημεῖα als wunderbare Vorgänge kein Ausweis, keine Legitimation Jesu sind" (*Theol.*, 397). Therefore, the miracles as events are "im Grunde entbehrlich" (409). The significance of the miracles lies "gar nicht im mirakulösen Vorgang" (396), and they are only "Bilder, Symbole" (397) for what Jesus means to the believer. The miracles have no meaning in themselves, but the meaning lies hidden behind them and can only be "seen" with the spiritual eyes of faith. "Sie sind im Grunde nichts anderes als Worte, verba visibilia" (412). The glory which was seen in Jesus (1 : 14) has nothing to do with miraculous power (397) but is the meaning of Jesus which was only recognized by the Church after his death, i.e., it can only be said that Jesus' earthly life had glory in the light of the glory of Jesus' exaltation (376). As far as John's attitude towards tradition is concerned, it must, of course, be

---

[1] *Theologie des Neuen Testaments*[6] (1968).

said : "Jedenfalls sieht er die Aufgabe der Verkündigung der Gemeinde nicht in der Weitergabe der historischen Tradition von Jezus" (412). Bultmann even doubts that John saw the Cana miracle as a historical event (*Jh.*, 83, 4).

Obviously, however, the miracles were one of the most difficult obstacles Bultmann had to overcome in his existential interpretation of John. An exegete such as Bultmann could not deny that John sometimes emphasizes the miracles. He breaks his interpretative principle of "nichts als ein Mencsh" and admits this : "so wird doch der menschlichen Schwäche unter Umständen das σημεῖον konzediert" (*Jh.*, 173). The miracles can give "den ersten Anstoss zur Aufmerksamkeit auf Jezus, zum Anfang des Glaubens" (*Theol.*, 397) although a faith based on miracles is "kein wirklicher Glaube" (*Jh.*, 83, 7).

Käsemann more or less reversed the position of Bultmann, first in two articles, one of which treats the prologue, and then in 1966 working it out in a booklet in which he discusses the central issues of Johannine theology in such a profound and provocating way that the scientific debate will be stimulated for years.[1] He revived the old liberal interpretation of F.C. Baur, A.v. Harnack, E. Hirsch and others against which Bultmann had reacted. According to this interpretation, the Jesus of John is an "über die Erde schreitende Gott" (*Jesu*, 22). Käsemann argues that the "flesh" of 1 : 14a should not be stressed because Jesus is not depicted as a real man in the Gospel but rather as a divine epiphany (Prol., 175). He does not need food, knows everything, and performs the most miraculous wonders (22f.). The "flesh" does not mean that God *became* a man but only that he changed his place from heaven to earth for a while and appeared in human form in order to communicate with us (27). "In Wahrheit ändert er nicht sich selbst, sondern nur seinen jeweiligen Ort" (28). The human traits of Jesus in the Gospel are not signs of his humility but only "das unabdingbare Mindestmass der Ausstattungsregie" necessary to manifest God in the world (23f.). Of course, the Passion became a "Problem" for the Evangelist. It is not integrated in the Gospel but follows like an afterthought which could not be neglected because it was so important in the tradition. "Fast möchte man sagen, sie klappe nach, weil Johannes sie unmöglich übergehen ... konnte" (19). John reinterpreted

---

[1] Aufbau und Anliegen des Johanneischen Prologs, in : *Exegetische Versuche und Besinnungen* II (1964) 155-180; *Jesu Letzter Wille nach Johannes 17*[2] (1967). In this book he repeats more extensively and with some modification the theory first advanced in his essay "Ketzer und Zeuge" (1951).

it to fit his divine Jesus : for him it is not a sign of humiliation but of glory, Jesus returns to the Father. The obedience of Jesus in Jn. is "die Manifestation göttlicher Herrschaft"; his Passion is described as "Siegesweg" (38). The conclusion : the Christology of Jn. is a representation of "naiven Doketismus" (52).

The miracles are one of the most important links in Käsemann's argument. "Wunder sind auch für Johannes nicht entbehrlich und nicht bloss Konzessionen an menschliche Schwachheit. Dann brauchten sie nicht aufs äusserste gesteigert zu werden ... und wäre übersehen, dass sie ausdrücklich als Demonstrationen der Herrlichkeit Jesu beschreiben werden ... Gott manifestiert sich auf Erden nicht ohne Wunderglanz" (43f.). The glory of Jesus (1 : 14) is certainly not only his eternal meaning but in the first place his miraculous power (45). The earthly glory of Jesus is no anticipation of the glory of the exalted Christ but rather a projection of the glory of the preexistent Logos in the world (40f.).

He does not deny that there is also miracle-criticism in the Gospel. But this is not because John has anything against miracles; he only wants to avoid Jesus being forgotten on account of his gifts (45). The meaning of the miracles has to be seen, but this must be combined with the demonstrative element in them : "Wie wenig Johannes im Irdischen das Wahre sah, wie sehr er es bestenfalls Abglanz des Himmlischen sein liess und deshalb alle Wunder für ihn Zeichen und Hinweise auf die im Logos selber erfolgende Offenbarung blieben, als 'Beweise' göttlicher Macht im Raum des Vorläufigen hat auch er sie gelten lassen... Solche Beweise sind freilich doppeldeutig und, wenn isoliert, irreführend, wie gegen die vorjohanneische Überlieferung eingewandt wird." The word that Jesus is bread, light, life, etc. is "bestätigt" by the signs (96f.).

Because Jesus was no true man, historical tradition is not really important to John. The revelation which Jesus brought is not to be found *in* the flesh, in history; rather these are only the means through which the revelation came. Dogmatic reflection dominates the tradition in Jn. As far as John presents history, it must be said : "Die praesentia Christi ist ihr einziges Thema". The history is only the typical illustration of the divine truth (67). The narrative is not realistic but fantastic (82) — with the exception of the traditional sēmeia stories (66, 82). It is quite understandable then "dass hier mit der Überlieferung freier und gewalttätiger umgegangen wird als irgendwo sonst im Neuen Testament" (68). He rejects the statement of Barrett (72) that

John "takes pains to emphasize the historical reality of what he describes" and stresses that "Objekt des Sehens für Johannes nicht das ist, was wir den historischen Jesus nenen" (76).

2. John's Criticism of S : His Attitude towards Miracle-Faith

As we have seen, the traditions which John used had the aim of inspiring faith by proclaiming the miracles of Jesus. In attempting to evaluate John's redaction, one is first struck by the fact that he is apparently critical of this kind of faith. (a) He partly rejects it or regards it as of little value, (b) makes it clear that much has to be added to it, (c) but nevertheless maintains that the miracles have some significance as witnesses to Christ for those who need it.

A) *The Faith of the Masses*

At a first glance one is impressed by the fact that John frequently says many believed in Jesus because of his miracles. One is immediately inclined to think that this is a vital part of his message. On closer inspection, however, it becomes clear that what John means by πιστεύω in these instances is still far from full faith.

The first occurrence of the faith of the multitudes is 2 : 23 : "many believed in his name when they saw the signs that he performed." The following verse, however, adds that "Jesus for his part would not trust himself to them". The implication is that this faith is untrustworthy. According to 6 : 2 a large crowd followed Jesus after having seen his miracles. Their faith is strengthened by the multiplication of the bread so that they confess Jesus as the prophet (v. 14). But when they find Jesus again at the other side of the lake, he reproaches them that they do not seek him because they understood the meaning of the signs but only because they experienced the material miracles (26) and bluntly adds that although they saw, they do not believe (36). It seems that John did not wait until v. 26 to make it clear that he rejects the faith of the crowd but immediately stressed it by adding v. 15 to the source : the mob wanted to make Jesus "king" of a rebellion and Jesus hastily sought refuge in the mountains. In other words, what S probably intended as a positive confession is reinterpreted by John as a misunderstanding of Jesus. 4 : 45 says the Galileans received Jesus because they had seen the miracles he had performed in Jerusalem.

When one of them, a royal officer, comes to Jesus and entreats him to perform another miracle, Jesus complains to him about all the Galileans : "You will never believe without seeing signs and portents" (48). V. 45 then has a negative rather than a positive meaning : they received him *but only* on account of the miracles — finally they would reject him (6 : 66). It is probable that the problematic v. 44 has to be interpreted in this light : "A prophet is without honour in his own country", i.e., Galilee had an eye only for the miracles of Jesus.[1]

Further on in the Gospel there are a number of instances where the reaction to miracles is described by the word πιστεύω without any explicit criticism being added. We must note, however, that there are indications that John sometimes uses this word very loosely and intends to denote nothing more than an initial interest in Jesus with it. In 8 : 30f. it is twice stated that many believed in Jesus having heard his powerful words. Jesus puts their faith to the test by a word that is offensive to Jews (31f.); their reaction is that they want to kill him (37,40), and Jesus calls them the devil's brood (44). Another example is 4 : 39. The Samaritan woman told the villagers of Sychar about the miraculous knowledge of Jesus, and they were so interested that they walked over to invite him to stay with them for a while. After they had heard his word, they came to a true faith (42). But John already applies the word πιστεύω to their curiosity in v. 39 before they had even seen Jesus.

Now we are ready to examine 7 : 31 : "Among the people many believed in him. 'When the Messiah comes', they said, 'is it likely that he will perform more signs than this man ?'" This is no confession but only a careful question which reflects a very superficial way of thinking, supposing that signs can be added up as mere portents. The significance of this "faith" is rather that it occasions the action of the Jews in the next verse.

The climax of the first half of the Gospel, in which the revelation before the world is described (cc. 1-12), is the raising of Lazarus. In cc. 11-12 it is stressed again and again that the result of this wonderful deed of Jesus was the faith of many. According to 11 : 45, great numbers believed, but some reported Jesus to the Pharisees. The fear of the Jewish authorities is that all will come to faith on account of the many signs which Jesus performs (48), and they decide to kill him (53). Jesus leaves the vicinity for a while, but when it becomes known that

---

[1] Bultmann; Schnackenburg; Brown.

he is back in Bethany, the believing multitude journeys there again so that the authorities decide to kill Lazarus as well (12 : 9-11). This is followed by the triumphal entry. John explains that the reason that the multitudes hailed Jesus king is that those who had witnessed the miracle had spread the news of it. In a panic, the Pharisees exclaim that the world has gone after Jesus (17-19). Miracle-faith is so strongly emphasized in these chapters that it is all the more significant that there are indications that John does not really appreciate it. The climax of the popular movement was that the people hailed Jesus Messianic King — does this not indicate that He is misunderstood as in 6 : 15 ? The conclusion of the first half of the Gospel commences with the following surprising words : "In spite of the many signs which Jesus had performed in their presence they would not believe in him" (12 : 37). How could John have written these words shortly after having depicted the wide impact of the raising of Lazarus ? Some say John means all the preceding miracle-faith was in fact unbelief,[1] but this cannot be the case as this unbelief is *contrasted* to the weak faith of the many in v. 42. Part of the explanation is that v. 37 evaluates the total result of the earthly work of Jesus and means that although large numbers believed in him, the Jewish nation as a whole rejected him. But this can hardly be the full explanation because the numbers were not so small ! 12 : 12 literally says that all the pilgrims (ὁ ὄχλος) greeted Jesus as Messiah, and the impression this made on the Pharisees was that the world was following Jesus (19). The full solution is that when the final conclusion about the life of Jesus has to be drawn, the existing faith is negligible both because of low quality and of limited quantity. The low quality of the faith is stressed by vv. 42f. : nevertheless many of the leaders — and, therefore, many more of the ordinary people — believed in Jesus. But why was this then neglected in v. 37 ? The reason is given explicitly : their faith was so weak that they did not even confess it, "for they valued the glory of men rather than the glory of God." This attitude is the decisive obstacle to come to a true faith according to 5 : 44.

Thus the ending of the first half of the Gospel which may be called the book of signs, is that the signs were answered by unbelief. The point of the repeated mentioning of the faith of the crowds in the last two chapters is not that the sēmeia had good results but that the

---

[1] J.P. Charlier, La notion de signe dans le IVe évangile, in : *RSPhTh* 43 (1959) 438; L. Schottroff, *Glaubende*, 252. This interpretation leads to grave misunderstandings.

"faith" of the people caused the hatred of the authorities and therefore the rejection of Jesus (note that the "faith" is all three times followed by the reaction of the leaders).

The conclusion is that the miracle-faith of the masses is not held up as an example to the reader. John does not call it unbelief, but neither does he regard it as true faith — much has still to happen to it.

B) *The Critical Addition*

Jn. 9 presents a dramatization of the full scale of the development of faith, beginning with a miracle and ending with a complete confession. This gives us the opportunity of evaluating the role of miracle-faith. We have it here fully. The man born blind not only experiences the miracle himself but differs from the Jews of 12 : 42 who seek the glory of men : even before the hostile Jewish authorities he maintains that the miracle must prove that Jesus is a prophet (16) and authorized by God (33) so that he is excommunicated (34). Unlike those of 2 : 23ff. he is not unfaithful or untrustworthy so that Jesus is willing to entrust himself to him personally (35ff.). But this was also necessary because he does not yet understand who Jesus really is (36). One is not saved by a miracle-faith unless it leads one to a personal meeting with Jesus.

This is proved by 3 : 1ff. Nicodemus came as near to faith as could be expected that a good Jewish theologican would come on the basis of the miracles and he made a confession similar to that of 9 : 33 : the signs are a divine legitimation of Jesus as teacher. C. 3 is closely connected with 2 : 23ff. but this only means that Nicodemus is yet another example of one who was impressed by the miracles, not that he is one of those untrustworthy believers of 2 : 23 for it is not stated that he "believed"; he is more serious because he personally comes to Jesus; he is not untrustworthy because later it is twice mentioned that he stood up for Jesus (7 : 50; 19 : 39). Nevertheless, c. 3 portrays him as still totally on the side of the "flesh" (6) : he does not understand a thing (4, 7, 9) and does not believe (12). He will not be saved before he has been regenerated by the Spirit, which means the same as the personal meeting with Jesus of c. 9 because Jesus comes in the Spirit (14 : 18).

Jn. 4 — the Samaritan woman and her co-villagers, impressed by Jesus' miraculous knowledge (19, 29, 30), achieved a certain degree of "faith", but they only came to a true faith after having heard Jesus Himself (42) which is again identical to receiving the Spirit, for the Spirit works through the word (6 : 63).

1 : 50f. — we have seen (p. 39) that v. 51 is probably a deliberate addition by John to S. In the light of the foregoing it becomes completely intelligible. In S Nathanael believed in Jesus on account of his miraculous knowledge (49), and Jesus answers that his faith will grow when he sees more impressive miracles. John could not leave it at that and added : "You shall see heaven wide open, and God's angels ascending and descending upon the Son of Man." The Gospel reports no angelophanies, and, therefore, deeper vision is intended here : they shall see reflected in the miracles the unity of Son and Father. The growth of faith is reinterpreted by John : it will take place not by seeing more astonishing miracles but by insight into the deeper meaning of the miracles, e.g., that Jesus is "the real bread which ascended from heaven" (6 : 41). The addition is basically the same as in the foregoing instances, for the Spirit gives the insight. The fulfilment of this promise of Jesus to the disciples already commences in 2 : 11, and, as we shall see, the "critical addition" is included in their faith on the basis of the sēmeion mentioned there; the same applies to 20 : 31.

A mere miracle-faith is inadequate, but this does not mean the miracles cannot be a real help on the way to faith.

C) The Testimony of the Miracles as a Second Best

In 10 : 38 and 14 : 12, Jesus says in nearly identical words that men should believe his word ($\pi\iota\sigma\tau\epsilon\acute{u}\omega$ + dative referring to the words just pronounced), but if they do not, they should believe on account of his "works". That is to say, the word should be sufficient to convince, but if that is not the case with some, as a result of their human weakness, Jesus gives the works as second best.[1] (The same is implied by 10 : 25). This does not mean, however, that the miracles are a weak support for faith because the word $\check{\epsilon}\rho\gamma o\nu$ characterizes them as the works of God (5 : 17ff.). God knows the weakness of men and gave the miracles along with the Scriptures and John the Baptist as witnesses to Jesus (5 : 31-40, especially 5 : 36). But the theme of testimony also reveals that the miracles are second best because according to 8 : 14 the testimony of Jesus' word is actually sufficient. Does all this mean that John used the miracles as "arguments for faith" as in the orthodox apologetics? This is not quite true. John refuses to isolate the miracles. This is, for instance, revealed by the fact that he always uses the word $\check{\epsilon}\rho\gamma o\nu$ when referring to the testimony of the miracles. As we shall see (part

---

[1] Cf. A. Schlatter, Der Glaube im Neuen Testament[2] (1896) 122.

4 B), this word sometimes refers to both the miracle and the spiritual
work of Christ which it signifies, to both the deed and the word. It is
certainly the case in 5 : 36 and probably also in 10 : 38 and 14 : 12. In
other words, the ἔργα of Jesus on account of which the Jews should
believe are not only the miracles but also the signified spiritual "works"
of the living Christ bringing people to life in the Church.

That John's criticism of isolated proofs for faith is an important
theme, is forcefully borne out by the Thomas episode. The climax of
the Gospel is Thomas' confession in 20 : 28 : "My Lord and my God",
and the answer is the last saying of Jesus : "Because you have seen me
you have found faith. Happy are they who never saw me and yet have
found faith" (20 : 29). This is not only a beatitude for the whole
Church of John's time but also an exhortation to them not to remain
in such an attitude towards Jesus, needing and demanding proofs in
order to believe. The distinction is made here not only between all the
disciples who saw and the later believers who did not, but also between
Thomas and the other disciples. They also saw the hands and the side
of Jesus (20 : 20) but are not reproached like Thomas to whom Jesus
says : "Be unbelieving no longer, but believe" (27). Why is this ?
Because only he *demanded* the legitimation (25). John is not unwilling
to narrate the appearances (and miracles) but finally emphasizes that
it is a lesser way of coming to faith if they are needed as authentication
of Jesus.

Now we have treated virtually all the texts in the Gospel in which
miracle and faith are related to each other, with the exception of 4 : 53
and 4 : 48. Thus far, we have not found a single instance where John
does not throw a critical light of some sort on this relation, but 4 : 53
is an exception[1] : the royal officer believed upon hearing that his son
had recovered. This is a full faith because the pericope describes the
faith growing step by step : the man's question implies some faith (47);
then he believes "the word" which Jesus spoke to him and started the
return journey (50); this faith was affirmed and completed by the
observation of the miracle itself. There is no indication that the man
saw any deeper meaning in the miracle and that the "critical addition"
is therefore incorporated in his faith. From v. 53, it seems that John
has taken over the message of S without modification. Thus, it becomes
fully conceivable why he had to make the harsh addition v. 48 :
"Jesus said to him : 'Without seeing signs and portents you will

---

[1] Bultmann; Schottroff, *Glaubende*, 266.

certainly never believe'." The human weakness which needs the support of the miracles is deplored. The Galileans are contrasted to the Samaritans of the preceding pericope, who believed the word of Jesus without seeing signs (4 : 42). John would have found support for his addition in the traditional pericope because v. 50 provides an example of faith in Jesus' word without any guarantee. What is expressly stated in v. 48 is again that the way of the miracles is not the best one. With the rest of the Gospel in mind it can be added that it may also be implied that a miracle-faith is not yet a full faith.

Can one say that actually the miracles are dispensable because the ideal is that one should believe without them? This is going too far. 4 : 48 stresses that some will *never* believe without miracles. God knows this, and in his mercy grants men the needed support. Therefore, Jesus did perform miracles, and this is accepted by John. Jesus says : "If I do not perform the works of my Father, do not believe me" (10 : 37). The basic reason that John is critical of the testimony of the miracles is not that he does not want to give the support for faith but that he wants to make it clear that the support should help one further towards a direct relationship with Christ.

D) *Conclusion and Prospect*

John is critical of his source's use of miracles to inspire faith.[1] As far as this "apologetic" theme is concerned, we can hardly go further than the statement of Bultmann that the miracles are a concession to human weakness. This theme is no central part of John's theology. But why were the sēmeia then given such an important place in the Gospel? At least as far as structure is concerned, they form the back-bone of the first half of the Gospel, and in the conclusion it is stated that this was a book of sēmeia (20 : 30f.). The answer to this question is, of course, that the miracles are interpreted. We have seen that this implies a criticism of miracle-faith but the important question is whether the interpretation is also a criticism of the miracles themselves or whether it needs them. Are the miracles interpreted because other-wise they would have no meaning or are they interpreted because they are revelation themselves? Faith should not live by miracles but by

---

[1] Vs. R.T. Fortna, Source and Redaction in the Fourth Gospel's portrayal of Jesus' Signs, *JBL* 84 (1970) 152 : "At the outset it should be emphasized how fully dependent on the source John is, how completely he takes over and affirms its attitude towards the signs."

the word — but does the word need the miracle ? Criticism of miracle-
faith need not imply criticism of miracles because the defectiveness of
the faith may be due to the blindness of men rather than to the miracles.
It is clear that thus far we have moved only along the surface, and a
full solution will need deeper investigation.

3.   JOHN'S METHOD OF SYMBOLICAL EXPLICATION

Before we tackle Johannine theology for the solution of this problem,
we may first arm ourselves with some concrete observations about
John's method of redacting the tradition. How did the tradition function
in John's preaching and writing ? What was the primary source of the
symbolical interpretations — the traditional miracle stories or some
other elements in "Johannine theology" ? Is the symbolism really an
interpretation of the deeds of Jesus, or are his deeds only illustrations
of the truths expressed in the symbolism ? Bultmann takes the second
position. As far as John is concerned, the miracles need not have
happened. They are only "Bilder", illustrations for what he wants to
say in any case. After the interpretation preceding the raising of
Lazarus, the miracle as such has become "höchst überflüssig" (Jh.,
301, 3). In fact, according to his source criticism, much of the symbolical
material literally has another "source" than the miracle stories, i.e.,
the Offenbarungsreden which John used (161; 103, 4).

To begin with it is significant that not all the sēmeia are interpreted.
In the case of the walking on the water this is certain; with the healing
of the boy it is nearly certain; the healing at Bethesda causes some
doubt, but it is, in any case, not made clear that it has symbolical
meaning. As we shall presently see, the possibility of symbolical
interpretation lies at hand especially in the second and third of these
examples. But John felt no need to make it clear that he has noticed
it. There is no necessity that a deeper meaning must be seen behind
the deeds of Jesus, for in themselves they are meaningful.

The miracle of the wine is also not explicitly interpreted, but from
the way in which the story itself is told, it is quite clear that John
intends the reader to see deeper meaning. The mentioning of the hour of
Jesus (2 : 4), i.e., the hour of his glorification, indicates that the reader
must expect to find glory (11b), i.e., the revelation of the meaning of
the glorified Christ, in the miracle. When it is expressly added in v. 6
that the water which was changed into wine was in water-jars "of the

kind used for Jewish rites of purification", one can hardly refrain
from thinking that this deed of Jesus has the same significance as the
next one, the cleansing of the temple, i.e., that Jesus fulfills and
replaces Jewish regilion.[1] (This is an important line of thought in the
first four chapters, cf. 1 : 17 ; 3 : 1ff. ; 4 : 20ff.). The picture seems to be
completed by v. 9 where it is added that the steward did not know
πόθεν the good wine came. πόθεν usually has a typical Johannine
Christological meaning in the Gospel : Jesus came from above and,
therefore, the world does not know "whence" he came (7 : 27 ; 8 : 14 ;
9 : 29f. ; 19 : 9). The Samaritan woman asked Jesus πόθεν he would
attain living water (4 : 11). The impression is created that as the water
and the bread (c. 6), so also the wine is a symbol for the revelation
which Jesus brings of which man does not know the πόθεν [2]. The
water of Jewish religion is replaced by the wine of the revelation of the
Truth in Jesus. It is possible to go further with the symbolism. The
death of Jesus is also part of what happens in the "hour" of glorification. Does the wine then, like the wine of the Eucharist, allude to the
blood of Jesus which will replace the Jewish purification rites ?[3] The
Eucharistic symbolism connected to the bread in c. 6 would be a parallel.
It is impossible to decide with certainty — and this is significant.

It is not accidental that we doubt again and again. The interpretation
is not given separately from the story so that we can be certain, but it is
hinted at in the narrative. Literal meaning and deeper meaning cannot
be clearly distinguished ; the deed of Jesus and its meaning are not
separated. John narrates the healing of the boy without any conscious
allusion to deeper meaning, but he would not have objected to anyone
(such as Dodd, p. 324) who saw in the thrice repeated "your boy lives"
(4 : 50, 51, 53) a reference to the spiritual ζωοποιεῖν of Jesus discussed
in the next chapter, because for him, the deeds of Jesus have meaning
even if he does not say it. The same applies to the healing at Bethesda.
Who shall decide whether the physical ἐγείρειν (5 : 8) is a symbol of the
spiritual ἐγείρειν of God in v. 21 ?[4] History and divine meaning are
not on different levels.

---

[1] Barrett; Dodd, 299; Brown, 104; Hoskyns; Westcott; vs. Bultmann; Bernard;
A. Smitmans, *Das Weinwunder von Kana* (1966) 278.

[2] Bultmann; Schnackenburg; Hoskyns.

[3] Affirmed by Barrett and Hoskyns; denied by Bultmann and Schnackenburg, 342;
doubted by Dodd, 298.

[4] Haenchen, *Probleme*, 50; Dodd, 324. This way be corroborated by the fact that
v. 21 provides the only instance in Jn. of the use of the verb in a spiritual sense.

This can be contrasted to the hermeneutical method of Philo Alexan-
drinus. He clearly distinguishes between the literal meaning and the
deeper meaning which can be discovered by means of allegorical
exegesis. He regards them as alternatives, and along with the books
which contain "historical" exegesis of the Pentateuch, he even wrote
a separate commentary for the allegorical interpretation of the Law.
At the end of his allegorical interpretation of the story of the tower of
Babel he says those who interpret the story literally may perhaps be
right, but they should also open their eyes for allegory because the
literal meanings of the words of the Law are only like the shadows of
the realities of the deeper meanings.[1] When he finds the literal meaning
offensive, he frequently explains it away by allegory. Because of this
sharp distinction between the two, Philo can give totally different
interpretations of the same historical fact in different contexts. For
instance, in one case he takes the snake into which the staff of Moses
turned as symbol of sinful passion, while elsewhere it is the divine
word.[2] The content of the interpretations is not in the first place derived
from the history but from Philo's religious philosophy. W.F. Howard
wrote[3] : "We therefore distinguish between the allegorizing method
which treats the story as a mere transparency through which we can
see the real meaning, and the method of the Fourth Evangelist who
describes what he believes to be veritable fact, but with a keen eye to
the deeper revelation which the story may contain." In contrast with
John, Philo "preserved the religious value by sacrificing the history
upon the altar of allegory."

In the two final sēmeia, narrative and interpretation are remarkably
interwoven. The healing of the man born blind is followed by a long
legal process which must be of John's hand. In the first place it is clear
that the process demonstrates the reality of the miracle. The neighbours and Pharisees doubt whether the man who is now seeing has
really been blind, but he and his parents testify that it is true. The
real conflict between the Pharisees and the healed man, as a result of
which he is excommunicated, is that they refuse to accept the fact of
the miracle while he refuses to deny it. Bultmann (255,1) agrees that the
trial proves the fact of the miracle, but it causes him no problems in
his conception of John's theology because he regards the bulk of the

---

[1] *De confusione linguarum*, 190; cf. G. Delling, Wunder — Allegorie — Mythus bei
Philon von Alexandreia, in : *Gottes ist der Orient* (Festschrift für O. Eissfeldt, 1957) 53.

[2] Respectively *All.* II 90 and *Migr.* 83; cf. Delling, 50f.

[3] *Fourth Gospel*, 186.

trial as part of the σημεῖα = *Quelle*. In the second place, however, the process at the same time dramatizes the symbolical meaning of the miracle, that Jesus is the true light. The blindness of the Pharisees is revealed by this light (9 : 39) not because they do not see the deeper meaning of the miracle but simply because they rejected it as such. The blind man received vision by this light not only because he had a personal meeting with Jesus, in which his eyes were opened to see who Jesus really was, but also because he stuck to the fact of the miracle in spite of persecution. The level of fact is not abandoned for the sake of symbolism.

As in 2 : 4, so also in 11 : 4 the reader is prepared for the symbolical meaning of the raising of Lazarus by connecting it to the "hour" of Jezus. He says Lazarus became ill "so that the Son of God may be glorified by it". On the symbolical level this already points to the fact that the glory of the glorified Christ will be revealed by the miracle, i.e., that he gives life to the world (cf. vv. 25f.). This may however, not be separated from the meaning of the statement on the historical level, i.e., that the illness of Lazarus will lead to the crucifixion (= glorification) of Jesus. And this is part of the narrative : because of this miracle, the Jews decided to kill Jesus (45ff.). We have already experienced that in this chapter more so than in others it is impossible to make a complete source-critical division between the source and the redaction. This is mainly because the narrative and the interpretation are not separable. Dodd (363) wrote : "The interweaving of narrative and dialogue is complete". The dialogues "not only discuss high themes of Johannine theology, but also promote and explain the action of the narrative... Word and action form an indivisible whole." Bultmann feels that after the symbolical explication of vv. 25f., the miracle itself has become superfluous. In fact, however, the marvellousness of the miracle is repeatedly emphasized in vv. 28-44.[1] Neither Mary nor the Jews believe that Jesus can do anything after death has set in ; therefore, they mourn as unbelievers and warn Jesus not to open the grave because there will be a stench. Vv. 28-44 may be traditional for the greater part, but why has John not abbreviated them if he found the miracle superfluous ? Bultmann (309) could not overlook this and wrote : "Die breite Ausführung in 11 : 28-44 zeigt nämlich, dass die Auferweckung des Lazarus nicht nur Symbol für Jesu Wort V. 25f. ist ; sie könnte dann viel kürzer erzählt sein." To this point we can agree,

---

[1] Cf. Windisch, Erzählungsstil, 185 : "Die Erzählung ist natürlich in erster Linie als Epiphaniegeschichte zu werten." Similarly Wendland, *Literaturformen*, 306.

but his explanation does not give the real answer : "Vielmehr gibt
11 : 28-44 ein Gegenbild zu 11 : 17-27 : der primitive Glaube derer
wird gezeichnet, die des äusserlichen Wunders bedürfen, um Jesus
als den Offenbarer anzuerkennen." The narrative is certainly more than
a symbol but not because it is needed as "Gegenbild" but reversely,
because the narrative and the interpretation, the deed and its meaning,
overlap to such an extent that the deed is more than a mere symbol
which points away from itself but important enough to be narrated at
length. (This will later be affirmed by the investigation of the concept
δόξα in v. 40.)

It can, however, not be denied that John actually had to make
additions to the text of the source in order to reveal the symbolical
meaning he saw in it. The most interesting way of looking into his
"workshop" is by studying these additions under the aspect of their
relation to the traditional story. Do they arise from the story or are they
imported from outside ?

Firstly, the miracle of the wine. We have conjectured that John
inserted the three phrases on the basis of which the symbolical interpretation becomes possible. The first one is v. 4b : "My hour has not
yet come." In S Jesus already refused to react immediately to the
request of Mary so that the addition is in fact only an interpretation
of this refusal as being a result of the fact that Jesus' hour for the complete revelation of glory (11b) had not yet come. In v. 6 John added that
the water-jars were "of the kind that were used for Jewish rites of
purification." It was Jewish law that hands had to be washed before
and after meals, and as we have seen (p. 53), stone water-jars would
have been especially suitable for purification purposes. Therefore,
John would probably have thought this addition was a historically
correct explanation of the water-jars of his source. It seems that John
also added the parenthetical phrase in v. 9, in which it is said that the
steward did not know πόθεν the wine came. According to v. 10 this
must have been the case. It is also instructive to compare the traditional
meaning of the miracle with its Johannine interpretation. In S the
wine was probably taken as sign of the Messianic time : in Jesus the
eschatological "marriage" between God and his people is realized.
John goes even further than S in "realizing" eschatology and concen-
trating all in Jesus. For him the wine is not only a symbol for the
eschatological time but also for Jesus himself. The quantity of the
wine was enormous, and accordingly, God's gift to the world in Jesus
was a πλήρωμα of "grace upon grace" (1 : 16). Jewish expectations

are not only fulfilled as in S, but the grace of Jesus is so abundant that Jewish religion is replaced (2 : 6). This miracle story illustrates 1 : 17, which says : "The law was given through Moses, grace and truth came through Jesus Christ." Thus, the Johannine redaction has added to the pericope an element of antithesis against Judaism which was not present in the traditional story. But is this a totally new addition? S did contain an antithesis between the best wine and the poorer wine (10). The intention is not that Judaism is the poorer wine but that the whole world is like poor wine when contrasted to the eschatological "new wine" of God. It is, however, a very small step from here to the antithesis between Judaism and Christian revelation. John has not really "added" a new interpretation : he only intensified the meaning of the original pericope, probably to suit the circumstances of his community. (We shall see in part 7 that there is a historical explanation why the redaction is polemical against Judaism whereas the traditional story is not : S wanted to convert the Jews but John polemized against them.)

We now turn to the miracle of the bread. Probably John inserted ἵνα μή τι ἀπόληται in 6 : 12 to hint at the interpretation of the bread as spiritual bread which is contrasted to ἡ βρῶσις ἡ ἀπολλυμένη in v. 27. These words do not, however, introduce something new on the historical level but only emphasize what Jezus said in v. 12. Of great importance is 6 : 4, which is almost certainly from John's hand : "It was near the time of Passover, the great Jewish festival." It prepares for the symbolical discourse. In the first place, manna (31ff.) had a prominent place in the Jewish Passover liturgy, e.g., Joshua 5 : 10-12 was read where it is said that the last manna fell during the Passover feast at Gilgal.[1] In the second place, the discourse refers to Jesus' death by using Eucharistic symbolism, and the Eucharist was the Christian Passover.[2] John wrote more than half a century after the death of Jesus. One would be inclined to think that he made this insertion without having any reason for it on the level of fact, being interested only in its significance on the symbolical level. But Mk. 6 : 39 says the people sat down upon the "green grass", and Jn. 6 : 10

---

[1] B. Gärtner, *John 6 and the Jewish Passover* (Con. Neot. 17, 1959) 15ff.

[2] The theory of Bultmann, Bornkamm and others, that vv. 51c-58 are a later addition by an ecclesiastical redactor, has not found acceptance in the modern discussion. Jeremias initially accepted it (*ThBl* 20, 1941, 44) but later rejected it under the impression of Ruckstuhl's arguments (*ZNW* 44, 1952-3, 256f.). Also E. Schweizer rejected his earlier view that the verses are secondary (*EvTh* 12, 1952-3, 353ff.).

mentions that there was "plenty of grass". Springtime, the time of the Passover, falls at the end of the rainy season and appears to be the best season for abundant grass.[1] It seems probable that John would have thought is *was* springtime. In any case his interpretation builds on earlier interpretations of the miracle. We have seen that the Marcan account includes references to the Eucharist as well as to the time of Israel in the desert (the time of the manna).[2] The bulk of the long discourse in c. 6 is, of course, Johannine, but a traditional sequence of events seems to be followed. As in Mk. 6, the feeding miracle is followed by the walking on the water. In Mk. 8 the feeding miracle is also followed by a crossing of the lake by boat, and then the Jews' request of a sign is mentioned, which is also the next event in Jn. 6. In both the chapters a discussion about bread follows (Mk. 8 : 14-21 ; Jn. 6: 32-65). In Mk. 8 : 27-30 and Jn. 6 : 66-69, Peter's confession is reported, and then the work of the devil in the disciples is mentioned in both (Mk. 8 : 33; Jn. 6 : 70). It is scarcely deniable that even in this high flight of symbolical interpretation, John must still in some way or other be keeping in mind what he had heard about the life of Jesus; he has not abandoned the level of fact for the sake of theology.

A final example is 9 : 7, where John seems to have added the explanation ἀπεσταλμένος to the name Siloam. He prepares the reader for the symbolical interpretation that Jesus is the real light which gives sight to men by saying the name of the pool by which the blind man received vision, was "sent" (as Jesus was sent from the Father). There was a pool in Jerusalem called Shiloah in Hebrew, and this word at least sounds like a derivation of šlḥ, "to send".

The conclusion is that John would not have thought that he was imposing a "Johannine" interpretation upon the works of Jesus, but he would have been convinced that he was interpreting the real meaning which was intended by Jesus. Basically, the symbolism is not added to the tradition but derived from it. The psychological way in which John treated the tradition seems to have been more or less as follows : he pondered on the stories of S until it struck him that, e.g., the water-jars of Cana would have been there for purification purposes, and therefore it was water of the Jewish religion which has changed into the wine of Jesus; or that Jesus had probably multiplied the bread in springtime, i.e., near the Passover, and therefore the bread should, according to the divine intention as revealed in history, be interpreted

---

[1] Dodd, *Hist. Trad.*, 211, note 3.

[2] Pp. 45, 57.

in connection with the manna and the Eucharist. Of course he had a
theology which he did not put out of his mind when he interpreted the
miracles. The whole discourse of c. 6 is not derived directly from the
feeding story. But it is based on the story. John is not only saying what
the deed of Jesus means to him, but he says what he thought it really
meant. How he could possibly have thought that his deep symbolism
had been intended in the actions of Jesus is the problem of his hermeneutical principle which has to be treated later; his ways of thinking are
very strange to our western mind. In any case, thus far the material
has left the impression that John does not seek divine meaning behind
the history on a different level but *in* the history. There seems to be a
striking unity between event and meaning. What this really means
will have to be discovered by penetrating deeper into John's theology.

4. The Relation between Event and Meaning in John's Theology : The Basic Concepts connected to the Miracles

The words "sign", "work", and "glory" proved to be very suitable
for an investigation of this matter.

A) Σημεῖον

The seventeen occurrences of this word in the Gospel may be divided
into four groups : (a) seven times from the lips of Jews : 2 : 18; 3 : 2;
6 : 30; 7 : 31; 9 : 16; 10 : 41; 11 : 47; (b) five times as object of the
Jews' perception : 2 : 23; 4 : 48; 6 : 2, 14; 12 : 18; (c) four times in the
commentary of the narrator (and not as the object of anybody's
perception) : 2 : 11; 4 : 54; 12 : 37; 20 : 30; (d) once in the mouth of
Jesus : 6 : 26.[1] In (a) and (b), the word means nothing more than it
means in S, i.e., "miracle", only here and there accompanied by the
idea of legitimation which is also basic in S. In the mouth of Jesus, it
clearly has a richer meaning, while this meaning is also indirectly included in three of the four instances of (c).

We investigate (d) and then (c). After the multiplication of the bread
and the crossing of the lake, the multitude seek Jesus, and when they

---

[1] 4 : 48 is also a saying of Jesus, but it should rather be counted under (b) because it is
a complaint about the Jewish way of looking at miracles and the Old Testament term
σημεῖα καὶ τέρατα is used in which the possibilities of the word sēmeion to mean
more than "miracle" is expressly excluded by the word τέρας.

find him, Jesus reproaches them (6 : 26) : "In very truth I know that
you have not come looking for me because you saw signs but because
you ate the bread and your hunger was satisfied." These words connect
the narrative to the symbolical discourse. Jesus says the people have
not really seen the signs; otherwise, that would have been their reason
for seeking him. "See" must have more than its ordinary meaning
because according to vv. 2 and 14, the people *have* seen the sēmeia.
Deeper vision is implied : they have only seen the miraculous events
and have not understood the miracle as symbol of the bread of life; they
are not striving for the "food that lasts" (v. 27). In other words,
σημεῖον means more than "miracle" here; it means symbol, sign
pointing towards meaning. This is a quite normal use of the word.
The meaning of sign indicating something else frequently occurs in
classical Greek as well as in the LXX, where it is usually connected with
the symbolical acts of the prophets (Heb. '*oth*).[1] On the other hand it is
clear that σημεῖον means not only "symbol" here. Then Jesus' complaint would have been that the people had not *understood* the sēmeia.
Now it is that they have not *seen* them. Jesus does not want the people
to avert their eyes from the sēmeia to their meaning but to see the
meaning *in* them. The word sēmeion always refers to a miracle elsewhere in Jn., and, as would thus have been expected, this original
meaning is not excluded by the new dimension which is added to the
word here. Jesus does not ask the people to see his deed as symbol but
as miracle-with-meaning. Both levels are referred to in one word.
"See", then refers not only to deeper vision or understanding as
Bultmann (161) thinks but is physical vision which at the same time
discovers meaning.

We now turn to group (c). Sēmeion means no more than "miracle"
in 4 : 54, but in 2 : 11 the deeper dimensions of 6 : 26 are probably
indirectly present. V. 11b shows that the performing of the sign was at
the same time revelation of glory, and as we shall see, the glory is
connected with the deeper meaning which John sees in the miracle
of the wine. 2 : 11 qualifies all the following sēmeia in the Gospel
because it is not only said that Jesus performed a sēmeion or the
first sēmeion but ταύτην ἀρχὴν τῶν σημείων (the others are mentioned) and ἀρχή not only means "first" but also the beginning, the
root, the "Ausgangspunkt" which determines how the rest will be.[2]

---

[1] Is. 7 : 3; 8 : 18; 20 : 1-6, 18; Ez. 12 : 6; 4 : 3; 24 : 24, 27. There is no single indication
in Jn. that he has the prophetic signs in mind when using sēmeion as "sign".

[2] Michel, Der Anfang der Zeichen Jesu, 20.

The expression ποιεῖν σημεῖα is twice used to summarize the whole life-work of Jesus, in 12 : 37, the conclusion of the first half of the Gospel describing the public ministry, and in 20 : 30, the conclusion of the whole Gospel. It is clear that in the eyes of John the main part of the earthly work of Jesus was not simply the performance of miracles. Miracle-faith is criticized; the discourses and dialogues fill more space than the miracle stories; the real theological résumé of Jesus' earthly work is the final prayer (c. 17), and it does not mention the miracles separately but makes it clear that Jesus' work was to reveal the Father - and the same applies to the prologue. Therefore, one is immediately inclined to think ποιεῖν σημεῖα must mean more than "to perform miracles." There are a few indications which may affirm this. In c. 20 John reports two appearances of Jesus before the disciples. Immediately following them he writes in v. 30 : "There were many other signs that Jesus performed in the presence of his disciples." The concept sēmeion is widened to include the appearances. John never directly says the resurrection is also a sēmeion, but it is significant that when the Jews ask Jesus for a sēmeion in 2 : 18, he answers by referring to his resurrection. As a result of its connection with the meaning of the miracles as expressed in the words, the concept sēmeion has acquired striking elasticity. According to 20 : 31, the description of the sēmeia has the aim of inspiring a full faith. For John, full faith cannot be based on mere miracles but only on the full revelation. Therefore ποιεῖν σημεῖα must in the last analysis include all that the Gospel of John preaches about Jesus, both the works and the words. Again the historical tradition and the spiritual interpretation are bound together by one expression.

It remains striking that the word sēmeion was chosen for the final characterization of the revelation brought by Jesus. An important reason for this is probably that the way in which John interpreted the miracles was also the way in which he interpreted the whole life, death, and resurrection of Jesus. As with the miracles, John sought to see divine meaning in all the different aspects of the story of the earthly Jesus. Examples can be multiplied : the washing of the disciples' feet alludes to the forgiveness of sins; the cleansing of the Temple to the replacement of the Jewish cult; the water of the well to the living water; Jesus' being lifted up on the cross to his exaltation (3 : 14); the resurrection and appearances to the spiritual coming of Christ to his followers (14 : 18); etc. Therefore, John could qualify his whole Gospel as describing sēmeia. The sēmeia should provide us with a key to the basic hermeneutical principle of John.

In conclusion, we compare the groups (a) — (d). The extended meaning which occurs four times in the last two groups implies some criticism of the normal meaning in the thirteen other occurrences : it should be recognized that a sēmeion of Jesus is more than a mere miracle. The important point is, however, that the criticism is not a rejection of the original meaning but only a deepening of it. The basic meaning of sēmeion in Jn., i.e., "miracle", is maintained in these four instances. Therefore, the general opinion that sēmeion in Jn. means "sign" in the proper sense of the word is not correct.[1] Sēmeion is the central concept of S. From the semantic point of view John has not radically reinterpreted the traditional concept but he rather built on it. Therefore, the impression is created that, whereas he had his doubts about the kind of faith which S could inspire, he had no scruples about building his idea of revelation on that which revelation was in S, namely, demonstration of divine power.

B) *Ἔργον*

This is the only alternative word for a miracle in the Gospel. It does not occur in S material, and it appears that, in contrast to the word sēmeion, John himself chose it and used it according to his own theological ideas about the miracles. As could be expected, it usually seems to have a wider meaning than sēmeion, but in a number of instances it means no more than "miracle" : there can at least be no doubt about 7 : 3, 21; 10 : 32, 33. The setting for the full meaning of the word is provided by 4 : 34 and 17 : 4, the first and last occurrence in connection with Jesus and also the only instances of its singular use in connection with him. In both cases, it denotes the total life-work of Jesus, the revelation of the Father, i.e., the works as well as the words. In 14 : 10-12 the plural erga (ἔργα) occurs thrice. In v. 10 the ῥήματα of Jesus are said to be erga of God. Erga must here have the wider meaning of "works of revelation" so that the words may be included.[2] This is affirmed by v. 12 where it is said Jesus' followers will do greater works than he did. This cannot mean they will perform more miraculous wonders because how can one outdo the raising of Lazarus ? In the

---

[1] Vs., e.g., K.H. Rengstorf, art. sēmeion, *ThW* VII 247f. : "Zugleich zeigt sich, dass das johanneische sēmeion die erga Jesu nicht als 'Wunder' kennzeichnet, sondern als 'Zeichen', die eine bestimmte Erkenntnis ermöglichen." Dodd (142) goes too far in saying John would have considered such non-miraculous acts as the cleansing of the temple or the washing of the disciples' feet also as sēmeia.

[2] Vs. Barrett, Bernard, and Hoskyns, who say the *erga* are miracles.

farewell discourses, the task of the disciples is the preaching of the Gospel. The *erga* of 4. 12 are, in the first place, words. On the other hand, as far as the *erga* of Jesus are concerned, the wider meaning does not replace the concrete meaning of "miracles" as Bultmann thinks but only includes it in the broader context. This is indicated by v. 11 where the *erga* are again contrasted to the words ($\mu o \iota$) and mentioned as bearing an alternative witness to Jesus. This can only be explained if the erga are at least partly a reference to miracles.

So the word *ergon* indicates how closely the works and words are related, but it also more specifically reveals much about the relation between event and interpretation. We turn to 5 : 17ff. According to vv. 20ff., the real *erga* of the Son which he will perform in unity with the Father are $\zeta \omega o \pi o \iota \epsilon \hat{\iota} \nu$ and $\kappa \rho \acute{\iota} \nu \epsilon \iota \nu$, i.e., the spiritual works which are symbolized by for instance the last two sēmeia. Already in vv. 17-19 the work of Jesus is the theme. The Jews persecute Jesus because he has healed the paralysed man on the Sabbath, and he answers that he always works in unity with the Father (17, 19, 20a). This $\dot{\epsilon} \rho \gamma \acute{a} \zeta \epsilon \sigma \theta a \iota$ refers to the miracles of Jesus, for it explains why he performed the miracle on the Sabbath : the Father works continually, and, therefore, Jesus also has to work on all days. V. 20b also indicates that the miracles have been the theme in the foregoing verses : the spiritual works are distinguished from them as $\mu \epsilon \hat{\iota} \zeta o \nu a \ \check{\epsilon} \rho \gamma a \ (\tau o \acute{\upsilon} \tau \omega \nu$ refers to the miracles). Vv. 17-20a show that the miracles of Jesus are a direct imitation of the works of the Father, or rather, "What the Father does, the Son also does" (19b), i.e., they are identical to the works of the Father ($\acute{o} \mu o \acute{\iota} \omega s$ does not mean "in the same way" but "also".) Now the difficult problem is the relation between the works of vv. 17-20a and those of vv. 20b ff. Are the works of the Father which are reflected in the miracles according to v. 19 identical to the spiritual works of giving life and judging performed by Father and Son ? If this is the case, it would mean that the miracles not only symbolize the spiritual work of Christ but are such a direct reflection of it that one can say they are identical with it. This would be the strongest expression of the unity between event and meaning which we have encountered thus far. It should first be admitted that this identification is not explicitly made. The miracles and the spiritual works are both called *erga* in v. 20, and they are compared, but comparison implies distinction : the spiritual works are greater. Vv. 20ff. are no direct symbolical explication of the miracle. The healing of paralysis is not $\zeta \omega o \pi o \iota \epsilon \hat{\iota} \nu$ or $\kappa \rho \acute{\iota} \nu \epsilon \iota \nu$. On the other hand it appears that the idea of the unity of all the works

of Father and Son forms the background of the whole passage. The
works of the Father are not divided, and if the miracles are said to
reflect them in vv. 17-20a and if they are then defined as giving life in
vv. 21ff., then surely it is manifest that the miracles reflect the giving
of life.[1] The giving of life is also described as ἐγείρειν in v. 21, and the
healing word in the miracle story, was ἔγειρε (8). In the immediately
preceding miracle story the healing word ζῇ is thrice repeated, and it is
not impossible that John saw this as a reflection of the ζωοποιεῖν since
vv. 17ff. discuss not only one miracle but miracles in the plural (16b,
19b, 20b). Therefore, one could conclude that this passage implies that
symbolic deed and symbolized reality are actually identical. But if this is
the case, it is still so unclear that corroboration is necessary. This is
afforded further on in the chapter in v. 36 and especially in c. 9.

5 : 36 — the discussion of Jesus' spiritual works (21-30) is followed
by an exposition of the threefold witness of the Father to the Son
through John the Baptist, the *erga*, and the Scriptures (31-40). In v. 36
Jesus says : "The works which the Father has given me to fulfil, the
very works that I am doing, testify on my behalf that the Father has
sent me." The miracles must be at least partly intended because the
testimony of the *erga* is contrasted to the words of Jesus in 10 : 25, 38 ;
14 : 11. But the meaning of spiritual works has not been lost. According
to v. 36 the Father "*gave*" the works to the Son, and this is also the
expression used about the spiritual works in vv. 22, 26, 27. If only
miracles were intended, the "fulfil" (τελειόω) of v. 36 would be a
rather ponderous word, but it *is* used in 4 : 34 and 17 : 4 of the total *ergon* of Christ. Therefore, v. 36 indicates that the visible and invisible
erga of Christ form such a unity that they can be mentioned in one
word.[2] With this in mind, it seems probable that the wider meaning
which *erga* has in 14 : 10, 12 is not excluded in 14 : 11. The same may
be true of the *erga* of 10 : 38 — note that the faith based on them is
clearly described as a full faith. The works of Christ to which John
appeals for testimony are then not only the miraculous works of the
earthly Jesus but also the works of the exalted Christ which can be
seen in the Church.

All the lines of thought are brought together in 9 : 3-5. Jesus says
the man has been born blind in order that the *erga* of God may be
revealed in him. In the first place, the historical miracle is meant

---

[1] Dodd, 323; Brown, 218; W. Thüsing, *Die Erhöhung und Verherrlichung Jesu im
Johannesevangelium* (1960) 59.

[2] Barrett ; Bultmann ; Bernard ; Strathmann.

because in v. 4 Jesus says he must do these works before night falls, i.e., before his death, and in the context, this means Jesus must perform the miracle even though it is the Sabbath (14), a parallel to 5 : 17. According to v. 5, however, the *erga* which have to be completed while Jesus is in the world are the giving of spiritual light, that which is "revealed" (3b) in the miracle. This is why v. 4 can say "we" have to do the works : the exalted Christ performs the spiritual works through the Church, a parallel to the *erga* of the disciples in 14 : 12.

Hence, the "work" of the miracle is at the same time the imparting of spiritual light.[1] Dodd (140) aptly speaks of the "intrinsic unity of symbol and thing symbolized. ... The healing of the blind by Christ *is* the cleansing of the soul from error." The miracles are more than symbols of the spiritual work of Christ because they share in its reality ; they are rather like the moving images of this work seen through frosted glass.

No wonder Bultmann had some trouble interpreting this concept. He strongly emphasizes 14 : 10 which would indicate that "die ἔργα nichts anderes sind als die ῥήματα" (*Theol.*, 413). The instances where the word clearly denotes the miracles represent a "Sprachgebrauch der von dem des Evglisten zu unterscheiden ist" (Jh. 218, 7). In 9 : 3 and 10 : 32 the miracles are only *erga* insofar as they are symbols of the spiritual works of Christ. What, then, about the contrast between word and work in 10 : 38 and 14 : 11 ? He agrees that these verses seem to contradict him but says their correct interpretation is that Jesus "von einem Autoritätsglauben, der das über Jesus Gesagte hinnimmt, auf einen Glauben verweist, der Jesu Wort als die ihn treffende Anrede, also als sein Wirken, versteht" (*Theol.*, 413). But how can the word of Jesus himself be "das über Jesus Gesagte" and how could John have implied that, in comparison with this, the "Wort als ... treffende Anrede" is second best ?

C) *Δόξα*

Glory is the primary concept by which John denotes what revelation is to him. The gist of the prologue is that "we have seen his glory" (14c). Glory and glorification are frequently used in connection with the departure of Jesus, but after the prologue *doxa* (*δόξα*) occurs only thrice in connection with the life of Jesus — and in all three cases, it is said to be revealed in a miracle, once in the first (2 : 11) and twice in

---

[1] Hoskyns; Westcott; Schlatter; Thüsing, *Erhöhung*, 62.

the last (11 : 4, 40). Obviously, this concept must be an important key to the full meaning of the miracles.

In 1 : 14de the glory which was seen in Jesus is defined as : δόξαν ὡς μονογενοῦς παρὰ πατρός, πλήρης χάριτος καὶ ἀληθείας. Πλήρης is indeclinable and refers to μονογενοῦς and not to δόξαν, but as μονογενοῦς explains the quality of the *doxa*, the *doxa* is in fact described as revelation of grace and truth. Χάρις is God's generous love, and in v. 16, it is that which man receives from this love, in Johannine terms : life. 'Αλήθεια is the divine reality as revealed in Jesus (18), also called light by John. Therefore, the glory is the revelation of the life and light of the Logos (4), of that which is symbolized by the miracles. After the interruption of v. 15, v. 16 explains v. 14 : "For out of his fulness we all received, grace upon grace." The full vision of the glory was only possible where the gifts of Christs were received. The vision is the vision of faith; the glory is much more than miraculous power. While the prologue is the first introduction, 1 : 51 is the final introduction to what follows in the Gospel narrative. Jesus promises the disciples the same kind of vision : they will "see" the unity of Father and Son.

It seems understandable that Bultmann (83) categorically says the *doxa* of 2 : 11 is "nicht die Macht des Wundertäters" but the revelation of the Father and that the miracle story is "nur Bild dafür". But why then is the *doxa* of Jesus' life only mentioned in connection with miracles ? 11 : 40 — when Martha objects to having the stone removed from before Lazarus's grave, Jesus says : "Did I not tell you that if you believe, you will see the *doxa* of God ?" (Because of the unity of Father and Son, the glory of the one is identical to that of the other.) In the first place, this glory must be much more than miraculous power, because Martha has to believe to see it while the miracle itself was seen by all present. Jesus explicitly refers Martha to what he has told her, and this is the symbolical explication of the miracle in vv. 25ff. where πιστεύω occurs four times. Hence, to see the glory means to comprehend the miracle with the vision of faith. On the other hand, Martha has not yet seen the glory when she believes Jesus' words but *will* see it only when Jesus performs the miracle. Jesus promises her this vision to encourage her faith when she shows doubts about his power to conquer death by warning him of the stench. Indeed, we have seen (p. 109) that the whole context of vv. 28-44 illustrates the marvellousness of the miracle. That this interest does not belong only to S is shown by vv. 41f., which are probably Johannine. Jesus prays loudly in order that the crowd may believe he has been sent by the Father. But how will they come to this faith ? By the fact of the miracle which will prove that the Father heard Jesus. Therefore, it is not correct to say with Bultmann that the glory is *not* the miraculous power. The glory is not only the miraculous because it includes the meaning of the miracle. But the vision of faith by which the glory is beheld is simultaneously the vision of historical fact.

It may be pointed out in passing that "see" frequently has this double aspect in the Johannine writings. We have already examined 6 : 26 where the seeing of the sēmeia implies both physical vision and comprehension in faith. According to 14 : 8f., Philip asks Jesus : "Lord, show us the Father and we ask no more", and Jesus answers : "Have I been all this time with you, Philip, and you still do not know me ? Anyone who has seen me has seen the Father." On the one hand, this vision is physical because its object is the earthly Jesus with whom Philip has shared company for a long time; on the other hand, more than ordinary vision is, of course, necessary to "see" the Father in Jesus. In the farewell discourses Jesus repeatedly promises the disciples that they will see him again (14 : 19; 16 : 16, 17, 19), referring both to the resurrection and to his coming in the Spirit. According to 1 Jn. 1 : 1-3, the eternal life was revealed, and it was seen with the eyes and felt with the hands. The object of such vision is concrete, but in it, the invisible eternal life is seen (2). Again I have to disagree with Bultmann because he denies the concrete basis of John's thought. He says (45, 1) the vision in the verses mentioned above is not "Wahrnehmung mit den sinnlichen Augen" but "vom Innewerden nicht sinnlich sichtbarer Sachverhalte ausgesagt."[1]

In 11 : 4 Jesus says in reference to the illness of Lazarus that it has come "for the glory of God, that the Son of God may be glorified by it." Of course, the glory must here have the same double aspect as in 11 : 40. This is also affirmed by the close parallelism with 9 : 3 where, as we have seen, a similar unity between event and interpretation is implied.

The first miracle story is concluded by 2 : 11, which is actually a

---

[1] I can agree with O. Cullmann who stressed the "simultanéité de 'voir avec les yeux' et 'contempler par la foi'" — Εἶδεν καὶ ἐπίστευσεν, in : *Aux sources de la tradition Chrétienne* (Mélanges M. Goguel, 1950) 58; also with F. Mussner, *Die Johanneische Sehweise und die Frage nach dem Historischen Jesus* (1965), who says John intends seeing "mit den Augen des Glaubens" (24) but this vision is not identical with faith because the "gläubige Sehakt bleibt ja radikal an den σάρξ γενόμενος gebunden" (21) and therefore the eyewitnesses are inevitable (23).

general rule for all the signs : "Jesus worked this first of the signs at Cana-in-Galilee and he revealed his glory and his disciples believed in him." The middle phrase about the glory is probably Johannine as 11 : 4, 40 certainly are. If not, "glory" in any case means much more in the present context than it could have meant in S. 2 : 11 indicates that this miracle is the first fulfilment of that which was anticipated in 1 : 14 and 51. Therefore, the glory is the grace and truth which replaced the law of Moses (1 : 17), the invisible divine reality which was "revealed" ($\phi\alpha\nu\epsilon\rho\delta\omega$, cf. 9 : 3; 1 Jn. 1 : 2) in Jesus. On the other hand, the revelation of the glory is here parallel to the performance of the sēmeion, and sēmeion basically means miracle so that the glory cannot be separated from the miracle as fact. The revelation of the glory is mentioned before the faith of the disciples : the miracle does not become revelation of glory only after being contemplated in faith.

The foregoing may shed some light on 1 . 14abc : "The Word became flesh and dwelt among us and we saw his glory." V. 14de indicates the deeper dimensions of the glory, and this line could be drawn right through to c. 11. There it has appeared, however, that the line has a double aspect. Now the natural question is whether this line can again be drawn back from c. 11 over 2 : 11 to 1 : 14c, and whether it can be said that the glory of the Word also has a physically visible aspect. This might be indicated by the use of the strong word $\sigma\alpha\rho\xi$. If the question has to be answered in the affirmative, it would mean that the historical emphasis of v. 14ab and the theological emphasis of 14de are bound together into a unity by the concept *doxa* with its double aspect in 14c (see part 5 B).

D)   *Conclusion*

Each one of the three concepts *sign, work* and *glory* led us to the same insight : the surprising unity of event and meaning. They illustrate this unity from three different points of view. Somewhat schematically it may be said that sēmeion illuminates the unity from below, *doxa* from above, and *ergon* from the side. A sēmeion is basically a miracle, but also a miracle-with meaning; *doxa* is primarily the grace and truth, but not revealed without powerful miracles; in *ergon*, the two levels are represented with more or less equal weight. Our investigation of the three concepts has become somewhat monotonous, so frequently did we arrive at this same unity. But this is perhaps an adequate reflection of John's meditative way of continually circling around the central truths, an illustration of how essential this unity was to him. Hoskyns

(p. 34f.) wrote : "The gospel stubbornly refuses ... to be divided into history *and* interpretation. The history invades the interpretation, and the interpretation pervades the history... Its author's major purpose was to maintain and to insist upon this unity. The commentator is, therefore, continually brought back to respect this deep-seated interlocking of history and interpretation. Separate the two, and the extremity of violence is done to the text. What Jesus *is* to the faith of the true Christian believer, he *was* in the flesh : this is the theme of the Fourth Gospel, and it is precisely this unity that constitutes the Problem of the Gospel." John's whole intention is perverted in the wide-spread opinion which is expressed for instance by Dibelius as follows : John puts into words "nicht was Jesus war sondern was die Christen an Jesus haben."[1]

Real symbols, such as the letters on this page, have to be interpreted or else they are meaningless; they are not the realities for which they stand. On the contrary, the sēmeia actually are these realities and their interpretation merely has to reveal this. To repeat the example of the image seen through frosted glass : one may not recognize the person whose blurred image one sees until one has a moment to interpret some of the recognizable features of the image — then this interpretation only helps one to understand what one *is actually seeing*. With this in mind, John's method of symbolical explication becomes understandable : he contemplates the "blurred images" of the traditional miracle stories until he finds significant features by which he can recognize what he really sees. Because he believes the deeds of Jesus to be the eternal deeds of God, he finds meaning in what seems to us to be insignificant details about these deeds, e.g., springtime, water-jars, etc.

A final illustration may be drawn from the Gospel itself. The washing of the disciples' feet by Jesus (c. 13) is interpreted symbolically just like the miracles : it signifies the cleansing from sins. But "signifies" is too weak a word because when Peter objects, Jesus says : "You do not know now what *I am doing*, but one day you will" (7), and, "You (plural) *are* clean" (10). The deed of Jesus *is* what it symbolizes.

This unity is however not the solution of the problem of the Fourth Gospel but only a definition of it. On what basis could John write in this way ? Is the complete unity of history and eternity not a clear sign that this is not realistic history any longer, that John is a docetist ?

---

[1] *RGG*² III 350; similarly W.G. Kümmel, *Einleitung*, 160; Strathmann, 22f.

Käsemann agrees that both sides of the miracles have to be emphasized, the miraculous as well as the significant, and he has little trouble with this unity because he sees it situated above the level of reality : Jesus is no real man. In order to answer these questions we are compelled to enter deeper into the Christology of John : how could he maintain that he is writing history while he is actually writing, to a large extent, about the present Christ ?

5.   JOHN'S HERMENEUTICAL PRINCIPLE :
THE GLORIFICATION OF JESUS AND THE GLORY IN THE FLESH

A)   *The Glorification of Jesus*

According to C.H. Dodd (pp. 139f.), the texture of John's thought is determined by Platonic philosophy according to which the visible world is a copy of a world of invisible realities. Something like visible bread is only a μίμημα or symbol of the archetypal bread, the ἄρτος ἀληθινός, "the reality which lies within and behind every visible and tangible loaf, ... its inner essence, and the transcendental real existence which abides" while all concrete bread decays. "From this we can understand [John's] characteristic use of symbolism — I mean in particular the way in which the symbol is absorbed into the reality it signifies." This unity is based on the Platonic unity of archetype and symbol. In this context, Dodd (141) understands the concept sēmeion, and he uses this symbolism as hermeneutical key to the interpretation of the entire Gospel. He regards the Gospel as written for educated Hellenists and thinks our closest sources for the kind of philosophy the author assumed are Philo and the Hermetic literature (133). This, however, is questionable. Although these philosophical writings were also influenced by the general pre-gnostic atmosphere in which John lived, they basically differ widely from John "da im Johannesevangelium jegliche philosophische Gedankenbildung fehlt" (Bultmann).[1] Dodd's way of explaining the unity is very attractive, but apart from his general considerations, there is no specific evidence for Platonic symbolism in the Gospel, while there is, as we shall see, much evidence for another explanation of the symbolism.

We can agree with Dodd that the sēmeia are of primary importance to find the key to the relation between the earthly Jesus and the exalted

---

[1] *RGG*³ III 846.

Christ in John. The central definition of what happened in the sēmeia is that they were revelation of *doxa*; the usual word for Jesus' exaltation is δοξάσθαι — the concept of glory is the hinge on which the Christology of John turns.

Jesus' departure from the world and return to the Father is usually referred to as his glorification : 7 : 39; 11 : 4; 12 : 16, 23, 28; 13 : 31f.; 17 : 1, 5. Jesus is glorified because he re-enters into the glory which he had in his preexistence (17 : 5). But because his glorification is identical with that of the Father (13 : 31f.), he is also glorified in his departure because his laying down his life is the completion of his earthly work by which he glorified the Father (17 : 4). Actually, however, his work cannot be completed before his exaltation because only then can he live in his followers (14 : 20) so that he can be glorified by their unity (17 : 10ff.), the "fruit" of their Christian life (15 : 18), their missionary work (14 : 12f.; 12 : 23f., 32). The first step by which all this becomes possible is that Jesus' exaltation implies the coming of the Paraclete who helps the followers to understand the revelation of Jesus' life (14 : 25f.; 16 : 12-16). An essential element in the total glorification of Jesus is that the Paraclete "glorifies" (16 : 14) him by revealing the true meaning, i.e., glory, of his earthly life.

The earthly revelation was limited because the disciples' understanding was weak : "There is still much more that I could say to you but you would not be able to bear *(βαστάζειν)* it now" (16 : 12). This is partly because of their grief (16 : 6) but primarily because of their lack of insight. Throughout the farewell discourses, the disciples are portrayed as those who do not understand and ask stupid questions : 13 : 36f.; 14 : 4f., 8, 22; 16 : 17f., 29. 16 : 12 is contrasted by 16 : 13: "However, when he comes who is the Spirit of truth, he will guide you into all the truth." The Paraclete is not in the first place "Comforter" but Teacher of truth. 14 : 25f. also implies that the earthly revelation was limited : "This I have told you while I am still with you; but (δὲ is adversative) the Paraclete, the Holy Spirit whom the Father will send in my name, will teach you everything and remind you of all that I have told you." The contrast between the two verses indicates that v. 25 actually means "this and no more" and that the Spirit, therefore, really brings new teaching. On the other hand, Jesus goes out of his way in 16 : 13f. to stress that the Spirit will not speak on his own authority but only draw from what belongs to Jesus. What this means is clarified by 14 : 26 : he will only teach by reminding of the revelation of Jesus. Because he only teaches what he takes from Jesus (16 : 14), the teaching and reminding cannot be different but must be identical.[1] His new teaching is not really addition to the revelation of Jesus for it is only explication of its real meaning. The identity of teaching and reminding is related to the unity of history and interpretation in the Gospel. This unity is also expressed by 15 : 27 where the testimony of the Paraclete through the disciples is mentioned : the Paraclete will bear witness to Christ, "and you also bear witness because you *are (ἐστε)* with me from the first." The present tense probably indicates that the communion with Jesus continues after his death. Therefore, the testimony is not only based on the companionship with the historical Jesus but at the same time (one word !) also on the communion with the Spirit.

That explication is an essential part of the work of the Paraclete is affirmed by 16 : 23a, 25 : "In that day you will ask me no questions... This *(ταῦτα)* I have told you in veiled speech *(παροιμίαις)* ; an hour is coming when I will no longer speak to you in veiled speech but tell you of the Father in plain words." The "day" and the "hour" refer to the time when Jesus will return to his disciples (22), i.e., the time of the Spirit. He will help them to understand the revelation so that they need not ask stupid questions as during the present evening any longer. ταῦτα does not refer to Jesus' symbolical discourses but to his whole earthly revelation because it is contrasted to the total spiritual revelation. The earthly Jesus was "veiled" and had to be "re-vealed" by the Spirit.

There are three explicit indications of what this meant in practice. According to 12 : 16, the disciples "did not understand" the Messianic significance of Jesus' entry into Jerusalem at first, "but after he had been glorified, they remembered that this had been written about him and that this had happened to him." The glorification of Jesus implies the coming of the Spirit and, therefore, insight into his Messianic glory. As in 14 : 26 the teaching and reminding of the Paraclete are equivalent, so here the insight comes not as addition but by way of "remembering." 2 : 22 and 13 : 7 have to be interpreted in a similar way : the Paraclete gave insight into the symbolical meaning of the cleansing of the temple and the washing of the feet. Again in agreement with 14 : 26, the former uses the word "remember" and the latter, "understand."

Obviously, John regarded himself as guided by the Paraclete, and this was the authorization for his reinterpretation of the Gospel tradition. He admits that he is to some extent writing about Jesus as

---

[1] Hoskyns; Westcott; Bultmann.

he was perceived not by the eyewitnesses but by the later Church. Of course, this is partly the case in all the Gospels and not the least in S, where there is e.g. no "Messiasgeheimnis". The important difference, however, is that whereas this reinterpretation was usually a natural and unconscious process, John is conscious of the fact that he is actively participating in it and makes it a central theological theme.

There are a number of examples in the Gospel where John is explicitly not writing about the earthly Jesus but about the exalted Christ. In Jesus' dialogue with Nicodemus in c. 3, the first person singular on the lips of Jesus switches to the third person in v. 13, and it is stated that the Son of Man *went* up into heaven. Already in v. 11, the first person singular starts changing to the first person plural, which betrays that gradually the speaking of the earthly Jesus about himself becomes the testimony of the Church about the exalted Christ. In 4 : 23 and 5 : 25 Jesus refers to the time when the Spirit will be there with the words : $\text{ἔρχεται ὥρα καὶ νῦν ἐστιν}$. At the time of the earthly Jesus, this hour was not yet present as is clearly shown by 4 : 21 ; where it is only stated that the "hour is coming". But in John's way of writing about the earthly Jesus, this hour is already proleptically present because the earthly Jesus and the exalted Christ overlap. It should be understood in this light that whereas the events of the glorification are normally referred to in the future tense in the farewell discourses, the past or present tenses are sometimes used : 13 : 31 ; 14 : 17, 19 ; 15 : 27. In the final prayer, Jesus partly prays as if he is already the Advocate in heaven interceding for his followers. According to 17 : 11, he literally says : $\text{οὐκέτι εἰμὶ ἐν τῷ κόσμῳ}$; cf. also vv. 10, 22.

This prolepsis is one of the themes of 17 : 1-5 where it is discussed in terms of past and future glory : (v. 1) Jesus asks the Father to glorify the Son, (2) "for Thou hast given him authority over all mankind, to give eternal life to all whom Thou hast given him. (V. 3 is parenthetical.) (4) I have glorified Thee on earth by completing the work which Thou gavest me to do ; (5) and now, Father, glorify me ..." V. 2 says that Jesus had the authority to (ἵνα explicates by denoting purpose) impart eternal life during his earthly existence ; this is the same as revealing God's Name and glorifying God (cf. vv. 3, 4. 6). Therefore v. 2 means the same as v. 4 : Jesus glorified the Father on earth. But according to vv. 1 and 5, this glorification still has to take place. The future glorification of v. 1 has to follow the past glorification of v. 2 (καθὼς denotes reason)[1] for else the imparting of life mentioned in v. 2 cannot be

---

[1] Arndt-Gingrich.

effectuated; v. 2 needs v. 1; it can only be pronounced in the light of
v. 1 for not until the final glorification does it come true. V. 2 is equivalent to v. 4 and v. 1 to v. 5, so that one would expect that v. 4 also
anticipates v. 5. This is indeed so, and it affirms the preceding. According to v. 4, Jesus has completed the work which the Father gave him.
But this is a proleptical way of speaking because 10 : 18; 14 : 31 teach
that part of the work which the Father gave him, is to lay down his
life. V. 4 could only be pronounced in anticipation of Jesus' final
glorification.[1] The earthly glory (v. 4a) anticipates the final glory. The
conclusion is that one would expect that every time John says the earthly Jesus revealed glory, this glory is a prolepsis of his final glory.[2]

This agrees with 2 : 4b and 11b : Jesus objected that his hour had
not yet $(ο\mathring{υ}πω)$ come but nevertheless revealed his glory. There are
only three other instances of $ὥρα$ with the possessive pronoun referring
to Jesus, i.e., of the hour of Jesus in the Gospel, and all three clearly
refer to the hour determined by God for Jesus' death : 7 : 30; 8 : 20;
13 : 1. According to 7 : 3, Jesus' brothers urge him to go and perform
miracles in Jerusalem. Jesus answers : $ὁ\ καιρὸς\ ὁ\ ἐμὸς\ ο\mathring{υ}πω$ (cf.
2 : 4b) $πάρεστιν$ (6), ... $ἐγὼ\ οὐκ\ ἀναβαίνω$ (8). According to v. 1, the
Jews wanted to kill Jesus, and in v. 7 Jesus says the reason why the
time is right for his brothers to go to Jerusalem but not for him is that
the world cannot hate them. Clearly the "time" of Jesus is the same as

---

[1] It is tempting to say only the cross is included in the *ergon* of v. 4 (Barrett; Thüsing,
Erhöhung, 48). When Jesus died, he had completed his earthly work and could say ;
$τετέλεσται$ (19 : 30). Then the cross is not part of the glorification of v. 5 but of Jesus'
earthly work. 17 : 4f. is the keystone of Thüsing's theory of two phases in the glorification, *viz.*, firstly Jesus' earthly ministry including the cross and secondly Jesus' returning
into the full glory of the Father, followed by the sending of the Spirit, etc. This distinction
compels him to argue that the cross is not included in the hour of glorification mentioned in v. 1 (76, 191). This is very questionable because the hour of glorification does
include the cross in 12 : 23ff. Throughout the farewell discourses, the distinction is not
between Jesus' cross and glorification but between his earthly life with the disciples
on the one hand and his departure-including-the-cross, i.e., his glorification, on the
other hand (17 :12f.; 16 : 4f.; 13 : 1, 33). This is the distinction between 17 : 4 and 5.
Hence, v. 4 does not directly include the cross but anticipates not only the cross but
the full glorification which must follow according to v. 5. The relation of v. 4 to v. 5 is
similar to that of v. 2 to v. 1. As we shall see (pp. 133f.), this separation of the cross from
the glorification leads Thüsing to a very "Pauline" interpretation of Jn. which results
in other more serious mistakes.

[2] Similarly W.F. Howard, *Christianity according to St. John* (1943) 26f., discusses
"proleptic emphasis" as one of the principles of the Gospel : "the end is seen from the
beginning."

his hour : it is the time of his death. ($\dot{\alpha}\nu\alpha\beta\alpha\iota\nu\dot{\omega}$ has a double meaning and also refers to the final "going up" as in 3 : 13; 6 : 62; 20 : 17.) 2 : 4b can hardly mean the hour determined by God for the performance of the miracle (Schnackenburg) because Jesus immediately performs it. Therefore, it is nearly certain that the hour of 2 : 4 is the hour of Jesus' departure. It is not quite correct to say it is the hour of death, and, therefore, the miracle is a sign of the forgiveness of sins by Jesus' blood (Hoskyns, Strathmann, Cullmann[1]). In 12 : 23, 27f.; 17 : 1 this hour is expressly defined as the hour of glorification (and in 13 : 1 as the hour of returning to the Father). Jesus' death is only part of what happens in this hour. John does not emphasize the cross and reconciliation separately as Paul does. Jesus' death is only the first step of the glorification, which also comprises the coming of the Paraclete and so the completion of the revelation. That this is the direction in which the interpretation of 2 : 4 must be sought is also indicated by the close parallel 7 : 1-13. What Jesus' brothers really want from him is : $\phi\alpha\nu\acute{\epsilon}\rho\omega\sigma\sigma\nu$ $\sigma\epsilon\alpha\upsilon\tau\grave{\sigma}\nu$ $\tau\hat{\omega}$ $\kappa\acute{\sigma}\sigma\mu\omega$ (4), but for this the time has not yet come, and when Jesus, nevertheless, goes up to Jerusalem, he does it $o\dot{\upsilon}$ $\phi\alpha\nu\epsilon\rho\hat{\omega}s$ $\dot{\alpha}\lambda\lambda\dot{\alpha}$ $\dot{\omega}s$ $\dot{\epsilon}\nu$ $\kappa\rho\upsilon\pi\tau\hat{\omega}$ (10). The "hour" of 2 : 4 is the time for the full revelation of glory. During the life of Jesus, this time had not yet come. Therefore 2 : 4b indicates that the Johannine evaluation of the miracle $\dot{\epsilon}\phi\alpha\nu\acute{\epsilon}\rho\omega\sigma\epsilon\nu$ $\tau\grave{\eta}\nu$ $\delta\acute{\sigma}\xi\alpha\nu$ $\alpha\dot{\upsilon}\tau o\hat{\upsilon}$ (11b) is a prolepsis of the final glorification. 2 : 4 warns the reader that the meaning of all the miracles is not limited to what would have been obvious during the life of Jesus, but their full meaning can only be grasped in the light of the fact that Jesus is glorified and therefore present, in the light of the Paraclete. Hence 2 : 4 implies an admittance of John that he has reinterpreted the miracles.[2]

That this is the key for all the miracles is proved by the fact that the introduction of the last miracle also refers to the glorification : the illness of Lazarus came "for the sake of the glory of God, so that the Son of God may be glorified by it" (11 : 4). We have seen that the glory revealed in the miracle (4, 40) partly refers to the symbolical interpretation that Jesus is the Life. On the historical level v. 4b means the miracle causes the Jews to kill Jesus. On the deeper level it reminds the reader that the full glory can only be seen in the light of the glorification.

---

[1] *Urchristentum und Gottesdienst*[3] (1956) 68ff.

[2] Some scholars are inclined to say the miracles are signs pointing to the cross, e.g., Charlier, Notion de signe, 443ff. No; they are signs revealing glory in anticipation of the glorification.

John regards his new interpretation of S as insight imparted by the Paraclete. We have seen that the teaching which the Paraclete imparts is not really a new addition because he teaches only by reminding. The Paraclete imparts the exalted Christ, but if he does this only by reminding of the earthly Jesus, it means that the two are one. And this is precisely the basic tenor of John's thinking. He refuses to distinguish between the Christ of his experience and the Jesus of the tradition. Therefore, he cannot but see the present Christ in every traditional narrative, i.e., interpret it symbolically. The Paraclete reminds of all the words of Jesus (14 : 26). This agrees with the fact that the symbolical interpretation of the miracles is always given as words of Jesus (cc. 6, 9, 11). The words which the Paraclete call to mind are not primarily historical words of Jesus but words of the exalted Christ, words which the earthly Jesus "would have spoken" because in fact the full revelation had already been given in him. The identity of "remind" and "teach", of the earthly and exalted Jesus, is the ultimate basis of the unity of event and interpretation.

Therefore, the Johannine symbolism is related to Jewish typology rather than to Platonic philosophy. The Jews regarded the past actions of God as revelation of how he would act in the present or future because they believed he is always the same and acts consistently. John regarded the miracles of Jesus as revelation of the works of the exalted Christ in the present because he believed Jesus to be God and therefore to be the same before and after his exaltation.[1]

B) *The Glory in the Flesh*

When 1 : 14 has to be interpreted in the light of this all-embracing unity of Jesus and Christ, of event and meaning, two questions arise. In the first place, after having established that the earthly glory is proleptic, one is inclined to think this is not partly but wholly so, because this would give a neater picture. This would mean the glory of 1 : 14 is not real but projected into the flesh at a later stage. In the second place, if one, nevertheless, wants to maintain that there was really glory in the flesh, the problem arises of how this highly "dogmatic" glory of John could be revealed in human history. Then the flesh of 1 : 14 seems not to be real but docetic.

The first possibility is favoured by many because then the Christology of John is not so "high" and may be harmonized with the Synop-

---

[1] Cf. Hofbeck, *Semeion*, 212-9.

tics where *doxa* is never said to have been visible in the earthly Jesus. (It is mentioned only in the transfiguration scene — Lk. 9 : 31ff.) The New Testament normally uses *doxa* only of the exalted Christ. The first possibility also enables one to harmonize with Paul because then the flesh of 1 : 14 may be interpreted as humiliation (Phil. 2). Bultmann carries this the furthest and stresses that the flesh was a total concealment of the Logos : He came in total "Verhülltheit"; Jesus was "nichts als ein Mensch." He says that Jesus' life only *becomes* revelation of glory in the light of the glorification; there was *no* glory visible in the earthly Jesus.[1]

There are, however, some objections to emphasizing the *sarx (σάρξ)* of 1 : 14. ‘Ο λόγος σὰρξ ἐγένετο is usually translated "the Word *became* flesh." This is not quite correct because "become" means to change into, but the Logos did not change into flesh for *logos* continues to be the subject of the further statements in 1 : 14. Γίνομαι has a very wide spectrum of meaning, and there are a number of possibilities for a weaker translation than "become", e.g., "come" or "appear". 1 Jn. 4 : 2 speaks of Christ ἐν σαρκὶ ἐληλυθότα (similarly 2 Jn. 7). The best paraphrase is probaly that "the Logos came on the human scene as flesh" (Barrett). This is affirmed by the following considerations. The significance of 14a-b is to explain how 14c, the vision of the glory, was possible. 14de is then, again, an explanation of what the glory was so that 14c is the centre of v. 14 on which the emphasis should be laid. The flesh does not conceal the glory but explains its visibleness; it does not imply humiliation but a demonstration of divinity. The flesh does not denote the nature of the Logos but his place, the human scene where he had to come for the sake of manifesting himself to men. This place is only a means to and end. 14b expresses its temporariness : the Logos only "pitched his tent" here for a while. Basically, 14a repeats what has already twice been stated in the prologue, namely, that the Logos came into the world like shining light, i.e., to reveal himself (5, 9-11).[2]

That the flesh only prepares the revelation of glory and stands in its shade is clearly shown by the rest of the Gospel. The "flesh" of Jesus does not really appear again while the demonstration of glory is frequently mentioned. Jesus is like a God on earth. He performs the

---

[1] *Theol.*, 401; *Jh.*, 376f.

[2] Schlatter saw that the flesh implies no "Erniedrigung". F.C. Baur, *Kritische Untersuchungen über die kanonischen Evangelien* (1847), 94ff., stressed that the flesh should not be emphasized.

most miraculous wonders. He speaks in such an unworldly way that the Jews repeatedly misunderstand him. Even when he is weary and thirsty, he need not drink or eat (c. 4). He knows the inner thoughts of all whom he meets. He addresses his mother as γύναι. He need not pray (11 : 42). When the soldiers find him in Gethsemane, they fall to the ground. The passion story is rather a story of triumph : Jesus keeps the initiative and even death is depicted as his own act after he had uttered the call of victory τετέλεσται (19 : 30). There are some traits of humility in the Johannine portrayal of Jesus, but they are dominated by his divinity. The humanity of Jesus is assumed and has not yet become a problem, but it is not stressed at all. Through the centuries, the σὰρξ ἐγένετο has led its own life in the dogma of incarnation and of the true humanity of Jesus, which may be justified by Paul and the Synoptics but which is not in agreement with its Johannine context.

It is a favourite statement that the glory could not be seen by the world[1] and that their unbelief was caused by the flesh, the humanity of Jesus. In fact, however, unbelief is not depicted as reaction to the humility of Jesus but to the brightness of the divine revelation in him. The negative reaction of the world is first mentioned in 1 : 10f. after the statement that the light of the Logos had come into the world. The Jews want to stone Jesus after his explicit declaration of his unity with the Father (10 : 30-33). When Jesus has to explain their rejection of his words, he does not ascribe it to the veiled character of his speech but to the fact that they are the devil's brood (8 : 43f.). The reason for the rejection of the revelation by the world lies not with the revelation but with the world : the revelation is clear but the world, stubborn. This is particularly clear with the miracles. The "miracle-criticism" is not a criticism of miracles but of men. According to 12 : 37, Jesus performed many miracles, but the Jews did not believe in him. The explanation is given in the following verses — because of their blindness ! The miracles are God's testimony to Jesus, and they would have been convincing, were it not that the Jews were not of the sheep of Jesus (10 : 25f.). The reason that Jesus did not entrust himself to the multitude which believed on account of the miracles in 2 : 23 is not because there is anything wrong with the miracles but because Jesus knew

---

[1] Kittel, *ThW* II 252; Schnackenburg, 340; Dom J. Dupont, *Essais sur la Christologie de S. Jean* (1951) 289; W.G. Grossouw, La Glorification du Christ dans le quatrième évangile, in : *L'Evangile de Jean* (Recherches bibliques III, 1958) 140, who stresses that the glory can only be seen in the light of the cross.

what was wrong with man (v. 25). According to 15 : 24, Jesus blames the Jews that while he has performed among them works that no one else performed, their reaction was : νῦν δὲ καὶ ἑωράκασιν καὶ μεμισήκασιν καὶ ἐμὲ καὶ τὸν πατέρα μου. Although it should not be overemphasized, it cannot be denied that the Father is also object of the vision of the unbelieving Jews. This can only mean that the mighty works of Jesus are such a concrete revelation of the power of God that even the world sees something of the glory. The raising of Lazarus is the direct cause of the Jews to kill Jesus. What is rejected is not the weakness of the flesh but the brightness of the *doxa* as revealed in this final miracle. The Jews do sometimes allege the humanity of Jesus as reason that they do not believe in him (6 : 42; 7 : 27). But this is only a poor excuse by which they try to hide from the light of his divinity.

Therefore, the glory in the flesh is only partly a prolepsis of the glorification; partly, it is genuine divine epiphany visible even to unbelievers. This agrees with the result of our investigation of the three verses in which *doxa* is connected to the miracles, i.e., that the glory is partly the miraculous power as such. The voice from heaven in 12 : 28 may be taken to mean just what it says : "I have glorified it (my name), and I will glorify it again", i.e., glory *was* revealed in the earthly life of Jesus and will be revealed at his departure. Hence, the vision of 1 : 14c is, in the first place, the physical vision of the eye-witnesses from whom the tradition stems. It is true that the "we" of 1 : 14c is taken up by the "we" of the whole church in v. 16, so that it is clear that the Church is, as it were, looking through the eyes of the disciples and seeing deeper than they have seen. But it is not the function of the *sarx* to indicate that the vision had to be a deeper vision. This is indicated by 14de. The function of the *sarx* is the opposite, namely, to make it clear that the vision is, in the first place, physical vision because flesh implies "among us" (14b), visibleness, concreteness. We have to conclude that Bultmann's interpretation reverses the intention of 1 : 14 and, thus, of the entire Gospel. The Johannine Christology is so "high" that it is misunderstood when it is seen on the same level as that of the Synoptics or Paul.[1]

---

[1] W. Thüsing (*Erhöhung und Verherrlichung*) attempts to harmonize Jn. and the Christology of Phil. 2 as much as possible (222). He argues that because Jesus was not with the Father during his earthly life as before and after it (17 : 5), he had given up his preexistent glory with the incarnation which was "eine Art Erniedrigung" (207, 222). Therefore, the glory which John ascribes to his earthly life is only revealed "Zeichenhaft" in the miracles

In our rejection of any kenotic interpretation of John, we find ourselves on the course leading towards the second possibility mentioned
above, i.e., a docetic interpretation. The question which now has to be
answered is whether we can continue on this course or whether we
have to depart from it at some point. Käsemann went fairly far in this
direction, and we take him as partner in the discussion. It will hardly
be of any avail to object against him that John accepts the humanity
of Jesus and can therefore not be called docetic. He does not deny the
traits of humility in the Johannine Jesus (*Jesu*, 25) and admits John's
dialectical way of thinking to such an extent that he disagrees with
Harnack and others who went so far as to say the flesh of Jesus was
transparent and God could directly be seen in him (Prol., 174). The
docetism he intends was not yet so developed as to reject systematically
the humanity of Jesus, but it was a "naive Doktismus", a Christology
in which the glory of Jesus was spontaneously so strongly emphasized
that his humanity was endangered. We cannot deny that, as the
Gospel lies before us, the divinity of Jesus dominates his humanity.[1]
He is God who will always be present, the true light who conquers the
world, the Life of the world. John has one main dogma, i.e., the unity
of Father and Son, and this is demonstrated by the Gospel. We may
attempt to secure somewhat more room for the humanity of Jesus than
Käsemann, but this will at the most produce a difference in degree.

A fixed point, however, is that Käsemann denies that the earthly
glory anticipates the final glorification (*Jesu*, 40 — he says the two
stages of the glory are used as the strongest argument by those who
emphasize Jesus' humiliation, p. 36). Although he takes Jn. 17 as
basis for his interpretation, the farewell discourses and the Paraclete
(which we have found to be the key to the composition of the Gospel)
in fact play no role. He regards the cross as an afterthought (19) while
we found the departure of Jesus to be a vital necessity for the completion of the revelation. We can agree with Käsemann that John is

---

(227), and it is not the miraculous power (229); it has no "Eigengewicht ... sondern ist
ganz Beziehung auf die Verherrlichung" (233); it could only be seen in the faith which
became possible after the glorification (226, note 16). This mistaken interpretation of
the earthly glory is related to his basic distinction between the two phases of Jesus'
glorification (see p. 128). Because he regards the cross as belonging to the first phase
together with the earthly life (like Phil. 2), the earthly glory is made completely dependent
on the glorification and is interpreted in harmony with the humiliation of the cross.

[1] Cf. E. Schweizer, *Jesus Christus*, 165 : "Ja, die Betonung, dass wirklich Gott selbst
in ihm zu finden ist, ist mit solch letzter Konsequenz durchgeführt, dass das Menschsein
Jesu darunter in den Schatten zu geraten droht."

writing about Jesus as God always present, but the difference is that our investigation has led us to conclude that John was conscious of the fact that this high Christology is later interpretation. For John, the earthly Jesus had to die, and the Spirit had to come before the full glory of Jesus could be revealed. If John had thought Jesus was so glorious that this was not necessary, one would certainly be inclined to call him a docetist. But to the mind of John, the divinity of Jesus was not so manifest during his life that the divine Person of the Paraclete was no longer necessary; Jesus was not so unearthly that he did not need to die. In this way, John could secure room for the reality of the Gospel history. It was not absorbed into the dogma because it belonged to a different phase. The tradition is important to John because he not only uses it for a typical illustration of divine truth (*Jesu*, 67), but he regards it as a realistic report of events which have to be carefully interpreted for their divine meaning to be understood. Käsemann does not deny that the deeper meaning of the miracles had to be seen, but he says the reason is because the docetist John did not see "im Irdischen das Wahre" and regarded the earthly as "bestenfalls Abglanz des Himmlischen" (96). It seems to me that precisely the opposite is true : John interpreted the events from the life of Jesus not because they would otherwise be meaningless but because he regarded them as real revelation in the worldly sphere. Therefore, Käsemann goes too far when he says : "Die Mitteilung historischer, durch das Augenzeugnis der Apostel ausgewiesener Tatsachen nützt als solche gar nichts" (78). One goes too far in the reaction against him in saying the *sarx* conceals the glory. Käsemann is much nearer to the truth than Bultmann. But the flesh does imply at least so much earthliness that interpretation is necessary in order to see the full glory. The point of the flesh is not so much the true humanity of Jesus (cf. the impressive miracles which became possible because of the flesh) but the concrete visibleness of the revelation in Jesus. This is vital to John. Although not certain, it is probable that 1 : 14; 6 : 53ff. and 19 : 34 contain a hidden polemic against docetists. In any case, 1 John makes it clear that the Johannine type of theology could become antidocetic when it was denied that Jesus had indeed come in the flesh. But again the point is not the human lowliness of Jesus but the concrete perceptibility of the revelation — it was seen with the eyes and touched with the hands (1 Jn. 1 : 1ff.).[1]

---

[1] J.L. Martyn, *History and Theol.*, 117, agrees with Käsemann that Jn. is docetic.

Final conclusions may now be drawn. Basic to the theology of John is that there was *really doxa* in the *sarx*. Bultmann denies that the *doxa* is real, and Käsemann, that the *sarx* is real. Against both it has to be maintained that the history and the tradition was of vital importance to John. Although he may have treated it freely here and there, he had a basic theological appreciation of it because he regarded event and meaning as a unity. Bultmann broke this unity by situating the meaning behind the event. Käsemann does not deny the unity because he maintains, e.g., that the miracles are important both as works of power and as signs. But this "unity" is not really a unity of event and meaning because it is situated above the sphere of historical reality. History has become docetic, and the "unity" implies its partial dissolution in the dogma. This is too easy a unity. For John it was not so simple because there had to be a unity of meaning and *real* history. Therefore, he needed two phases for it, before and after Jesus' exaltation, and the Paraclete to weld them together.

It must not be denied that there are strong, latent tensions in the theology of John. He wants to be based on history, but the theological power of his developed Christology is so great that if the interpretor is not careful, history is in one way or another absorbed by theology. A strong anchor in history was necessary in order to keep the Johannine Christology from being blown away. This anchor is the reality of both the *doxa* and the *sarx*. If both are acknowledged, they mutually guarantee each other and form an immovable anchor.

But the reality of the glory and the flesh can only be secured by emphasizing both aspects of the glory, i.e., manifestation and anticipation. In other words, the glory of Jesus was connected to both his

G. Bornkamm, Zur Interpretation des Johannesevangeliums, in : *Geschichte und Glaube* I (1958) 104-121, thoroughly discusses *Jesu letzter Wille* and also finds Käsemann's fundamental mistake to be his neglect of the aspect of anticipation in the glory (113f.), One of the central themes in the recent book of W. Wilkens, *Zeichen und Werke* (1969), is polemic with Käsemann. In his former book (*Entstehungsgeschichte*, 1958) he argued that the author of the narrative material of the Gospel added the discourse material at a later date. In his latter book he attempted to distinguish between the theology of the two layers. He kept them apart as far as possible and, therefore, could not analyse the relation between the earthly and final glory, i.e., the aspect of anticipation. For him, the earthly glory is only the power of Jesus (32). The result is that although he raised a number of acceptable objections against Käsemann, he could not get to the root of things. His distinction of literary strata was not accepted in the scientific discussion for source-critical reasons, and it seems that here we have a theological reason for questioning it. His main objection against Käsemann is that the Gospel contains realistic history, of which the Passion forms an integral part (49, 59ff., 111, 131).

preexistence and his postexistence. As the Logos, Jesus had always had glory and this was manifested when he came to the earth for a while. But the full meaning of this manifestation was revealed only when the postexistent Christ came to live in his followers. If either aspect of the glory is denied, the anchor in history cannot keep the tension. If the manifestation of the glory is not acknowledged, the earthly revelation is, as it were, too light to counterbalance the weight of the theology so that the life of Jesus is dominated by the interpretation and misinterpreted as humiliation or even as mere humanity. On the other hand, if it is not acknowledged that the glory is also partly anticipation of the final glorification, the earthly glory is overemphasized and cannot be counterbalanced by the flesh so that the flesh is lifted up from the sphere of reality to that of docetism.

The point of John's theology, that to which he is driving, is to urge upon the reader that Christ wants to live in him through the Spirit who brings the word, i.e., through the word (14 : 23f.; 15 : 7). Both the earthly Jesus and the coming Lord are made present in the word. The vital point, however, is that the past and the future are not absorbed into this present but retain their reality. We have already seen that the presence of the glory in the glorified Christ does not imply denial of the historicity of the glory of Jesus. This is balanced by the statement of Jesus at the end of the final prayer (17 : 24) that his followers will see the complete glory in the future when they are where he and the Father are. The present glory which the believers experience in the word is reality because it is rooted in the past and future reality of the glory.

6. FINAL CONCLUSION ABOUT THE MIRACLES

We have already established that John accepts as a second best the testimony of the miracles as such. Their primary importance, however, is that they have symbolical meaning. Now the question is whether an event must be miraculous in order to reveal meaning. In principle, it does not seem to be so because the washing of the disciples' feet and the water from the well are interpreted in the same way as the miracles. But why does John then present a selection of the most miraculous wonders which we know from the early Christian tradition ? In the light of the foregoing it seems fair to say John chose wonderful miracles because he wanted to balance the mighty glory of the exalted Christ, i.e., of the interpretation, with an equal weight of earthly glory. This balance was necessary for the unity of event and interpretation. The interpretation is mighty and, therefore, the event should also be mighty. Otherwise it may have seemed that the "interpretation" is actually projection of theology into the event. Now it is clear that the glory of the present meaning is really interpretation of the event because it had already been manifestation of glory. This can also be seen from the other side : because the miracles were so wonderful, they attracted the attention and inspired powerful interpretation. Perhaps one can say the three miracles which are not really interpreted are the least astonishing ones (the boy in Caphernaum, the man at Bethesda, and the walking on the water), while the three which are elaborately inter- preted are the most astonishing ones (the feeding of the thousands, the man born blind, and Lazarus — "life", John's primary concept for salvation, is kept for this most marvellous miracle). Probably the miracles formed the corner-stone in the development of John's sym- bolical method before this method was applied to non-miraculous events and even to Old Testament ideas like the Shepherd and the Vine — thence, the aptness of the word sēmeion to characterize the Gospel (20 : 30). John would hardly have magnified the miracles because for him the whole point of the miraculous is the historical reality of the glory. We do not know whether S and the other traditions available to him also included less marvellous miracles than the seven reported in the Gospel. Probably they did. John frequently mentions in passing that Jesus performed other miracles (2 : 23; 4 : 45; 6 : 2; 20 : 30). Then John deliberately selected the greatest ones.

Thus, the miraculous events were revelation of glory in themselves, and the meaning was seen in them — event and meaning are a unity. But this unity is a two-edged sword and explains both John's basic acceptance and his criticism of S. On the one hand, one cannot have the interpretation without the miracle (as Bultmann wishes), but on the other hand, one can also not have the miracles without the interpreta- tion. If one does not see the meaning, one does not see the miracle, the sēmeion (6 : 26). Therefore, the miracles can also be dangerous because their miraculous aspect may distract the attention from Jesus himself. John warns against this but, nevertheless, emphasizes the miracles because he trusts that under the guidance of the Spirit, their effect will often be that they not only attract the attention but also lead on to deeper insight, i.e., to the living Christ who *is* himself everything he imparted in the miracles.

Excurs: *The Theological Literature on the Sēmeia*

The point of view taken here of John's evaluation of the miracles may be further clarified by comparing it with various other points of view in some of the literature.

Many of the interpreters try to modernize John and then, of course, have little eye for his first century way of emphasizing the miraculous as manifestation of glory. I shall discuss them more or less in an order of decreasing negativity as to the role of the miraculous. J. Becker (Wunder und Christologie, *NTS* 16, 1970, 130-48) wrote an interesting article in which he studied the miracles in Jn. using the same three methods which have been applied in the three chapters of this book. He interprets Jn. dualistically (144) and says that John thinks : "Die Christologie der Semeiaquelle bleibt auf der Seite des Todes stecken" (146). He goes further than Bultmann and argues that the miracles are less than symbols : they are meaningless. John does regard them as real events but narrates them with the purpose of intensifying the offence of Jesus' flesh : they conceal the glory of Jesus and so heighten the paradox of his "Heilsanspruch" (147f.). Luise Schottroff (*Der Glaubende und die feindliche Welt*, 1970) is virtually in complete agreement with Becker. She interprets John strictly according to Gnostic dualism and emphasizes that the miracles as much as the flesh of Jesus are completely "innerweltlich" (255) and, therefore, the opposite of real revelation. John only reproduces the thoughts of the sēmeia source to show that they break down when heavenly realities have to be dealt with, to demonstrate their uselessness (256). What is startling is that at the end of the book she investigates the healing of the son of the royal officer and concludes that this is an exception and the faith of 4 : 53 is a good faith (266) ! Becker and Schottroff chose an obvious way of avoiding the inconsistency of evaluating the miracles as concession like Bultmann. They are already refuted, however, by the mere fact that John used S as source. Schottroff (268) admits that Gnostic literature never mentions the miracles. G. Sass (*Die Auferweckung des Lazarus*, 1967) also goes further than Bultmann. He thinks John deliberately retold and developed the traditional story in such a way that the reader could no longer misunderstand it as a historical event but had to see that it is a symbolical illustration (25, 56, 64). The interpretation of K.L. Schmidt (Die johanneische Charakter der Erzählung vom Hochzeitswunder in Kana, in : *Harnack-Ehrung*, 1921, 32-43) is very similar to that of Bultmann. He says that John "dem Mirakulösen

keinen Wert zuerkennt" (40) and therefore his emphasizing of the
miracles is a concession for the "Gemeindefrömmigkeit" (37). For
John himself the miracles are only allegories (40). J.P. Charlier (La
notion de signe dans le IVe Ev., in : *RSPhTh* 43, 1959, 434-48) concludes from 12 : 37 that miracle-faith is unbelief (438). A sēmeion is
"une manifestation voilée de la doxa du Christ" (442), and, therefore,
one must "dépasser le signe pour arriver à la réalitè qu'il manifeste"
(439). The miracles do not reveal the Messianic power of Jesus (447) but
lead the believer to the foot of the cross (443). P. Riga (Signs of Glory,
Interpretation 17, 1963, 402-24) equates the signs to parables (405);
they are "enigmatic" and "essentially obscure"; "man must have
faith to see in the sēmeia the "works of God" (410).

The articles of E. Haenchen are valuable, and I have frequently
referred to them. He says John does not doubt the historicity of
the miracles (Der Vater der mich gesandt hat, *NTS* 9, 1962-3, 208-16,
here 209), and John admits that they are frequently necessary to
inspire faith (Probleme, 29); but Haenchen denies the unity of event
and meaning by saying that John valued the miracles "nur als Hinweise auf das eigentliche Heilsgeschehen" (54) from which they are
"tief verschieden" (Vater, 209). S. Hofbeck wrote a dissertation on the
concept sēmeion in the Gospel (*Sēmeion*, 1966). Revelation can only
be found "hinter" the miracles (105). Therefore, "ein Geschehen aber
wird erst zur Offenbarung wenn der Glaube das Geschehen als Offenbarung wahrnimmt" (127). The "Offenbarung hat nichts Demonstrati-
ves an sich" (176); the miracles conceal the glory (185), thence, faith
based on them is a misunderstanding. In this commentary R.E. Brown
wrote an appendix on the sēmeia in which the aspect of meaning
slightly dominates the aspect of manifestation; for instance, he says
about the raising of Lazarus : "the restoration of physical life is
important only as a sign of the gift of eternal life" (529). Nevertheless
he agrees that a miracle-faith can be one step in the right direction
(528). We have seen that Hoskyns describes the Johannine "unity" in
an admirable way in his beautiful commentary, but he becomes just
too theological when he writes about the miracles : "They are not
narrated as prodigies, or wonders. ... They are quite properly signs
or parables of the nature of (Jesus') work" (190). Dodd also stresses
the "unity" but the danger of his Platonistic interpretation is that the
"symbol is absorbed into the reality it signifies" (140). It is symptoma-
tic that he denies the demonstrative aspect of the miracles, e.g. :
"The new age which Jesus inaugurates is not to be defined in terms of

crude miracle on the phenomenal level, the plane of *sarx*, but in terms of that order of being which is real and eternal" (336). He thinks the *erga* which bear witness to Jesus cannot be the miracles because mere miracles would not impress the educated Hellenistic readers that John has in mind (332, 361f.).

Only a few interpreters one-sidedly emphasize the demonstrative aspect. M. Inch (Apologetic Use of "Sign" in the Fourth Gospel, *Evangelical Quarterly* 42, 1970, 35-53) only stresses that John developed and incorporated the miracle stories "to demonstrate the persuasiveness of Jesus' Messianic claim" (39). John wants to convince unbelievers (35). W. Wilkens (*Zeichen und Werke*, 1969) attempts to prove that John laid even more emphasis on the demonstrative character of the sēmeia than his source (30-45). The basis of his argument is a very questionable source criticism. As strongly as he trusts literary criticism on the basis of little more than *aporias*, so strong is his scepticism about form criticism. He thinks John treated his tradition very freely so that he explains much that can better be explained by the development of tradition as deliberate changes by John — for instance he regards *all* the peculiarities in the pericope on the feeding of the five thousand as such (36). Then, of course, it seems that John enlarged the miraculous.

Finally, I mention a number of men whose evaluations of the role of the miracles in the Gospel seem to me to be more or less correct. As would be expected, Barrett, the trustworthy companion in all Johannine research, wrote a balanced paragraph on the sēmeia (62-65). Schnackenburg incorporated an excursus on the sēmeia in his learned commentary. John stresses the "massive 'Materialität'" (354) of the miracles but at the same time sees deeper meaning in them : "In dem aus göttlicher Macht gewirkten Geschehen erfährt der Glaubende etwas vom göttlichen Wesen Jesu, schaut er die Majestät des Gottessohnes, ahnt er auch den lichtglanz der himmlischen Welt, den er mit leiblichen Augen noch nicht sehen kann" (340 — a beautiful expression of the "unity"). He undervalues the manifestation of the glory, however, when he says the flesh conceals the glory so that it can only be seen in faith (340). It is disappointing that although he accepts the sēmeia source-hypothesis, he makes no real use of it in the excursus. The result is that he cannot explain the apparent tensions in the Gospel and has to speak about a "Gebrochenheit" in the Johannine sēmeion-concept (346). E. Schweizer (Die Heilung des Königlichen, *EvTh* 11, 1951-2, 64-71) agrees that John has nothing against the miraculous and thinks he even elaborated it, but he urgently warned that Jesus should not be replaced by his gifts (69f.). L. Cerfaux (Les miracles signes messianiques de Jésus et œuvres de Dieu, selon l'Evangile de S. Jean, in : *L'attente du Messie*, Recherches bibliques, 1954, 131-38) says miracle-faith is accepted as a first step (134) and stresses the "unity" by saying the spiritual power of Christ revealed by the miracles does not lie on another level, but "le miracle est cette Puissance elle-même en acte ; voir le miracle, c'est atteindre et contempler la Puissance spirituelle" (136). The following scholars are also in basic agreement with the foregoing : D. Mollat, Le sèmeion johannique et le sèmeion hellenistique, *EThL* 38 (1962) 856-94, here 890-2 ; O. Michel, Der Anfang der Zeichen Jesu, in : *Die Leibhaftigkeit des Wortes* (Köberle-Festgave, ed. Michel, 1958), 15-22, here 18 ; H. Conzelmann, *Grundriss der Theologie des Neuen Testaments* (1968) 376-8 ; R.H. Fuller, *Interpreting the Miracles* (1963) 98f. ; A. Richardson, *The Miracle Stories of the Gospels* (1941) 116. In the preface to his book in which he attempted to reconstruct the "Gospel of Signs", R.T. Fortna said he hoped to publish another book in which he would work out the *Redaktionsgeschichte* called forth by his source criticism. For the time being, however, we have to be satisfied with a short article which appeared two years after he had written the mentioned preface (Source and Redaction in the Fourth Gospel's Portrayal of Jesus' Signs, *JBL* 84, 1970, 151-66). He actually only discusses the relation between miracle and faith so that he could not reveal John's basic theological reasons for emphasizing the miracles, i.e., the "unity", the glory, etc. The fact that he lacked this may be the reason for his underestimation of John's criticism of miracle-faith (see p. 105 above). He, nevertheless, agrees that in contrast to the source, John saw faith as a "complex phenomenon" (163) which had to grow towards deeper insight.

7.   A HISTORICAL RECONSTRUCTION OF THE CHANGE OF THE "SITZ IM LEBEN" OF S INTO THAT OF JOHN : THE JEWS IN THE GOSPEL

It seems probable that S incorporated missionary preaching for the Jews. The decisive difference between S and John is not that John is not Jewish any longer. It seems to me that John is hardly less Jewish than S. This, at least, is indicated by the arguments of those who regard the entire Gospel as a missionary book for Jews, e.g., W.C. van Unnik and J.A.T. Robinson. John based his Gospel on the Jewish sēmeia-theology of his source. A great part of the Gospel consists of discussion with Jews and answering of Jewish objections. The title χριστός plays an important role, and in contrast to Paul, it nearly always has the full Jewish meaning of "the Messiah" (only in 1 : 17 and 17 : 3 is it a proper name). The Jewish synagogues are mentioned in connection with the persecution of the Church (16 : 2) and not the Gentile courts as in Mt. 10. Indeed, while pagans are frequently referred to in the Synoptics, they hardly occur in Jn. The Jews are criticized on every page whereas heathen practices, such as idolatry, are not mentioned. Thus, the arguments may be multiplied. This may suffice because this is not what has to be proved here.

The point is that the significant difference between S and Jn. is that John writes about the Jews in such a hostile way that the Gospel rather seems to be the opposite of a missionary book for Jews. John usually generalizes and calls all the different groups of Palestinians appearing in his Gospel οἱ Ἰουδαῖοι. Sometimes it has a neutral meaning, but usually it is almost a technical title for the hostile religious authorities.[1] The Johannine Jesus dissociates himself from them by speaking of "your law" (8 : 17; 10 : 34, cf. 15 : 25) and even calling them the devil's brood (8 : 44). He continually argues with them. Their arguments, however, are not really answered but only reported to expose their blindness; they are not the sheep of Jesus (10 : 26). The Jews of the diaspora where the Gospel was written would not have dissociated themselves from "the Jews" in the Gospel because they usually designated themselves with this title.[2] Clearly, the language of John about the Jews was scarcely designed to convert them, rather to be polemical.[3] Jewish feasts are called "the feast of the Jews" as though the Jews are a strange nation — the break between Church and synagogue seems to be complete.

The change of the *Sitz im Leben* could, of course, simply have had a geographical cause : the contents of S was originally preached in a region where Jewish missionary work was possible but was later also used in the Gospel of John, who lived in a town where the synagogue was too hostile for missionary work. An objection against this is that it seems that the Gospel reflects a former *Sitz im Leben* of Jewish

---

[1] Cf. Schnackenburg, 275.

[2] W. Gutbrod, *ThW* III 372.

[3] This is affirmed by the most interpreters, e.g. Schnackenburg, Messiasfrage, 259ff.; Brown, LXXIII; Kümmel, *Einleitung*, 159; E. Grässer, Die antijüdische Polemik im Johannesevangelium, *NTS* 11 (1964-5) 85.

missionary work by means of sēmeia. In practically all cases where the miracles as such are mentioned in the Gospel, it concerns Jewish belief and unbelief. (This will presently become clearer.) One would prefer an explanation of how the situation could have changed in the city of John, if there is one.

A fixed point is provided by the word ἀποσυνάγωγος, which occurs thrice in Jn. (9 : 22 ; 12 : 42 ; 16 : 2) and nowhere else in the New Testament. In 9 : 34, it is described as the expulsion (ἐξέβαλον) of the former blind man by the Jewish authorities. According to v. 22, it was an official Jewish institution. The problem is what this was because before 70 A.D. only the first and second grades of the synagogue excommunication were in practice. But this was no expulsion because the persons thus excommunicated were not yet cut off from all the religious practices of the community, and the excommunication was not permanent but aimed at ameliorating the person. In Jn. the Jews are so hostile that it seems clear that the expulsion was complete and permanent; in 16 : 2 it is even mentioned in immediate connection with the killing of Jesus' followers.

Therefore, another explanation must be sought, and it may be found in the development of Jewish history after the fall of Jerusalem in 70 A.D. As a result of the war, all of the leading groups amongst the Jews lost their influence, except for the Pharisees who organized themselves in Jamnia for the study of the Torah. The Temple, which had been the centre of Judaism, was destroyed, and the Pharisees made the Thorah the new centre. They decided about matters on which there was difference among Jews and so created more conformity, e.g., the teachings of the Sadducees were rejected. Previous to this, the Jewish Christians were still basically accepted as Jews, e.g., in 58 A.D. when Paul came to Jerusalem (Acts 21 : 18ff.), it was still customary for Jewish Christians to offer sacrifice in the Temple. Paul could attempt to convert Jews in every city. But naturally this would become more and more difficult as a result of the new conformity. During the first decade after the war, the attitude of the Pharisees towards Jewish Christians was still mild under leadership of Johanan ben Zakkai.[1] In 80, however, he was succeeded by the authoritarian Gamaliel II, who convinced the other rabbis that a curse against the *minim* (heretical Jews, especially Christians) had to be inserted into the *Schemone Es're*, recited by the Jews as the chief prayer in the synagogues. This was the

---

[1] Cf. H. Mulder, Ontstaan en Doel van het Vierde Evangelie, *GThT* 69 (1969) 244.

final break between the Church and Judaism. The exact date is unknown but it must have been between 85 and 90. All the earlier measures taken against Christians by Jews were *ad hoc* decisions; this was the first official decision by the central authorities which corresponds to Jn. 9 : 22. It is true that expulsion is not explicitly mentioned in connection with the curse of the *minim*, but it would have been the practical result.[1]

Gamaliel II made his decisions known to all the synagogues of the Diaspora by means of official letters. Also in John's town Jews interested in Christianity would have been forced to sever their ties either with the Church or with the synagogue. The synagogue would have attempted to win back its former members. The Jews developed missionary power so that, e.g., Ignatius and the letter of Barnabas had to warn the Christians against the Jews in the second century.[2] The *Dialogue* of Justin also shows how the Christians had to answer hostile Jewish objections against the Messiahship of Jesus. A number of those mentioned by Justin are similar to those of the Jews in Jn.[3] The reaction of the author of Revelation on the hostility of the Jews was that he called them "the synagogue of Satan" (Rev. 2 : 9; 3 : 9).

In such a situation John writes his Gospel. In many respects it seems that the present circumstances in John's town are reflected by his way of describing the confrontation between Jesus and the Jews. Of course, he is not explicitly writing about the present but about history. But as one of the essential principles of this theology was that he saw the present Christ in the historical Jesus, so he saw the present conflict already reflected in the historical one. In his theology the historical Jesus and the exalted Christ living in the Church are identical, and, therefore, he is concerned about the essential unity of the persecution of Jesus and of the Church. He writes history as a two-level drama, at the same time alluding to the present. He also had a firm factual basis for doing this. For instance, it holds true for both the present and the time of Jesus' life that the Jews are hostile and that their influential leaders are the Pharisees.

---

[1] There is a wide unanimity among scholars that this is what John must have meant; cf. the following, also for more detail : W. Schrage, *ThW* VII 846-50; Bill. IV 629 ff.; Martyn, *History*, 31-39; Barrett, 229; K.L. Carroll, The Fourth Gospel and the exclusion of Christians from the Synagogues, *BJRL* 40 (1957-8) 19-32, here 22; C.H. Hunzinger, *Die jüdische Bannpraxis im neutestamentlichen Zeitalter* (Diss. Gött., 1954) 68ff.

[2] Mg. 8 : 1; 10 : 3; Phld. 6 : 1, cf. F. Neugebauer, *Die Entstehung des Johannesevangeliums* (1968) 14.

[3] R.H. Strachan, *The Fourth Gospel*[3] (1946) 51.

According to 12 : 42, a number even of the Jewish authorities felt
attracted to Jesus "but would not acknowledge him on account of the
Phasisees for fear of being banned from the synagogue." 19 : 38 says
essentially the same about Joseph of Arimathaea, and according to
9 : 22, the parents of the man born blind refused to confess that Jesus
had performed the miracle for fear of expulsion from the synagogue.
These are unmistakable allusions to Jews in the town of John who
were torn between their faith in Jesus and a natural desire not to desert
Judaism. By means of the example of the man born blind, John
encourages them openly to confess Jesus and to sever their ties with the
godless synagogue. It cannot be proved, but is is an interesting question
whether c. 9 is not a fairly exact reflection of the regular course of events
in John's town. A Jew is touched by the message of Jesus as the blind
man by his healing power. His heretical leanings are detected by his
neighbours, and they betray him to the *Gerousia*, the ruling body of
Jewish elders in the town. He and his parents are summoned, and when
he refuses to curse Jesus as a sinner, he is expelled.[1] John's encourage-
ment to Jews in similar difficulties is that after the man had broken
with the synagogue, he could "bow down and worship" Jesus
(προσεκύνησεν, 9 : 38) without any reservation and thus receive the
full blessing of the living Christ.

So although the Gospel is no missionary book, John does have some
Jews in mind who are still members of the synagogue. What is his
attitude towards the others who are not interested in Jesus ? Clearly
John is not optimistic about the chances of their conversion. The
community from which this Gospel arose experienced so much hostility
from outside that they isolated themselves from the world and had
only a limited missionary interest. They love each other but not those
outside (14 : 34). The first letter does not reflect any interest in the
conversion of heathen but rather stresses that the believers should
separate themselves from the world (1 Jn. 2 : 15). The Paraclete does
bear witness through the believers, but it is characteristic of the
negative attitude towards unbelievers that the testimony is not said
to lead them to Jesus but to convince them of their sins because they
hate Jesus and refuse to believe in him (16 : 8). It can best be compared
to the testimony of the former blind man before and against the "blind"
Pharisees. This pessimism concerning the world is related to John's

---

[1] J.L. Martyn (*History and Theol.*, 1968) emphasizes that the history described in
Jn. really takes place on two levels, 30 and 90 A.D. (10-57, 68, 77 etc.). He commences
his investigation with the two levels of Jn. 9.

emphasis on predestination. When "the Jews" did not believe in spite of the sēmeia, it is because God has blinded them so that "they could not believe" (12 : 37-40); they do not accept the testimony of the works because they are, in any case, not of the sheep of Jesus (10 : 25f.); they *cannot* hear the word of Jesus (8 : 43). The Jews who saw the signs did not believe because only those given to Jesus by the Father can come to him (6 : 36f.). It is not enough to be impressed by the signs, but one must be regenerated by the Spirit, whom the Jews "cannot receive" (3 : 1ff.; 14 : 17). (I do not deny that in the Gospel as a whole, predestination is counterbalanced by emphasis on man's free choice.) It is striking that again and again this rather negative predestinarian point of view is connected with pessimism about the missionary value of the sēmeia. This is probably a reflection of John's local experiences. Before 80 the preaching of S had success, and Jews were converted. But after the change of leadership in Jamnia, the Jews became hostile, and the preaching of miracles was hardly effective any longer. The Gospel account may even betray that great numbers of Jews who previously had had some interest in the preaching of the powerful Jesus later turned their backs upon the preachers. Does the Gospel not relate that masses of Jews had a certain degree of faith in Jesus on account of the miracles (2 : 23; 4 : 45; 6 : 2; 7 : 31; 11 : 45-12 : 19) but that this faith was shallow (6 : 26) and untrustworthy (2 : 24) so that the final result of the miracles was negligible (12 : 37)? On the basis of these experiences, John values the preaching of miracles much lower than S : they will hardly inspire faith and even when they do, this will not be the kind of faith which can withstand the hostility of fellow Jews. The world is left to the Paraclete (16 : 8-11), and the attention is rather concentrated on strengthening the persecuted community of believers.

For indeed the changes in the synagogue and the hostility of their brothers would have been distressing for the Jews in the local Christian congregation. There are hardly any signs in the Gospel that it is also addressed to Gentile Christians so that it seems that the greater part of the congregation was Jews. The synagogue not only expelled them but also organized propaganda to convince them that Jesus was not the Messiah. They may even have had the power of persecution. 16 : 2 mentions the killing of Christians. In normal circumstances under Roman rule this would, of course, not have been possible. But one has to keep in mind Paul's stoning by Jews in Lystra according to the account of Luke (Acts 14 : 19). Moreover, the Jewish religion was *religio licita* so that Jews had the protection of the court and stood under no compulsion to offer sacrifice to the Roman emperor. As long as a Jewish Christian was not expelled from the synagogue, he would have had the same privileges. But after expulsion he would probably have been liable to punishment. The correspondence between Plinius, the governor of Bythinia, and Trajanus proves that this was the case early in the second century. The Jews might have had the power to cause the execution of a Christian by repoiting his expulsion to the the Roman court. Then their propaganda to win back former members would have been strengthened by the threat of persecution.

No wonder that even in the important farewell discourses nearly a chapter is devoted to dealing with the hatred of the Jews (15 : 18-16 : 11). The believers should not be distressed because their Master was also hated and killed, and in death he conquered (16 : 7-11). "In the world you will have trouble. But courage ! The victory is mine; I have conquered the world" (16 : 33). A great part of the Gospel counters Jewish propaganda, not to convert the Jews but to strengthen the Christians. The true Israelite is he who believes in Jesus (1 : 47, 49). In cc. 5-10 various Jewish objections against Jesus' Messiahship are unmasked as symptoms of the darkness of the world.

The natural result of this history was that, on the one hand, the miracles were basic, and, on the other, they were criticized. They are basic because as one of the foundations of the tested faith of these Christians, their testimony, of course, has to be maintained; also because they refute the propaganda of the Jews according to their own dogmatics (3 : 2; 9 : 16, 31-3). On the other hand, however, after the changes in the synagogue, the experiences with the preaching of the sēmeia were disappointing. It became clear to John that in the new situation miracles could not be the main content of his Gospel. Faith has to be radically deepened in order to withstand persecution. Jews impressed by Jesus must "stay in his word" in order to become faithful disciples (8 : 31 — cf. the importance of the word μένειν in the gospel). The tradition was not enough; deeper insight was sought. This appreciation of deeper knowledge must have been strengthened by the climate of pre-Gnostic Jewish wisdom-mysticism which is reflected in the Gospel.

The danger of such a development is that theology can dominate tradition, and the earthly Jesus can be lost out of sight. But what is striking about the Gospel of John is that whereas, e.g., the author of Revelation reacted to persecution by turning to apocalyptic, and Paul could write theology without stressing the life of Jesus, John's theology even in its highest flights, is still entirely concentration on Jesus. His congregation had much written tradition about Jesus, but, nevertheless John wrote a Gospel. Much of it was not taken over from tradition literally, but he was convinced that he was writing about the Jesus who had lived on earth because he believed that he was guided by the Paraclete who imparted insight into nothing but the true meaning of the historical life of Jesus. The Paraclete's teaching was reminding so that even the discourses are replete with traditional themes. The fact that the sēmeia were basic for his congregation must have been one of the most important anchors attaching him to the earthly Jesus. The strong Christological concentration of S pointed the way for the development of his theology.

This strong connection of the development with Jesus called forth the danger of docetism. If this highly developed theology had to be tied down to the earthly Jesus, the danger was that the *sarx* of Jesus would not have enough weight to keep him from being lifted from the sphere of reality. This was a real danger. It is not accidental that docetists appear in the vicinity of John (cf. 1 Jn.) and that the Gospel was a favourite with Gnostics in the second century. The Johannine theology can be understood as leading towards docetism. But this is a misunderstanding. Again, the importance of the miracles in the whole conflict in John's town must have been one of the main anchors attaching the Johannine Jesus to the reality of the flesh because the point of the miracles is the historical reality of the manifestation of the glory.

The two striking characteristics of Johannine theology with which we have dealt in this book seem to balance each other. In one dimension, John's thinking has a very wide range; in another, it is very concentrated. In theological character, John's thinking ranges from historical realism to word-mysticism, comprising all in a magnificent unity. In content, however, the Johannine theology is very limited because like S it only concentrates on Jesus. The word of Zinzendorf eminently suits John : "I have but one passion. That is he and only he."

INDEX

B) Index Locorum

Old Testament

Gen.		**13 : 22**	83	**2 Kgs.**	
41 : 55	54	18 : 15, 18	81f.	5 : 10ff.	60
		34 : 10	81	**Job**	
Ex.					
4	64f.	**1 Kgs.**		9 : 8	58
18 : 13-27	57	4 : 42ff.	57	**Ps.**	
		17 : 18	53	28 : 3	58
Num.		17 : 23	55	74 : 9	83
14 : 11	65			106 : 30	59
		2 Kgs.		**Mal.**	
Dt.		4 : 35	52	4 : 5	81
13 : 2	63				

Apocrypha and Pseudepigrapha

Sap. Sal.		**1 Macc.**		**Bar. Syr. Apoc.**	
19 : 3	60	4 : 46	82	29 : 5-8	54
Sir.		14 : 41	82	**Coptic Apoc. Elijah**	
24 : 5f.	58			163ff.	85

Qumran Literature

1 Q S 11, 9ff.	81	1 Q p Hab. 7, 1-5	51	4 Q Test. 5ff.	81
1 Q Sa 1f.	57				

New Testament

Mt.		6 : 14f.	84	: 15	86
4 : 23	46	: 35-44	57, 71f.	: 16	46, 86
8 : 5ff.	80	: 51	74	9 : 7	85
11 : 5ff.	46, 86	7 : 32-37	15, 46, 93	11 : 20	46
12 : 25	51	8 : 1ff.	33, 57, 71f.	13 : 11, 16	46
: 27	56	: 11ff.	86	24 : 19	86
: 28	56	: 22-26	15, 93f.		
24 : 26	85	9 : 7	85	**Jn.**	
		: 14-28	93	1 : 14	120, 122, *130f.*, 133
Mk.		10 : 21	51	: 19ff.	87
1 : 24	46	13 : 4	65	: 35-51	*39, 61,* 74f. 78, 92
: 29-31	94	13 : 22	63, 85	: 42	51
2 : 8	51			: 47f.	51
: 22	54	**Lk.**		: 50f.	*42, 103,* 120
3 : 27	46	4 : 18-27	86		
5 : 1-20	93	7 : 11-17	93		

Hellenistic Literature